THE EPISTLE OF
PAUL TO THE ROMANS

from

THE MOFFATT
NEW TESTAMENT
COMMENTARY

Based on *The New Translation* by the

REV. PROFESSOR JAMES MOFFATT
D.D., LL.D., D.LITT.

and under his editorship

Religious Books in the Fontana Series

The Epistle of Paul to the Romans

C. H. DODD

COLLINS
fontana books

First published by Hodder & Stoughton May 1932
First issued in Fontana Books 1959

SENATVI ACADEMICO
VNIVERSITATIS ABREDONENSIS
ΕΥΧΑΡΙΣΤΗΡΙΟΝ

CONTENTS

INTRODUCTION

COMMENTARY

CONTENTS

INTRODUCTION

The Epistle to the Romans is the first great work of Christian theology. From the time of Augustine it had immense influence on the thought of the West, not only in theology, but also in philosophy and even in politics, all through the Middle Ages. At the Reformation its teaching provided the chief intellectual expression for the new spirit in religion. For us men of Western Christendom there is probably no other single writing so deeply embedded in our heritage of thought.

I. AUTHENTICITY AND INTEGRITY OF THE EPISTLE

Of the fourteen epistles which bear the name of Paul in our traditional Canon of the New Testament, one, the Epistle to the Hebrews, is certainly not by Paul. There are others whose authenticity has been, and in some cases still is, a subject of controversy. But no serious criticism admits any doubt of the four great epistles, those to the Romans, the Corinthians (two), and the Galatians. It is upon these that our knowledge of Paul as a writer and an historical personality primarily rests. They are sufficient to give a quite unmistakable impression of a strongly marked individuality. The authenticity of the Epistle to the Romans is a closed question.

This is not necessarily to say that it has reached us in the exact form in which the apostle sent it out. Like other ancient writings, the Pauline epistles were exposed to the vicissitudes of manuscript transmission. Moreover, there is evidence sufficient to convince many critics that in the process of forming the *corpus* of Pauline writings the epistles were to some extent manipulated. Thus, we know from internal evidence that Paul wrote more than two letters to Corinth; and many critics think that our 2 Corinthians is composed out of two of these letters, with possibly a fragment of a third. Thus it is not inherently unlikely that the Epistle to the Romans also may have undergone some such editorial treatment.

Two questions relating to the integrity of the epistle have been discussed, both affecting the last two chapters.

9

1. *The Shorter Recension*

There is evidence that in the second and third centuries MSS.
were current which contained a shorter version of the epistle,
though no such MS. has survived.

(i) The position of the doxology (xvi. 25–27) varies. Apart
from two MSS. which omit it altogether, it is found (*a*) after
xvi. 23 in many of the earliest MSS., (*b*) after xiv. 23 in many
MSS. chiefly later, (*c*) in both these places in a few MSS., and
(*d*) after xv. 33 in the Chester-Beatty papyrus (known as P46).
This, the earliest extant MS. of the Pauline epistles, (third
century), came to light piecemeal between 1930 and 1936, when
it was published. The doxology is thought not to be from Paul's
own hand, for reasons set forth in the commentary. It may
have been composed by an editor as a suitable conclusion for so
stately a work, or perhaps (as has been conjectured) as a conclusion to the whole Pauline corpus in an edition in which
Romans came last. But whether by Paul or not, we may fairly
assume that it was intended to stand at the end, and therefore
that the archetypes of those MSS. which have it after xiv. 23, or
xv. 33, finished the epistle at those points, the missing portions
having been supplied by scribes who copied them from MSS.
containing the complete epistle as we have it.

(ii) There exists a system of early Latin chapter-headings
(*breves*) which gives Rom. xiv. 15–23 as chap. 50, followed by
chap. 51 which is the doxology. Further, an ancient Latin
concordance to the Pauline epistles similarly refers to chaps. 50
and 51. This proves that the Latin version for which the *breves*
and the concordance were compiled lacked xv.–xvi. This version
was certainly older than the Latin Vulgate of the fourth century,
and probably as early as the second century.

(iii) There is evidence that some early texts lacked the words
' at Rome ' in i. 7 and 15, reading in the former place ' to those
who are in the love of God.' It is a plausible conjecture, that
the shorter recension lacked all reference to Rome, whether at
the beginning or at the end.

If then we leave aside for the moment the isolated evidence
of P46 we are left with two quite distinct recensions of the
epistle, and the question arises, whether the longer or the
shorter recension represents the original form of the epistle as
Paul wrote it.

(i) It is possible that Paul wrote a general epistle for circulation among churches where he had not had opportunity to preach, and that he subsequently adapted it for sending to Rome (on the occasion indicated by xv. 22–29). In that case, we have no means of determining the date or circumstances in which this hypothetical general epistle was written. The very specific statements of i. 8–13 show that the writer had in view, if not some definite church, at least a definite group of churches. Otherwise the opening of the letter would be artificial, not to say insincere. And supposing this general letter to have been subsequently adapted for Rome, the Romans, reading the warm expressions of i. 8–13, would unwittingly be reading what had been written without any thought of them in mind; which one is loth to believe. Further, xiv. 23 is a most unlikely close for such a letter, even with the addition of the doxology. It does not bring the argument of chap. xiv. to a conclusion worthy of the level on which it has been conducted. As the commentary will show, xiv. 23 is actually in the middle of a paragraph, which does not end until xv. 6. The plan of the epistle, which is more shapely than is usual in Paul's work, demands some such conclusion to its great argument as is found in xv. 7–13.

(ii) The alternative theory is that Paul wrote the longer recension and that it was later cut down. As it is unlikely that Paul mutilated his own work, we must suppose that someone else did the cutting. Some think it was Marcion, the second century heretic, whose method of dealing with such documents was drastic (he criticized ' with a penknife,' we are told). With his aversion for the Jewish and Old Testament elements in Christianity he may well have taken exception to some of chap. xv. On the other hand it is possible that the cutting was done by an orthodox editor for different reasons. There is little in xv.–xvi. particularly suitable for reading in church, and an abridged version would serve the purpose and economize labour and materials. If we ask why the cut was made so clumsily at xiv. 23, there is perhaps no answer but the illimitable stupidity of editors. At the same time we cannot rule out the possibility of accidental mutilation. The end of a roll of papyrus, and the last leaf of a *codex*, were all too easily damaged or lost, and many MSS. of ancient works lack their original ending.

(iii) But we have still to consider the evidence of the Chester-Beatty papyrus, in which the doxology follows xv. 33. Its archetype therefore presumably closed the epistle, quite suitably, with the words, ' The God of peace be with you all!' The argument of the epistle has been rounded off, and the recipients (in this case the Romans beyond doubt) have been informed of the apostle's intended movements. There would be no great difficulty in accepting this as the form of the epistle which left the apostle's hand. But we should still have to account for the existence of chap. xvi., which no one, I think, seriously doubts to be (substantially at least) Paul's own composition.

2. *The Destination of Chapter XVI*

Even before the discovery of P46 it had been suspected that chap. xvi. formed no part of the original Epistle to the Romans. The chief reasons for such suspicions are as follows:

(i) It is surprising that Paul should send such a host of greetings to individuals in a church to which he was a stranger; still more surprising that these include three 'fellow-workers' and two 'fellow-prisoners' of Paul, together with three men whom he calls 'my beloved,' and a lady whom he calls 'my mother.' Had Paul's friends, it is asked, migrated in a body to Rome?

(ii) The exhortations in xvi. 17–20 are strikingly different both in matter and in form from the rest of this epistle. Their pastoral tone recalls that of the letters to the Galatians, Corinthians, and Philippians, who were Paul's own flock. Moreover the dissensions here referred to do not seem to find any place in the epistle elsewhere. Paul's fear of disunion in the Roman church, it would seem from xv. 1–13, was due to the tension between Jewish and Gentile elements; but the false teaching against which he warns in xvi. 17–20 does not seem to be Jewish (see notes).

(iii) To these we may now add the evidence of P46 that some MSS. (strictly, that one MS.) brought the epistle to a close at xv. 33.

The hypothesis which has been offered is that chap. xvi. is a short letter, introducing Phoebe, warning against false teaching, and sending greetings, to some other church, which has been wrongly tacked on to the Epistle to the Romans. The church usually suggested is Ephesus, for the following reasons:

(a) Paul had lived longer at Ephesus than anywhere else since he set out on his travels, and so would be likely to have many friends there.

(b) Epaenetus, the senior member of the church in Asia

(xvi. 5), was more likely to be found at Ephesus than anywhere else.

(c) Aquila and Prisca were last heard of at Ephesus (1 Cor. xvi. 19), and at Ephesus there was a ' church in their house.' Moreover, according to 2 Tim. iv. 19, they were still at Ephesus when Paul was in prison at Rome. This is quite likely one of the genuine portions of the Pastoral Epistles.[1] But, even if it is not, it is evidence for a tradition in the church of Ephesus.

(d) The tone of the warnings in xvi. 17-20 would be more natural in a letter to Ephesus, and the false teachings attacked may well have been of a kind similar to the gnosticism which a little later is found at Colossae (not far away). According to Acts xx. 29-30, Paul warned the elders of Ephesus the last time he saw them against perverse teachings; and this speech, as it occurs in close connection with ' we-passages,' probably reflects some actual reminiscence of what was said, from one who was present. The Pastoral Epistles again are good evidence that at a somewhat later period there were serious troubles with gnostic teachers at Ephesus and these troubles may well have begun in Paul's own time. Thus xvi. 17-20, which is surprising in a letter to Rome, would be entirely appropriate in a letter to Ephesus.

There is much to be said for the Ephesian hypothesis, and it has been very widely accepted. Nevertheless, it is not without difficulties.

(a) Chap. xvi. makes a very odd impression, if it is taken as a complete letter. 'A letter consisting almost entirely of greetings,' as Lietzmann observed, ' may be intelligible in the age of the picture postcard; for any earlier period it is a monstrosity.' It is sometimes suggested that what we have is a mere fragment: the letter to Ephesus is for the most part lost; the greetings have survived. That is to support a hypothesis with another hypothesis, and not a very likely one. Again it has been suggested that the letter which was sent to Ephesus with these greetings was no other than chapters i.-xv. Paul wished to introduce Phoebe to the Ephesians, and took the occasion to send them a copy of the letter he had just written to Rome, adding the introductory note for Phoebe and greetings to individuals. This is the most attractive form of the hypothesis. As Paul wished the Colossians to read the Epistle to the Laodiceans, so he may have wished the Ephesians to read that to the Romans. But it would perhaps have been simpler and less misleading to enclose

[1] See P. N. Harrison, *The Problem of the Pastoral Epistles.*

the epistle in a covering letter, with a request like that of Col. iv. 16.

(b) Such a long series of greetings to individuals, in a church which Paul knew, would be quite exceptional. There are no individual greetings in the Epistles to the Thessalonians, Corinthians, Galatians, or Philippians. The only epistle to a church, which contains greetings to individuals, is the Epistle to the Colossians—that is, an epistle to a church to which Paul was a stranger. This may be accidental, but it looks as if Paul preferred not to single out for special greeting individual members of a church where all were his friends.

(c) The unusual expression, "All the churches of Christ salute you (xvi. 16)", needs some explanation. As I have shown in the notes, the moment when Paul was in touch with delegates of all his Gentile churches, and was writing to the capital of the Empire, is the one moment which provided a natural occasion for such a greeting. Addressed to Ephesus it is less natural.

(d) If the Epistle to the Romans ended at xv. 33, then its conclusion stands alone among Pauline epistles. For, although a letter might quite appropriately close with the words of xv. 33, as a matter of fact every other epistle of Paul ends with some form of the 'grace,' which is found at xvi. 20 or 24 (the MSS. varying).

These difficulties are not fatal to the Ephesian hypothesis; but they make it appear not wholly satisfactory. We may therefore re-examine the traditional association of this chapter with the letter to Rome, and ask whether there is any positive evidence that points to that destination.

(1) We have already seen that Paul did send greetings to individuals in churches which he had not visited; though, so far as we know, he did not do so in writing to churches where he was known to all. Now, he had particular reasons for wishing to establish personal contacts with Rome, and may well have chosen for that reason to send greetings to any members of the church there with whom he had any connection, even indirect. It is not necessary to assume that he had known personally every person mentioned. Yet it is not so absurd as it might seem, to suppose that many of his friends had actually migrated to Rome. There was an astonishing amount of travel in the Roman Empire of the first century. People engaged in trade were especially mobile. All roads led to Rome. Moreover, some at least, perhaps many, of the friends greeted are Jewish Christians; and there was a special reason why Jews whom

Paul had met elsewhere might about this time be found in Rome. In the year 49 [1] the Emperor Claudius banished Jews from Rome. Many of them must have dispersed themselves over the eastern provinces. Five years later, that is to say, four or five years before the date of the Epistle to the Romans, Claudius died. Apparently the edict of banishment lapsed, for early in the reign of Nero the Jews were again numerous in the city, and in favour at court. Thus it is entirely possible that Paul had met many Jews, temporarily exiled from Rome, who were now back there. This applies particularly to Aquila and Prisca. They were in business as tent-makers; and they were well-to-do, since they had a ' church in their house.' We may put them down as people in a large way of business—just the sort of people who travelled widely in this period. Aquila had originally come from Pontus. He lived in Rome till 49. He then conducted business at Corinth, stayed there for a time, and then went to Ephesus, where, we cannot doubt, a branch of the business was opened. But there is no reason to suppose that the Roman establishment was closed down. All that Aquila and Prisca would need to do when they left would be to instal a *procurator* who was not a Jew, and he could carry on business as usual. At Ephesus they may have been involved in the troubles described in Acts xix. 23–40—in which they may have ' risked their lives ' for Paul (Rom. xvi. 4). Like Paul, they may have been forced to leave Ephesus. The edict of banishment being no longer in force, it is likely that they would return to Rome; but, again, the establishment at Ephesus need not have been closed; and if 2 Tim. iv. 19 compels us to assume that they were at Ephesus again about 64, there would be nothing surprising about it. Thus they could have a ' household ' (which in their case would consist mainly of their business and industrial staff) at Ephesus and at Rome at the same time; and each household would contain a body of Christian slaves and dependents. There is possibly some collateral evidence for their connection with the Roman church. The Cemetery (or ' Catacomb ') of S. Priscilla on the Via Salaria goes back in its earliest parts to the first century. It includes a burial-vault of the family Acilius or Aquillius, which may be the nucleus of the whole. A consul Acilius Glabrio was a Christian in the time of Domitian. Now Priscus and Prisca are surnames in this family, and it is not unlikely that the slave of an Aquillius should receive

[1] For the date see Edward Meyer, *Ursprung und Anfänge des Christentums*, III., pp. 37–39, 462–463.

the name Aquila. It may be, then, that Aquila and Prisca were freed slaves of the Acilii, and closely associated with those members and dependents of the family who were buried on the Via Salaria. It is not a strong link, but it is a link between them and known facts about the church of Rome.

There are other names in the list which it is possible inferentially to connect with Rome.

(a) Rufus. The name is common enough; but it is worth observing that Mark xv. 21 identifies Simon of Cyrene as ' the father of Alexander and Rufus.' It is a fair inference that Rufus was well known to the church for which the Gospel according to Mark was primarily written, i.e. the church of Rome. See note on xvi. 13.

(b) The household of Narcissus. There was a Tiberius Claudius Narcissus, a freedman of the imperial house, who exercised great influence under Claudius, and was put to death shortly after the accession of Nero. We may assume that his ' household ' of slaves would pass, with his other property, to the Emperor; and they might then, as often happened in such cases, retain the distinguishing name of *Narcissiani*. There is an inscription which seems to confirm this. It was a suggestion of J. B. Lightfoot (*Philippians*, p. 175) that some of these *Narcissiani* were among the ' saints of Caesar's household ' referred to in Phil. iv. 22. The suggestion has been widely accepted, and seems probable.

(c) The household of Aristobulus. Lightfoot also suggested that these may have been former slaves of a grandson of Herod the Great bearing this name, who lived and died as a private person, in favour with the Emperor Claudius; and that they may on his death have passed into the imperial household. But this is a guess.

(d) Amplias, or, as the better MSS. have it, Ampliatus. There was in Rome a family of Aurelii who used this not uncommon surname. Christian members of the family are buried in the Cemetery of Domitilla on the Via Ardeatina, the beginnings of which go back to the first century. There is one tomb, decorated with paintings in a very early style, which bears the one word AMPLIATI in fine uncial lettering of the first or early second century. The position and character of the tomb suggest that it belonged to a person held in especial respect. It is quite possible that he is our ' Ampliatus beloved in the Lord.' In any case, we have early evidence of a Roman Christian family bearing this name.

(e) Nereus. The tradition of the Roman church associates Nereus and Achilleus with the Princess Domitilla, who was punished as a Christian under her cousin Domitian. The tradition can be traced back to the fourth century, and may be older. As the two names are always coupled together, it is not likely that the tradition of Nereus is simply based on the present passage. But more we cannot say.

Lightfoot and others have shown that all or nearly all of the names in this chapter can be found in inscriptions of the city of Rome, and an argument for the Roman destination of the greetings has been founded upon this fact. But no one who has had occasion to work upon even a fraction of the many thousands of Urban inscriptions can be impressed by such an argument. There are few Greek or Roman names which could be not traced in so vast a field. It is only where there is some indication of a connection between the name and Roman Christianity in the first century that the inscriptions help.

If we strike a balance between Ephesus and Rome on the basis of the names, we may say that Aquila and Prisca, and Epaenetus, are definitely connected with Ephesus, and no others. Aquila and Prisca, however, are equally definitely connected with Rome; and there is some evidence for connecting Rufus, Ampliatus, the household of Narcissus, and just possibly Nereus and the household of Aristobulus with that city. The balance is not distinctly in favour of Ephesus.

(2) The difficulty of the warning against dissensions and false doctrines (xvi. 17–20) is a serious one. I have, however, suggested in the notes some considerations which tend to make its tone, so different from that of the epistle in general, psychologically intelligible. As for its contents, it would not be true to say that the *only* danger which Paul apprehended for the Roman church arose from the extreme Jewish party. He clearly has in mind, from time to time, unethical interpretations of Christianity such as later found expression in some of the gnostic heresies, and directs against them his emphatic teaching about the ethical demands of the Gospel (e.g. vi. 1–14, viii. 5–13, xii. 2). Although he does not in the body of the epistle definitely indicate such tendencies as a peril to the unity of the Church, he may have felt impelled to give a warning against such a peril before closing.

It is clear that the arguments for Rome and Ephesus respectively come far short of proof one way or the other. Nor indeed is the evidence conclusive that i.–xv. constituted the original epistle. The recension lying behind P46 may have been only another, and more intelligent, abridgement, for there is even less of general interest in xvi. than in xv.

II. DATE, PLACE, AND OCCASION OF WRITING

If the integrity of the epistle may be assumed, this matter is easily settled. The letter was written before Paul had visited Rome, but after he had completed his missionary work in the eastern provinces, at a moment when he was about to go to Jerusalem (xv. 19–25). This cannot be the journey to Jerusalem mentioned in Acts xviii. 22, for at that time Paul was proposing to return to Ephesus, and therefore did not regard his work in the east as finished. Moreover, it is only in the course of the so-called ' Third Missionary Journey ' that place can be found for a divagation up to or over the borders of Illyricum (xv. 19; see notes). The journey to Jerusalem, therefore, which is in prospect must be the one described in Acts xx., and this is confirmed by the reference to the object of that journey in Acts xxiv. 17 and Rom. xv. 26–28, namely, to take to Jerusalem the proceeds of the relief fund raised in Greece and Asia Minor. The narrative of Acts is, happily, especially trustworthy at this point, since it belongs to those sections of the book which are based upon the diary of one of Paul's travelling companions (probably Luke, the author of the Gospel and the Acts). We may therefore conclude without hesitation, on the basis of Acts xx. 2–3, that Paul was in 'Greece' (i.e. the province of Achaia), and in all probability at Corinth, the capital of the province and the site of its most important church, or else at Cenchreae, its port. This is confirmed by Rom. xvi. 1.

The occasion of writing is equally clear from xv. 14–33 (see notes). It was not any internal conditions in the church of Rome that called forth the letter, but the development of Paul's own plans. Having finished his work in the east, he proposed to go west and start a mission in Spain. For this, Rome would be a suitable base of operations. He therefore projected a visit to Rome. Since he was by no means *persona grata* in certain Christian circles, he could not be altogether sure of a welcome. It was important for him to secure the sympathy of the church of Rome. He therefore sets before them a comprehensive and reasoned statement of the fundamentals of Christianity as he understood it, which is at the same time an *apologia* for the principles and methods of his Gentile mission. With this before them, the leaders of the church of Rome will be able to judge for themselves whether Paul is the dangerous innovator he was represented to be by his Jewish-Christian opponents, or a missionary whose work they can heartily support.

The epistle is thus the last writing of Paul as a free man and an active missionary that we possess.[1] It was written when he was at the height of his powers, at the close of his most successful period of work, and (in his own intention) at the opening of a new period of still wider enterprise. Events foiled his plans, and no doubt the Paul of the Captivity Epistles is a very different person from the Paul who might have written letters from Cartagena or Cadiz. Paul the restless traveller and pioneer missionary takes his leave of us in this great epistle, into which he has packed the ripe fruits of many years of thought and work, of preaching, controversy, and the cure of souls, of trial, suffering, and spiritual experience.

The absolute chronology of Paul's career cannot be fixed with certainty. The one quite certain date is that of Gallio's arrival at Corinth, which occurred while Paul was there (Acts xviii. 12): July, A.D. 51. Plotting out his journeys from this fixed point, we may say that the earliest date which is at all likely for Paul's departure from Corinth for Jerusalem is shortly before Easter, A.D. 57, and the latest, A.D. 59. The later of these seems to me the more probable. If it be accepted, then the end of Paul's two-year imprisonment in Rome (Acts xxviii. 30) brings us to A.D. 64. In that year, or early in the next, the Neronian persecution broke out, and, according to tradition, Paul perished under Nero. Thus the most probable date for the Epistle to the Romans is in the first quarter of A.D. 59, but a year or two earlier is possible.[2]

---

[1] Assuming that 1 Timothy and Titus are not authentic, or that any authentic portions of them belong to the period covered by the Acts of the Apostles, clear evidence for Paul's alleged release and second Roman imprisonment is lacking. See P. N. Harrison, *op. cit.*

[2] See my notes on Pauline chronology in the Oxford *Helps to the Study of the Bible*, (1931) p. 196.

III. THE CHURCH OF ROME

We have no direct information about the introduction of
Christianity to Rome. The city had a large Jewish population,
which made many proselytes. Under the Emperor Claudius
there were riots in the Jewish quarter which led to an edict
banishing all Jews from the capital. This was in A.D. 49. The
brief notice of this event in Suetonius' *Life of Claudius* (§ 25)
runs thus: ' He expelled the Jews from Rome because they
kept rioting at the instigation of Chrestus ' (*Judaeos impulsore
Chresto assidue tumultuantes Roma expulit*). Nothing further is
known of this Chrestus. The name was common among slaves.
He may have been an agitator of servile origin. But *Chrestus* is
an extremely common misspelling for *Christus* in Greek and
Latin (the pronunciation of *ē* and *i* scarcely differed in the Greek
of this period). It seems as though the general public, to whom
the Jewish and Christian religious term *Christus* was unintelligible, understood it as the familiar name *Chrestus*. Thus it is
quite possible that Suetonius' cryptic sentence is a garbled
reference to troubles that arose in the synagogue when Christianity got a footing in it. At any rate, it seems that there were
Christian Jews who were banished with the rest. A few months
later, Aquila and Prisca were at Corinth when Paul arrived
there. Nothing is said of their being converted by him; on
the contrary, Paul says that his first converts in Achaia were,
not Aquila and Prisca, but the house of Stephanas (1 Cor.
xvi. 15). The probability therefore is that they were Christians
at Rome.

We may take it, then, that by A.D. 49 Christianity had been
introduced into the city. The Roman tradition is that it was
Peter who planted the church there. But, in the earliest form
of the tradition, Peter and Paul are always named as joint
founders; that is to say, Peter is not regarded as founder in any
other sense than Paul: they both worked at Rome, and the
historic form which Roman Christianity took was the result of
their joint influence. That Peter, like Paul, died at Rome is
in all probability true, in spite of recent scepticism. It seems
to be implied already by Clement of Rome,[1] who wrote at a
time when there must have been many who remembered the
Neronian persecution. But it is very difficult, in view of what

[1] Clem v. 3–7.

we know of his life, to bring him to Rome before our fixed date, A.D. 49, when Christianity was already established there. When Paul visited Jerusalem seventeen years after his conversion (or possibly fifteen years, on our method of reckoning), Peter was still settled there. A little later he was at Antioch. On the most probable system of Pauline chronology,[1] these events fall in A.D. 48/49. It is thus unlikely that Peter in person founded Roman Christianity. The most probable account, in fact, is that which is given by the anonymous Roman writer of the fourth century who is referred to as Ambrosiaster: ' It is known that Jews lived at Rome in apostolic times, because they were subjects of the Roman Empire. Those of them who had become Christians passed on to the Romans the message that they should profess Christ and keep the Law. . . . Without seeing displays of mighty works, or any one of the apostles, they accepted the faith of Christ, though with Jewish rites.'[2] We may perhaps supplement this by the evidence of chap. xvi. It is probable that some of the persons greeted in that chapter had been members of Christian churches in the east before they went to Rome, and that they were engaged in missionary work there. Among them are Paul's ' fellow-worker,' Urban, and his ' fellow-prisoners,' Andronicus and Junia. The latter are expressly called ' apostles,' i.e. missionaries. They had been Christians before Paul was one, and may have been in Rome for some years.

From the epistle itself we can learn little about the Roman church. Unlike other epistles, it has no particular reference to the internal conditions of the church to which it is addressed, and Paul had no direct acquaintance with them. All that we can legitimately infer is that, like most churches outside Palestine, it was of mixed Jewish and Gentile membership, and that Jewish influence was probably stronger than it would have been in a church planted by Paul himself.

The church which Paul addressed must have been a large and important one. When the Neronian persecution broke out, the Christians of Rome were ' a large body ' (1 Clem. vi. 1), ' an immense multitude ' (Tacitus, Annals, xv. 44). Before the end of the first century the evidence of Christian burials is available in the earliest parts of the ' catacombs.' Under Domitian there were Christians among the aristocracy, and even in the imperial family. Perhaps the faith had penetrated

---

[1] See, again, my notes in the Oxford Helps to the Study of the Bible, pp. 196–197.
[2] Quoted in Sanday and Headlam's Romans, pp. xxv.–xxvi.; my translation.

upwards from the slaves and freedmen of ' Caesar's household ' who were Christians when Paul wrote to Philippi (Phil. iv. 22).[1] At any rate, we may infer that the church which in A.D. 64 could be represented as a public danger, and in spite of the persecution made such remarkable progress in the following decades, was already numerous and perhaps influential when Paul addressed the letter to it.

Of the reception of the epistle we know nothing. According to Acts xxviii. 15 (a good authority, since it is part of the ' we-document '), when Paul came to Rome as a prisoner he was welcomed with a kindness which was both gratifying, and, we should gather, not altogether expected as a matter of course. If the Epistle to the Philippians was written from Rome, then we can say that, while Paul was imprisoned in the city, influences adverse to him were at work in the Roman church (Phil. i. 15-18), and at one time he felt bitterly that there was scarcely anyone there whom he could trust (Phil. ii. 20-22). If the evidence of 2 Tim. iv. 16 can be accepted (whether from Paul himself, as is probable, or as representing the tradition of his churches), he was not supported at his trial by the local Christians. Thus it would appear that the object of the epistle was not completely attained.

IV. THE COMPOSITION OF THE EPISTLE

In taking the view that the Epistle to the Romans, as we have it, was written as a complete whole for the church of Rome about February, A.D. 59, we are not committed to supposing that its whole argument was there and then freshly minted for the occasion. It is rarely that an important book comes into being in that way; and this epistle is far from being an occasional letter directed to this or that particular problem as it arose, like most of Paul's correspondence. It gathers up a great deal of his thinking for years past. We can partly trace the process.

Whatever particular dates be assigned to the epistles to the Thessalonians, Corinthians, and Galatians, they all preceded the Epistle to the Romans. I have indicated in the notes several passages where a train of thought in Romans can be recognized at an earlier stage of its development in one of these

---

[1] Assuming that the Epistle to the Philippians was written from Rome, as I still think probable. See arguments for and against in the commentaries on Philippians, and on Colossians, Philemon, and Ephesians, in The Moffat Commentary.

other epistles. Thus the short eschatological passage, xiii. 11-14, points back to the more elaborate treatment of the same theme in 1 Thess. v. 1-10. The discussion of the ' body ' and the ' members,' in xii. 5-8, and of the problem of the scrupulous conscience, in xiv. 1-xv. 6, presupposes the fuller and fresher discussion of these themes in 1 Cor. xii. and viii.-x., without reference to which the passages in Romans are hardly to be understood in their full meaning. Still closer is the relation of this epistle to the Epistle to the Galatians. Not only is the general subject of the Galatian epistle—the opposition of ' faith ' and the ' Spirit,' on the one hand, and ' Law ' and ' works,' on the other—one of the main motives in Rom. iii. 21-viii. 39; the skeleton of the argument is similar, and there are places where the underlying connection of thought, implied in Romans, becomes clear only when we refer to Galatians. It is so, e.g., in the passage about Abraham in chap. iv., and in the passage about ' adoption ' in viii. 14-17 (see notes). The shorter epistle might almost have served as a first draft for the more elaborate argument of the longer. But there are subtle differences. Not only is the case presented less provocatively, but the attitude to the Law and to historic Judaism in general is less negative, and the thought is richer and more mature. The argument struck out in the heat of controversy has been reshaped by deeper reflection. The earlier epistles, in fact, give us glimpses of the workshop in which Paul's thought was hammered out. In Romans we have the finished product.

Again, I have pointed out in the Commentary that there are sections which stand out from the rest of the epistle by definite characteristics of style or matter. Thus chaps. ix.—xi. form a unity in themselves. They can be read and understood independently, and equally without them the epistle could be read through without any sense of a gap in the sequence of thought. It is probable that they represent a sermon or tract on the subject of the Rejection of Israel which Paul had composed earlier, and may have used frequently when he had to discuss that subject. Similarly, the discourse upon the universality of sin and retribution in i. 18-iii. 20 is different in style from the bulk of the epistle, and seems to contemplate a much more definitely Jewish audience. Without having the marks of an independent composition, like ix.-xi., it seems to follow the lines of a sermon or sermons which Paul must often have had occasion to deliver, probably when he was debating in the synagogue (Acts xviii. 4, xix. 8). The recognition of the fact that Paul probably used older materials in composing the epistle makes it a waste of time to examine particular passages in detail with a view to deducing from them information regarding conditions in the Roman church at the time.

But, whatever be the history of the ideas, and even of the language, of various parts of the epistle, everything in it has been fused into the unity of one great theme. From the statement of the theme in i. 16–17, the argument flows in an unbroken stream to its conclusion at xv. 13, after which there remain only personal and occasional matters to deal with. There are many parentheses, digressions, and excursuses, in Paul's manner, but all of them are strictly relevant to the stage of the main argument at which they are introduced, and in most of them points are brought out which are important for the next stage. The relatively informal manner of a letter is preserved, but it is clear that the argument was thought out as a whole. Paul evidently gave pains, as in no other epistle, to make his statement of his position comprehensive and coherent. For an analysis of the epistle see Table of Contents.[1]

V. THE THOUGHT OF THE EPISTLE

Any attempt to understand the epistle must begin with the recognition that it belongs to a world of thought different from our own, and different also from that of the Middle Ages and of the Reformation, when the Christian theology of the West received its traditional forms. There are two open doors into Paul's world. The one is the Old Testament, which all Christian readers of the epistle should know. The other is Greek thought, which, in spite of the decline of classics in the schools, still exercises an influence in our education. But Paul's immediate environment was not purely that of the Old Testament or of classical Greece. He is a writer of the Hellenistic Age, when a mixed civilization arose out of the interaction of Greek thought with that of various peoples of the Near East, including the Jews. The direct influence of non-Jewish Hellenistic thought upon Paul has, I think, been exaggerated. His main background is Judaism, though not altogether the Judaism of the Old Testament or of normal or orthodox Rabbinism, but partly the Hellenized Judaism of the Dispersion. So far as this

[1] A running paraphrase, intended to indicate the continuous movement of thought in the free medium of a letter, will be found as an appendix to my book, *The Meaning of Paul for To-day*.

epistle is concerned, three books may be said to stand more than any others for the formative influences upon his mind: Deutero-Isaiah in the Old Testament, the Wisdom of Solomon among Hellenistic Jewish writings, and 2 Esdras [1] among the productions of native, Aramaic-speaking Judaism. All these are readily accessible to readers of this commentary, and a careful study of them will be found most valuable for the understanding of the Epistle to the Romans. They are not (except in a limited sense) the 'sources' of Paul's theology; but they are a guide to the thought-forms employed by his powerful and original mind to express his interpretation of history and experience.

Of history and experience, I say. The emphasis on Paul's specific religious experience as the source of his theology served a most useful purpose in delivering the study of his epistles from an arid scholasticism; but it was one-sided. Even a cursory reading of this epistle will show how large a place in his thought is held by facts of history—the large sweep of the history of the People of God from the time of Abraham, and the particular historical events which led to the emergence of the Christian Church. Those particular events he first regarded from outside; for the Church had already been in existence for three or four years, probably, when he became a Christian. Then he came in, and his experience enabled him to look at the events from the inside. What he gives us is an interpretation, in the light of his experience, of a series of events in which he now saw a saving act of God, and which, so regarded, gave him a key to all history as divinely ordered. In Jewish thought of the 'apocalyptic' type, by which he was strongly influenced, history was held to be working up to a tremendous crisis, in which 'This Age' should pass away, and give place to 'The Age to Come'—the age of direct divine intervention in human affairs, the age of miracle. Paul held that with Jesus Christ the Age to Come had actually begun. **What is old is gone; the new has come** (2 Cor. v. 17).

Paul's theology therefore starts from objective facts in the real world, to which inward experience gives a meaning. But the experience itself is the result of the impact of the facts upon him. Jesus Christ had lived and died, and the Church had arisen, with a new and distinctive corporate life of its own. These facts had drawn Paul into their orbit. They mediated to him that touch of God upon his spirit by which he was made

---

[1] Not that he could have read this book, which was not completed before about A.D. 100. But it is the best representative of an aspect of Jewish thought which was evidently familiar to him.

a new man. He was bound to give to himself and to others some reasoned account of what had happened, partly because he was the sort of man who simply has to think things out. But also, now that the Crisis had come upon the world, he was impelled to show to all men within his reach, where they stood, and to bring them into the life of the New Age. Thus he became a missionary. His converts needed a firm intellectual basis for their faith, and he set out to instruct them. But many, whose opinions he could not but respect, thought that he was on wrong lines. Some of them were his old associates in Judaism, who refused altogether to accept his interpretation of events. Others were within the Christian Church, but shrank from the full consequences of their faith, as he saw them. He believed that they were accessible to persuasion, and so he developed certain lines of controversy and apologetic to meet the opposition. Thus he became a theologian.

In the Epistle to the Romans the controversial and apologetic aim is most prominent. Naturally the controversy often turns upon questions which have no more than an historical interest for us, in the form in which they were raised for Paul. Modern readers often turn away with the feeling that this is obsolete stuff. But a more patient consideration will often show that behind the temporary form of the questions discussed lie real and permanent interests. The discussion of the relation of Christianity to the religion out of which it sprang can never be obsolete while the Old Testament retains any place in Christian worship or instruction—that is, while Christianity remains an historical religion. Moreover, although the Jewish Law is a matter of indifference to us, yet the legalist conception of religion is by no means obsolete. In our time, as in Paul's, it besets the minds of many Christian people, and often gives a distorted view of the Christian religion to the general public. Paul's trenchant dealing with it, and his persuasive exposition of Christianity as a free life of the spirit, are still worth our consideration.

In such parts of the epistle, and indeed everywhere, Paul's thought needs translation. It is not only a matter of the translation of his Greek into intelligible English; for readers of this commentary that task has been performed by Dr. Moffatt, but the thought itself needs interpretation out of its antique categories into terms which have meaning for the mind of our time. This is the task of the commentator. The first part of it is to try to discover as exactly as possible what Paul meant, in his own terms. In such a commentary as this I have tried to avoid as far as possible lengthy disquisitions upon the first-century background. But some discussion of the meaning of terms in their original setting has proved indispensable. A hasty 're-interpretation,' before the primary meaning of the terms has been defined, can be most misleading. The second part is to try to indicate the bearing of what Paul meant, upon our own experience, our own questions, and our own thought.

My conviction is that most of it has a very real bearing on these things. It has far more than a merely historical interest. It deserves to be considered and estimated as a serious contribution to a philosophy of life tenable by modern men. If we approach the Epistle to the Romans in this spirit, then we have a further question to ask: not only, What did Paul say, and what did he mean? but also, Is it true? That question did not arise for the older dogmatic commentators, who assumed its answer. It does not interest those more modern commentators for whom the epistles are merely documents for the comparative study of religions. I believe it matters very much. Sometimes I think Paul is wrong, and I have ventured to say so. In the main, what he says seems to me to be profoundly true. Nor do I think that in ' re-interpreting ' it we need attenuate it to fit a theology, or philosophy, such as was popular not long ago, which recognizes the Divine only as immanent in a uniform evolutionary process. In much of the most recent thought there is a fresh emphasis on the idea of transcendence. In any case nothing compels us to reject at the outset Paul's assumption that there is a living God who stands outside the process, who calls men according to His purpose, and whose activity creates real crises in the lives of individuals and in the affairs of mankind. If we may believe that such a God broke decisively into the course of events at that point of history which is marked by the coming of Jesus Christ, then the structure of Paul's argument holds.

The optimism of a former generation shied at the gloomy view of mankind without Christ from which Paul's argument starts. To our disillusioned age, oppressed by the seemingly irremediable effects of all the evil that made the war, it may well seem no more than a sober statement of the *data* for our stiffest problems. The ideal with which he leaves us, that of a unity of the divisions of mankind in one body, functioning harmoniously because the pure sentiment for humanity is dominant in all its members, is the ideal to which our present

(a)

efforts must be directed. We may well give heed to what he
tells us, in between, of the divine resources available to solve
the problem and to realize the ideal. It all turns upon a crisis
of divine judgment and grace falling upon the world, and
repeated in every soul. It is something to find one man who,
with no optimistic illusions, is quite sure, and reasonably sure,
that when things are worst nothing can separate us from the
love of God. To get to know this man better is in itself a reward
for the effort to understand his greatest work.

(b)

St. Paul was a man with an ideal,
a fresh vision, a knowledge of the
resources available to attain that ideal
and an experience of God's intervention
in his personal life through Jesus
Christ, which made him a Christian
and gave them qualities of loyalty &
obedience to God whom (he says in Chap i
I serve with my spirit in the Gospel
of His Son I am set apart for the Gospel of God
(which he promised of old by His prophets in the
holy Scriptures) concerning His Son and am
Commissioned to promote obedience for His sake
among all the Gentiles.

Ergo jam ad argumentum ipsum transire satius fuerit; unde citra controversiam protinus constabit, praeter plurimas alias, et eas eximias dotes, hanc ei proprie competere, quae nunquam pro dignitate satis aestimetur: quod, si quis veram eius intelligentiam sit assequutus, ad reconditissimos quosque Scripturae thesauros adeundos habeat apertas fores.

JOHN CALVIN
*Argumentum in Epistolam
Pauli ad Romanos*

COMMENTARY

THE PROLOGUE
(i. 1–15)

i. 1–7: THE ADDRESS

Paul, a servant of Jesus Christ, called to be an apostle, i. set apart for the Gospel of God (which He promised 1 of old by His prophets in the holy scriptures) con- 2 cerning His Son, who was born of David's offspring 3 by natural descent and installed as Son of God with power by the Spirit of holiness when He was raised 4 from the dead—concerning Jesus Christ our Lord, through whom I have received the favour of my 5 commission to promote obedience to the faith for His sake among all the Gentiles, including your- 6 selves who are called to belong to Jesus Christ: to 7 all in Rome who are beloved by God, called to be saints, grace and peace to you from God our Father and the Lord Jesus Christ.

A Greek letter always began with some variety of the formula: ' M. to N., greeting.' It might naturally be elaborated in various ways. Thus: ' Theon to his most esteemed Tyrannus, many greetings '; ' Diogenes to Dionysius his brother, many greetings and health '; ' Isidora to Asklas her brother, greetings and perpetual health, as I pray.' Such openings are now familiar to us from many hundreds of private letters of New Testament times on papyrus discovered in recent years in Egypt. Paul's particular variation of the formula, at its simplest, is **Paul and Silvanus and Timotheus, to the church of the Thessalonians in God the Father and the Lord Jesus Christ: grace and peace to you** (1 Thes. i. 1). It is his custom to expand this in ways appropriate to the situation of his correspondents and his relations with them, as can be seen from a comparison of the openings of his several epistles. In the present case he is influenced by the fact that he is unknown to the church to which he writes, and has no authority over it, and by the fact that he wishes to win its sympathy for his proposed extension of missionary work. Thus he makes room in the address of the letter for a summary of his credentials as a missionary, and for a brief outline of the Christian faith which he preaches.

1 His credentials run thus: **Paul, a servant of Jesus Christ, called to be an apostle** (which we must understand in the sense of Gal. i. 1: **an apostle not appointed by men nor commissioned by any man, but by Jesus Christ and God** 4 **the Father**), **set apart for the Gospel of God concerning** 5 **Jesus Christ our Lord, through whom I have received the favour of my commission to promote obedience to the faith for His sake among all the Gentiles, including yourselves.** The **commission** of which Paul speaks, to preach to the Gentiles, had been formally recognized by the leaders of Jewish Christianity (Gal. ii. 7–9), who gave him a free hand in that field. But here as always he prefers to base his claims upon a direct divine call.

The Gospel Paul Preached

But the Romans might ask, What are the terms of the Gospel which you preach? Are they in accord with fundamental Christian teaching, as we have received it? Paul replies in advance to such a question by further parenthetic expansions 2 of the address of the letter. First, it is the Gospel which God promised of old by His prophets in the holy scriptures; that is to say, Paul's preaching of the Gospel loyally preserves continuity with the Old Testament tradition. It was necessary to say this, because it was represented in some quarters that by his attacks on the Law he was destroying the religious and ethical foundations on which the Christian religion was built (cf. also iii. 21 and note, p. 50).

3 Secondly, it presupposes certain beliefs about Jesus Christ —namely, that He is God's **Son, who was born of David's offspring by natural descent and installed as Son of God with power by the Spirit of holiness when He was raised from the dead.** This is scarcely a statement of Paul's own theology. He held that Christ was Son of God from all eternity, that He was ' in the fulness of time ' incarnate as a man, and that by His resurrection He was invested with the full power and glory of His divine status as Lord of all. This is put most fully and clearly in Phil. ii. 6–10; but there is no reason to suppose that it belongs only to the later period of Paul's theological thought. It is implied in this epistle, viii. 3, as well as in

2 Cor. viii. 9 and Gal. iv. 4. The present statement therefore
falls short of what Paul would regard as an adequate doctrine
of the Person of Christ. It recalls the primitive preaching of
the Church as it is put into the mouth of Peter in Acts ii. 22–34:
**Jesus the Nazarene, a man accredited to you by God
through miracles, wonders and signs performed among
you . . . you got wicked men to nail to the cross and
murder; but God raised Him by checking the pangs of
death . . . God has made Him both Lord and Christ,
this very Jesus whom you have crucified.** It is probable
that Paul is citing more or less exactly a common confession of
faith which would be known and recognized at Rome. The
statement is pretheological. It attests the facts that Jesus was
a real man, that He was acknowledged as Messiah, and that
after His resurrection, though not before, He was worshipped as
Son of God. These are the facts which it was the task of Christian theology to explain. Paul undertook the task, and so did
others along different lines. It is not, however, his present
purpose to expound his theology, but to place on record the
facts which he and his Roman readers alike regarded as fundamental.

i. 8-15: INTRODUCTION TO THE EPISTLE

**First of all, I thank my God through Jesus Christ for you
all, because the report of your faith is over all the** 8
**world. God is my witness, the God whom I serve
with my spirit in the Gospel of His Son, how un-** 9
**ceasingly I always mention you in my prayers, asking
if I may at last be sped upon my way to you by God's** 10
will. For I do yearn to see you, that I may impart 11
**to you some spiritual gift for your strengthening—
or, in other words, that I may be encouraged by** 12
meeting you, I by your faith and you by mine. 13
**Brothers, I would like you to understand that I have
often purposed to come to you (though up till now
I have been prevented) so as to have some results
among you as well as among the rest of the Gentiles.** 14
**To Greeks and to barbarians, to wise and to foolish
alike, I owe a duty. Hence my eagerness to preach** 15
the Gospel to you in Rome as well.

In Paul's time it was good manners, to judge from the papyri, to begin a letter, after the address and greeting, with some pious expression, usually a prayer for the well-being of the recipient, sometimes a thanksgiving to the gods. Thus: ' Ascles to his brother Serenus, greeting. Before everything I pray that you may be in good health, and that I may soon have you back. We were very sorry you missed the boat . . .'[1] ' Isias to Hephaestion her brother, greeting. If you are well, and things in general are going right, it would be as I am continually praying to the gods. I myself am in good health, and the child, and all at home, making mention of you continually. . . .'[2] A man writes to a popular official: ' Greeting, my lord Apion; I, Philosarapis, salute you, praying that you may be preserved and prosper with all your household. That not only we, but also our ancestral gods themselves, hold you in memory is clear. . . .'[3] A soldier writes from Italy to his father in Egypt: ' Apion to Epimachus his father and lord, greeting. First of all I pray that you are in health and continually prosper and fare well, with my sister and her daughter and my brother. I thank the Lord Serapis that when I was in danger at sea he saved me. . . .'[4] Paul adopted this convention. A study of the openings of his letters, to churches he knew well, will show how far from merely conventional his use of it could be. Here, where he writes as a stranger, the contents of his prayer and

8 thanksgiving are less profound and significant. He gives thanks that the faith of the Roman church is reported **all over the world**—that is, of course, among the Christian community everywhere, which no doubt felt a legitimate pride in knowing that it was well represented in the capital of the Empire; and

9-10 he prays that he may be able to visit Rome **by God's will** (literally, ' God willing '). The last phrase is also conventional in letters of the time (though a conventional phrase can be used with full sincerity). Thus the soldier whose letter I have just quoted says, ' I hope to be quickly promoted, if the gods will.' A pious and well-brought-up young man, no doubt.

11   Paul, then, is anxious to visit Rome. It was a natural enough ambition, to work in the capital of the Empire. Besides, Paul had to fight for his cause against opposition; if he could get a footing in the influential church of Rome, it would count for

[1] Olsson. *Papyrusbriefe aus der frühesten Römerzeit*, No. 80: my translation.
[2] Milligan, *Selections from the Greek Papyri*, No. 4: his translation.
[3] Grenfell and Hunt, *Oxyrhynchus Papyri*, No. 1664; their translation.
[4] Milligan, No. 36; his translation.

a good deal. Moreover, he was planning to open work in the west with a mission to Spain, and Rome would be the natural base of operations, as the nearest Christian church of any size. But the position was somewhat delicate. Rome was not one of his churches, and he did not **usually build on foundations laid by others** (xv. 20). He must therefore forestall any suspicion of intruding where he was not wanted. Thus he represents the coming visit as a matter of mutual benefit, **that 12 I may be encouraged by meeting you, I by your faith and you by mine.** At the same time he hints that Rome is, after 13 all, in his sphere of influence; for he is recognised as the apostle of the Gentiles (see i. 5), and Rome is undeniably a Gentile city.

He interprets his commission in fact, in the widest sense. **To Greeks and barbarians, to wise and foolish alike, I owe a duty.** The name **Greek** was applied at this period to anyone who by familiar use of the Greek language made himself a partaker in the Hellenistic culture which was widely diffused over the Roman Empire. The **barbarian** is properly one who speaks an unintelligible language. In 1 Cor. xiv. 11, Paul uses the word in its original signification: ' If I do not know the force of the speech, I shall be a barbarian to the speaker, and the speaker will be a barbarian to me ' (Moffatt translates: **I shall appear to the speaker to be talking gibberish**). Thus, in our period, it was applied to people who did not familiarly use Greek, and so were regarded as uncultured, like the Lycaonians (Acts xiv. 11) and the Maltese (Acts xxviii. 2: **natives** is literally ' barbarians '). Thus **Greeks and barbarians** means practically ' cultured and uncultured.' [1] Similarly, **wise** and **foolish** mean educated and uneducated. Paul, of course, thought of himself as in this sense **Greek** and **wise,** and his Roman correspondents would place themselves in the same category. The time was long past when a Roman playwright could say without prejudice, of his translated play, ' *Plautus vortit barbare.*' Greek language, letters, and fashions now ruled in the capital. Forty years later, when a Latin reaction was setting in, Juvenal wrote in disgust of Rome as *Graeca urbs*. Greek was from the beginning the language of the Roman church. Its earliest sepulchral inscriptions (which are extant from the seventies of the first century) are preponderantly in Greek. Only one Latin epitaph of a Roman bishop is known before the end of the third century. Thus in coming to

---

[1] Even to-day, ' Greece is not a nation: it is an idea,' as a Cypriot Greek once said to me.

Rome Paul would only be continuing the work he had been doing for years among ' Greeks.' His antithesis therefore of ' Greek ' and ' barbarian ' has little real force in this particular setting. It echoes the conviction expressed in Gal. iii. 28, Col. iii. 11, that Christianity transcends distinctions of race, sex, class, and culture. In principle his apostolic commission is as wide as this. Only in this very general sense does the double antithesis here suggest the motive for **my eagerness to preach the Gospel to you in Rome as well.**

THE GOSPEL ACCORDING TO PAUL
(i. 16–xv. 13)

i. 16–17: THE THEME OF THE EPISTLE:
THE RIGHTEOUSNESS OF GOD REVEALED

For I am proud of the Gospel; it is God's saving power 16
for everyone who has faith, for the Jew first and for
the Greek as well. God's righteousness is revealed
in it by faith and for faith—as it is written, *Now by* 17
faith shall the righteous live.

The dominant idea of the introductory section of the letter
has been the **Gospel,** and Paul's commission to preach it. To
expound and defend the Gospel, as he understood it, is the aim
of the epistle as a whole. He is **proud of the Gospel;** it is 16
worth preaching and expounding, for **it is God's saving
power,** as his long experience of missionary work had proved.
And it is **for everyone who has faith**—a maxim which, as he
will show at length, alone justifies its universal proclamation.
There were some who contended that it was only for Jews, or
for such Gentiles as would become Jews by conformity with
the Law. He will admit that the Jews have a certain priority:
it is **for the Jew first.** That is in the first instance a simple
matter of historical fact. The Gospel had been offered to the
Jews by Jesus. And that, Paul thought, indicated that it was
the will of God that they should have the first chance of accepting it (cf. xv. 9). According to the Acts of the Apostles, it was
his own normal practice, on opening work at a fresh place,
to approach the Jews first of all, wherever this was possible.
But it was **for the Greek as well.** The word **Greek** is
here used, not as it was used in verse 14, and as people in
general used it at the time, but as the Jews used it, meaning
adherents of the religions of the Graeco-Roman world, pagans,
or Gentiles.

What, then, is the content of the Gospel? It <u>is this</u>: **God's
righteousness is revealed in it by faith and for faith.** This
is, in fact, the theme of the epistle. It is important to determine
the meaning of the key-words, **righteousness** and **faith.** For

this, some study of the background of Paul's religious ideas and vocabulary will be necessary.

First, then, **God's righteousness.** There has been much discussion whether this is for Paul an attribute of God, or of men as saved by God; whether, that is, the Gospel reveals the fact that God is righteous, or communicates to men a righteousness of character which is divine in origin. No doubt it does both of these things. But the key to the problem is to recognize that in Paul's religious vocabulary the term **righteousness** stands, not only for a moral attribute (as in ordinary English, and Greek, usage), but also (in accordance with Hebrew usage) for an act or activity. When he says, therefore, **God's righteousness is revealed,** he means that a divine act or activity is taking place manifestly within the field of human experience—whereas much of His operation is **inscrutable** and **mysterious** (xi. 33).

Paul's background here as everywhere is the Old Testament. He read that book, as all Jews of the Dispersion did, in the Greek version known as the Septuagint. But he also understood the Hebrew original, and frequently betrays the fact that the meaning of a Greek word used by the Septuagint translators was determined for him by reference to the Hebrew lying behind it. Now the Greek word used here (*dikaiosyne*) is the ordinary term for ' righteousness ' (' the whole of virtue so far as it related to one's fellow-man,' as Aristotle defined it), or ' justice ' (' the science of giving every man his due,' as the Stoics defined it). But the corresponding Hebrew terms (*tsedheq*, *ts'dhaqa*), though they often coincide in meaning with the Greek term, attain that meaning along a different line of development. They are derived from a verb (*tsadhaq*) whose primary meaning seems to be rather ' to be in the right ' than ' to be righteous.' Its causative form (*hitsdiq*), generally translated ' justify,' means, not ' to make righteous,' but ' to put in the right '; and so, very often, ' to vindicate,' or ' give redress to,' a person who has suffered wrong. Thus a judge or ruler is thought of as ' righteous,' not so much because he observes and upholds an abstract standard of justice, as because he vindicates the cause of the wronged; his righteousness is revealed in the ' justification ' of those who are the victims of evil.[1]

In the faith of Judaism the ultimate act of vindication is the

[1] See Skinner's article, ' Righteousness in the Old Testament,' in Hastings' *Dictionary of the Bible.*

work of God, to whom His oppressed people look for deliverance. Thus, in Judges v. 11, the ' righteous acts of the Lord ' (literally, if we keep the usual translation, ' the righteousnesses ') means the acts of vindication or deliverance which Jehovah has wrought for His people, in giving them victory over their enemies.   Dr. Moffatt well translates: **how the Eternal upholds the right.** Here thought is on a rather crude and primitive plane (though not necessarily more crude than many of our prayers in war time).   But, in the developed thought of the prophets, this sense of ' righteousness ' as an act of vindication is still maintained.   Thus we read in Isa. li. 5: ' My righteousness is near, My salvation is gone forth, and Mine arms shall judge the peoples; the isles shall wait for Me, and on My arm shall they trust.'   (Note that Paul similarly brings ' salvation ' and ' righteousness ' together.)   Here Dr. Moffatt renders:

> *Swift and soon is My redress,*
> *My victory is dawning;*
> *Mine arms shall inflict judgment on the peoples,*
> *but the sea-coasts shall hope in Me.*

Again, in Isa. xlvi. 13: ' I bring near My righteousness, it shall not be far off, and My salvation shall not tarry, and I will give salvation in Zion, and My glory unto Israel ' (R.V.*m*.). Here Dr. Moffatt boldly renders:

> *I bring My triumph near, right near,*
> *My victory is hastening;*
> *I will grant Sion victory,*
> *and Israel the glory that is Mine.*

The word **triumph** does bring out one side of the meaning; but it is not a complete translation; for the Hebrew word always carries with it the idea of the victory of *right*.   Moreover, the promise of deliverance is addressed to those ' who know righteousness, the people in whose hearts is My law ' (Isa. li. 7. Moffatt: **ye who care for the good cause ... who lay My laws to heart**).   Here ' righteousness ' approaches the ordinary connotation of the word as we use it; yet in the previous verse it was used in the sense of ' vindication ': the transition from ' the good cause ' to ' the good cause vindicated ' is almost imperceptible in the Hebrew.   Similarly, in order to share in the promised redress the wicked must forsake his ways and the unrighteous man his thoughts, and return unto the Lord (Isa. lv. 7).   The vindication of right involves a real righteousness of the people on whose behalf it is wrought. Thus the 'righteousness,' or act of redress, has for its ultimate issue, not only a people delivered from wrongful oppression, but a people delivered from their own sin, a 'righteous' people in our sense. But always 'righteousness' is not primarily an attribute of God or of His people, but an activity whereby the right is asserted in the deliverance of man from the power of evil. It is in this sense that the same prophet calls Jehovah 'a just [righteous] God and a Saviour' (xlv. 21), and declares that 'in the Lord shall all the seed of Israel be justified [the verb *tsadhaq*], and shall glory': i.e. they shall be delivered from the power of evil. In all probability the familiar beatitude, 'Blessed are they which do hunger and thirst after righteousness,' contains the same meaning. For an English reader, as for a Greek reader, of the Gospels, that suggests 'those who ardently desire to be good'; but, in accordance with Old Testament usage, the original Aramaic beatitude would naturally mean 'Blessed are they who ardently desire the vindication of right, the triumph of the good cause'—the same people, in fact, who are referred to in Luke xviii. 7: **Will not God see justice done to His elect who cry to Him by day and night ?**

Now, in the prevailing thought of Judaism in the two or three centuries before Christ, it was assumed that in this present age the cause of right is in eclipse. Although 'the Most High ruleth in the kingdom of men' (Dan. iv. 17), yet for reasons best known to Himself He permits evil powers to hold sway. But in the good time coming—'the Age to Come'—the arm of the Lord would be bared for the discomfiture of evil and the establishment of good. Then His 'righteousness' would be revealed. That was where Paul stood as a Pharisee. The Gospel which he proclaims as a preacher of Christianity is that 'the righteousness of God *is* revealed.' The Age to Come *has* come, and the great vindication of right is taking place before our eyes. The present tense of the verb is all-important: it would be even better rendered 'the righteousness of God *is being* revealed,' for the Greek present is primarily a tense of continuous action. The revelation, as we shall see, is not yet complete; but it is real and even now in process.

This is the theme which is developed in the course of the epistle. First, the need for such a revelation is displayed in a sombre picture of the world under the dominance of sin, bringing its terrible retribution. This is not yet the revelation of righteousness, though it is preparatory to it. Next we have the righteousness of God displayed in ' justifying ' His people (cf. Isa. xlv. 25), i.e. in putting them in the right before Him (iii. 21–iv. 25). Then it is displayed in the ' salvation ' of men (cf. Isa. xlvi. 13, li. 5) from the power and dominance of sin (v.–viii.). Then, after an excursus which seeks to justify the ways of God with men, we have, finally, the revelation of His righteousness in the living of a good life by the people He has saved (xii.–xv.; cf. Isa. li. 7, lv. 7). Thus Paul finds in the Gospel of Christ the answer of history to the aspirations of the prophets after a decisive assertion and vindication of right against all evil in the world of men. The life and death of Jesus Christ, His resurrection, and the creation of the Church through His Spirit, constitute a decisive Act of God, an objective revelation of His righteousness.

The meaning, therefore, of the phrase, **God's righteousness is revealed,** might be given by some such paraphrase as this: ' God is now seen to be vindicating the right, redressing wrong, and delivering men from the power of evil.'

So much, then, for the term **righteousness** as used in Paul's statement of his theme. We have now to consider the term faith. The clause **by faith and for faith** is not very clear. Literally it is ' from faith to faith.' Commentators have tried various more or less subtle interpretations, but the probability is that we have no more than a rhetorical device to give emphasis to the idea of faith. There is a very similar repetition in 2 Cor. ii. 16: **to the one a deadly fragrance that makes for death, to the other a vital fragrance that makes for life** (literally, ' a fragrance from death to death . . . from life to life '). It would be difficult to find anything more than rhetorical emphasis in such expressions. So here the idea is simply that the revelation of God's righteousness is a matter of faith ' from start to finish,' as we say. That is the important thing for Paul. To corroborate it he quotes, after his manner, from the Old Testament: **Now by faith shall the righteous live** (Hab. ii. 4). For Habakkuk, ' faith ' meant faithfulness, fidelity. The righteous would preserve his life, in the troubles surrounding him, by sheer character—by honesty, integrity, trustworthiness. Whether the prophet meant that he would literally escape threatening destruction, or that, in spite of the worst that might happen, he would ' save his soul,' we need not stop to inquire. In any case, Paul understood the word ' faith ' differently.

The clue to his meaning is to be found where he quotes the same passage in Gal. iii. 11. It is worth while to follow the thought in that context. Paul has appealed to the Galatians to say whether the Christian experience they have had came to them **because you do what the law commands, or because you believe the Gospel message** (literally, ' from works of the Law, or from faith in the message '). Thus ' faith ' is something which can be contrasted with the acquisition of merit by compliance with a code of commandments. He goes on: **It is as with Abraham; he had faith in God and that was counted to him as righteousness.** Thus faith is the quality exemplified by Abraham. What Abraham's faith was, Paul discusses at length in Rom. iv., and he arrives at the conclusion that Abraham **gave glory to God and felt convinced that He was able to do what He had promised.** With this definition in mind, we may return to Galatians. Abraham was promised, Paul goes on, that in him all nations should be blessed. That cannot have meant that they would be blessed by the Law, for the Law brings a curse upon those who disobey it. It is only those who fulfil the impossible condition of perfect obedience to every command who can be saved through the Law: **he who performs these things shall live by them.** No one however does; so Paul held. What then? How can a man ' live '? **The just shall live by faith.** Paul therefore took the passage from Habakkuk to mean that, though it was impossible to gain life by obeying the Law, it was possible to do so by simple reliance on God, in the conviction that He is able to give the blessing He has promised to men—and it is implied that He can be trusted to do so, for ' God is trustworthy ' (1 Cor. i. 9; cf. 1 Cor. x. 13; 1 Thess. v. 24).

We may get further light on Paul's thought from 2 Cor. iii. 4–5 (where a literal translation will serve our purpose better than Dr. Moffatt's paraphrase): ' Such confidence we have in God through Christ. It is not as though we were self-sufficient, in the sense of reckoning that anything [we do] comes from ourselves: our sufficiency comes from God, who has made us sufficient as ministers of a new covenant.' The play upon the word ' sufficient ' here is an allusion to the ancient divine name Shaddai, of unknown origin, which Paul, in common with many Jewish scholars of his time, believed to mean etymologically ' He who suffices,' i.e. ' the All-sufficient.' Now, God was revealed to Abraham, we are told (Gen. xvii. 1; Exod. vi. 3), as El Shaddai (' God Almighty,' E.V., or, as the Greek trans-

FAITH IS UTTER RELIANCE on
the SUFFICIENCY OF GOD

lation of Aquila has it, ' God the All-sufficient '). Thus for
Paul the faith of Abraham was the response to the revelation
of God as the All-sufficient.

Putting all this together, we may say that for Paul faith is
that attitude in which, acknowledging our complete insufficiency
for any of the high ends of life, we rely utterly on the sufficiency
of God. It is to cease from all assertion of the self, even by way
of effort after righteousness, and to make room for the divine
initiative. By such faith a man enters into life, in every sense
in which that phrase can be used (and, as we shall see, Paul
uses it in a wide range of meaning). For the sake of clearness
I would add that it does not mean (as Habakkuk meant) fidelity
or loyalty to God; for that might be thought of as in itself
meritorious, and Paul would not have thought himself ' sufficient ' for such a thing, until through simple faith he had received
strength from God. Nor does it mean belief in a proposition,
though doubtless intellectual beliefs are involved when we come
to think it out. It is an act which is the negation of all activity,
a moment of passivity out of which the strength for action comes,
because in it God acts.

We may pause to observe that this is in harmony with the
use of the word *faith* in the Gospels. The fundamental statement is in Mark xi. 22–24: **Have faith in God! I tell you
truly, whoever says to this hill, ' Take and throw yourself
into the sea '** [cf. 1 Cor. xiii. 2], **and has not a doubt in his
mind, but believes that what he says will happen** [literally,
' is happening '], **he will have it done. So I tell you, whatever you pray and ask for, believe you have got it, and
you shall have it.** It is in this sense that Jesus says to Jairus,
in the presence of death, **' Have no fear; only believe '**
(Mark v. 36), and to the Twelve, terrified by the storm, **' Why
are you afraid like this ? Have you no faith yet ? '** (Mark
iv. 40), and to the father of a sick boy, **' Anything can be done
for one who believes '** (Mark ix. 23)—which is the correlative
of Mark x. 27: **Anything is possible for God.** In many
cases, indeed, where Jesus healed the sick, the ' faith ' they had
took the form of a simple trust in Him personally; but a reference to the fundamental text, Mark xi. 22–24, shows that He
accepted this as faith in God. It was the conviction that God
through His Messiah (cf. Matt. xi. 4–6, xii. 28) **was able to do
what He had promised** through the prophets. It is true
that Jesus in the Gospels characteristically contrasts faith with

fear, and not, like Paul, with ' works ': yet the contrast of faith with works is already implicit in such passages as Matt. xxi. 31-32, Luke xviii. 9-14.

The word **faith** occurs scores of times in the writings of Paul: it is one of the commonest terms in his vocabulary. But very seldom does he express the Object of faith. When he does so, it is indifferently ' faith towards God ' (1 Thess. i. 8) or ' faith towards Christ ' (Col. ii. 5). He could however use the latter expression only because it was for him tantamount to the former. There is no ultimate value in any religious attitude, unless it is directed towards the one and only God. ' God is trustworthy ' (1 Cor. i. 9, x. 13, 1 Thess. v. 24) is the fundamental postulate, to which our faith is the response. But, for Paul, the conditions under which such faith could be exercised are provided in Christ, and the God whose trustworthiness provokes our trust is the God who **has shone in my heart to illuminate men with the knowledge of God's glory in the face of Jesus Christ** (2 Cor. iv. 6). To say, as is sometimes said, that faith is for Paul the acceptance of the ' claims ' of Jesus Christ, is to get the whole thing out of focus. Whatever inward debates he may have had about the claims of Jesus before his conversion, he never alludes to them, and he never suggests that to become a Christian means to pass from faith in the One God to faith in Christ. The moment in which he ' saw Christ ' was the moment in which he found God and got faith in Him. That was how he felt. Of course, as a Jew he would have said that he had faith, meaning by that what other rabbis meant by it, which so far as we can gather from Jewish writings is, broadly, loyal attachment to the religion of Israel. The difference his conversion made, as he saw it, was not that his faith, formerly given to God, was now given to Christ, but that his faith in God was now for the first time the real thing—it was the faith of Abraham, as he would have said—a radical trust in God the All-sufficient, leaving no place for human merit of any kind. No doubt faith in the rabbinic sense included the belief that God would fulfil His promises, but always with the implied condition that the Law should be kept. What distress of mind this thought could bring to one who felt, with Paul, the impossibility of keeping the Law in its entirety, we can read in the Apocalypse of Ezra (2 Esdras in the Apocrypha). ' What profit is it unto us,' the writer asks, ' if there be promised us an immortal life, whereas we have done the works that bring death? '

(2 Esd. vii. 49). He speaks, indeed, of a man being saved ' by his works or by faith whereby he hath believed ' (ix. 7), and of God preserving ' such as have works and faith toward the Almighty ' (xiii. 23); but this ' faith ' is shown by other passages to be no other than loyalty to God as shown in faithful keeping of the Law. Thus it brings no comfort or peace of mind to the troubled seer: ' we that have received the Law shall perish by sin, and our heart also which received it ' (ix. 36). This apocalypse is nearer than any Jewish writing known to me, to Paul's pre-Christian outlook as we deduce it from his epistles. With such passages in mind—and, indeed, the whole discussion (2 Esd. iii.-x.)—we can understand why, in the compressed statement of this verse, Paul assumes that the righteousness of God can be fully revealed only if a way is found by which a man can live. The prophet declared that **by faith shall the righteous live,** and the revelation of righteousness here spoken of is a revelation **by faith and for faith,** and therefore fulfils the condition implied. To set forth all that this means is the purpose of the epistle.

I. THE UNIVERSAL SWAY OF SIN
AND RETRIBUTION

(i. 18–iii. 20)

The first great section of the epistle is preliminary to the working out of the main theme. The adversative conjunction but in i. 18 shows that the revelation of God's **anger** is contrasted, and not identified, with the revelation of His righteousness.

In contemporary Jewish thought the expected vindication of God's people was to be accompanied by a fearful judgment on the wicked. To crude minds, the wicked were simply the enemies of Israel, or pagans in general. More serious thinkers realized that Israelites who, though they possessed the Law, did not obey it were equally subject to the judgment. For some of them, like the author of 2 Esdras, the number of those who ' have works and faith towards the Almighty,' and so can count on being saved, was almost infinitesimally small. Others thought that the deficient virtue of Israelites might be helped out by the merits of the Fathers. But the common assumption was that some at least of the Chosen People would escape the judgment and share the blessings of the Coming Age because they deserved it and had a claim to it. Paul sets himself to destroy this assumption. Believing that the New Age has already dawned, he points to observable facts as indicating the character of the judgment. In the light of these facts it is indeed clear enough that the pagan world is sunk in iniquity and is suffering the retribution for it. But equally the facts do not give the slightest ground for supposing that the Jews are in any better position. If the author of 2 Esdras could find only a miserable handful of Israelites who really kept the Law, Paul can find none. If hypothetically any such could be found, they would be on the same level as Gentiles who live up to the standards of natural ethics; and a good pagan has more chance than a bad Jew.

Paul should not be understood as propounding a rigid theory of the total depravity of human nature. What he is mainly concerned to show is that attachment to the particular religious institutions of Judaism, divinely inspired though they are, gives no sufficient or exclusive claim to the divine favour. The moral universe is one; good is good and evil is evil, among Jews and Gentiles alike. The Law, rightly understood, gives a knowledge of good and evil. But in doing so it reveals a standard of goodness beyond human attainment. If salvation went by merit, then nothing but the attainment of this absolute standard would count, and no one would have any hope. That some Jews and some Gentiles attain a respectable standard is no doubt true, but in the last resort irrelevant. The blessing of God must be, not a recognition of goodness achieved, but a means of achieving it.

i. 18–32: SIN AND RETRIBUTION
IN THE PAGAN WORLD

18 But God's anger is revealed from heaven against all the impiety and wickedness of those who hinder the
19 Truth by their wickedness. For whatever is to be
20 known of God is plain to them; God Himself has made it plain—for ever since the world was created, His invisible nature, His everlasting power and divine being, have been quite perceptible in what
21 He has made. So they have no excuse. Though they

knew God, they have not glorified Him as God nor
given thanks to Him; they have turned to futile 22
speculations till their ignorant minds grew dark.
They claimed to be wise, but they have become fools; 23
they have *exchanged the glory of* the immortal *God for the
semblance* of the likeness of mortal man, of birds, of
quadrupeds, and of reptiles. So God has given them 24
up, in their heart's lust, to sexual vice, to the dis-
honouring of their own bodies,—since they have ex- 25
changed the truth of God for an untruth, worshipping
and serving the creature rather than the Creator
who is blessed for ever: Amen. That is why God 26
has given them up to vile passions; their women
have exchanged the natural function of sex for what 27
is unnatural, and in the same way the males have
abandoned the natural use of women and flamed
out in lust for one another, men perpetrating shame-
less acts with their own sex and getting in their own
persons the due recompense of their perversity. 28
Yes, as they disdained to acknowledge God any
longer, God has given them up to a reprobate instinct,
for the perpetration of what is improper, till they 29
are filled with all manner of wickedness, depravity,
lust, and viciousness, filled to the brim with envy, 30
murder, quarrels, intrigues, and malignity—slan-
derers, defamers, loathed by God, outrageous,
haughty, boastful, inventive in evil, disobedient to
parents, devoid of conscience, false to their word, 31-
callous, merciless; though they know God's decree   32
that people who practise such vice deserve death,
they not only do it themselves but applaud those who
practise it.

But God's anger is revealed from heaven.   The tense 18
again is the continuous present. A process is going on before
our eyes—the revelation of the Wrath of God. I should prefer
to keep the old translation here, because such an archaic phrase
suits a thoroughly archaic idea.   To render it into the terms
of ordinary intercourse is to bring the idea into a sphere to which
it does not belong.   The Greek word (*orgé*) does, indeed, mean
' anger '; but **God's anger** suggests the simple anthropo-
morphic idea that God is angry with men, and Paul's idea is not
so simple.

To begin with, Paul never uses the verb, ' to be angry,' with God as subject. Why not? If he speaks of ' the love of God ' he also says plainly that ' God loved us ' (2 Thess. ii. 16; Eph. ii. 4) and that we are ' loved by God ' (1 Thess. i. 4; Col. iii. 12); if he speaks of ' the grace of God,' he also says that ' God dealt graciously with us '—the noun *charis*, the verb *charizesthai* (Col. iii. 13); if he speaks of ' the faithfulness of God ' (Rom. iii. 3), he also says that ' God is faithful ' (1 Cor. i. 9, x. 13, 1 Thess. v. 24). Thus we take love, grace, and faithfulness, without hesitation, as describing—anthropomorphically, no doubt, in a sense—the personal attitude of God to men. The fact that God is never made the subject of the verb ' to be angry ' should make us hesitate to conclude that Paul thought of God's **anger** in the same way.

Again, while Paul has frequent occasion to make use of the theological concept of ' wrath,' there are only three places where he uses the expression ' the Wrath of God ': here, in Col. iii. 6, and in the parallel passage, Eph. v. 6. In Rom. ix. 22 it is not certain that the pronoun **his,** which occurs once only in the Greek, belongs to **anger** as well as to **might.** On the other hand, he constantly uses ' wrath,' or ' the Wrath ' in a curiously impersonal way. Thus we have ' children of wrath ' (Eph. ii. 3), ' vessels of wrath ' (Rom. ix. 22), ' day of wrath ' (Rom. ii. 5), ' the wrath to come ' (1 Thess. i. 10). ' The Law works wrath ' (Rom. iv. 15).[1] If we study other very numerous passages (e.g. in this epistle, v. 3, vii. 8, 13, etc.) where Paul uses the word here rendered ' works ' (or **produces**), it seems unnatural to understand Rom. iv. 15 to mean ' Law gives effect to the anger of God.' Again, there are several passages where ' the Wrath ' is used absolutely, almost as a proper noun, rightly represented by a capital letter in English: 1 Thess. ii. 16; Rom. v. 9, xii. 19, xiii. 5, and especially Rom. iii. 5, where Moffatt translates: **that it is unfair of God to inflict His anger on us,** but the literal translation is ' that God is unjust who brings upon [men] the Wrath.' I can find no place in Greek literature where the verb (*epipherein*) means to vent one's passions upon a person: it is frequently used with such direct objects as ' war,' ' an accusation,' ' punishment,' or the like. It would therefore be in place here if to Paul ' the Wrath ' meant, not a

---

[1] Note here that in Moffatt's translation, **what the Law produces is the Wrath, not the promise of God,** the words **not the promise of God,** which give the impression that both wrath and promise are in the same sense God's, are inserted by the translator, and have no equivalent in the Greek.

certain feeling or attitude of God towards us, but some process
or effect in the realm of objective facts.

Is there, then, any reason to suppose that a word which
originally meant, beyond doubt, the passion of anger could
come to have such a peculiar extension of meaning? To answer
this question we must go a long way back in the history of
religion. Professor Rudolf Otto, in his book *Das Heilige* (Eng.
trans., *The Idea of the Holy*), has done much to clarify our thought
upon the primitive basis of religious emotion and religious ideas.
He finds the raw material of religion in the sense of the ' numinous '—a shuddering awe before the *mysterium tremendum et
fascinans* which meets man in the midst of his experience of the
world. The negative side of this feeling, where it is sheer
desperate terror, is for the primitive evoked largely by such
things as thunder and earthquake, regarded, of course, not as
' natural phenomena ' (if anything is such for the primitive),
but as manifestations of the Mystery, in its menacing or destruc-
tive form. When religion reaches the point of personifying the
objects of numinous feeling, such phenomena are explained on
the analogy of the irrational passion of an angry man: they are
the anger of the gods.

Thus in the oldest parts of the Old Testament the anger of
Jehovah displays itself in thunder, earthquake, pestilence, and
the like. The prophets took up this idea, but rationalized it
by teaching that disaster is not an outbreak of irresponsible
anger, but an expression of the outraged justice of God. There
is no disaster but deserved disaster. Thus ' the Wrath of God '
is taken out of the sphere of the purely mysterious, and brought
into the sphere of cause and effect: sin is the cause, disaster
the effect. At the same time they taught that Jehovah was
loving and merciful, and desirous of saving His people from
disaster, by saving them from sin which is the cause of disaster.
Of course they did not rationalize away the ' numinous ' sense
of the Wrath of God, but they brought into relief the personal
relation of love and mercy in which God stands towards His
people, and which transcends wrath. While there is a tension,
not wholly resolved, between the wrath and the mercy of God,
it would be fair to say that in speaking of wrath and judgment
the prophets and psalmists have their minds mainly on events,
actual or expected, conceived as the inevitable results of sin;
and when they speak of mercy they are thinking mainly of the
personal relation between God and His people. Wrath is the
effect of human sin: mercy is not the effect of human goodness,

but is inherent in the character of God. When they speak of His righteousness, as we have seen, they find it consummated in a merciful deliverance of His people from the power and oppression of sin—in fact, from ' the Wrath.'

Thus the way is open for a further development in which anger as an attitude of God to men disappears, and His love and mercy become all-embracing. This is, as I believe, the purport of the teaching of Jesus, with its emphasis on limitless forgiveness and on God's fatherly kindness to ' the unthankful and evil.' In substance, Paul agrees with this, teaching that God loved us while we were yet sinners (Rom. v. 8) and that it is His kindness that leads us to repentance (Rom. ii. 4). But he retains the concept of ' the Wrath of God ' (which does not appear in the teaching of Jesus, unless we press certain features of the parables in an illegitimate manner: to find the character of God exhibited in the King who destroys his enemies is as illegitimate as to find it in the attitude of the Unjust Judge); he retains it, not to describe the attitude of God to man, but to describe an inevitable process of cause and effect in a moral universe, as we shall find in the verses which now follow.

It is to be noted that, if this sketch of the history of the idea is right, there is something impersonal about ' the Wrath of God ' from the beginning, and something incapable of being wholly personalized in the development of religious ideas. It is only to a God not yet fully conceived in terms of moral personality that the primitive numinous terror can be directed. The idea of an angry God is a first attempt to rationalize the shuddering awe which men feel before the incalculable possibilities of appalling disaster inherent in life, but it is an attempt which breaks down as the rational element in religion advances. In the long run we cannot think with full consistency of God in terms of the highest human ideals of personality and yet attribute to Him the irrational passion of anger.

18   Paul, then, calls upon his readers to observe the actual Nemesis or retribution for sin as exhibited in the facts of the world before them. ' The Wrath of God ' is being revealed **against all the impiety and wickedness of those who hinder the Truth by their wickedness.** In speaking of **those who hinder the Truth** he has in mind (as the following verses show) in the first place the pagan world; and the expression may refer primarily to the opposition offered by pagans to the spread of the truth of the Gospel. But behind this lies a

wider reference. The impiety and wickedness of men is hinder-
ing the truth about the nature of God, which is native to the
human mind, from having its due effect in the life of human
society at large. There is no other passage where Paul so
explicitly recognizes ' natural religion ' as a fundamental trait
of human nature. **Whatever is to be known of God is plain** 19-
to them; His invisible nature, His everlasting power and   20
divine being, have been made quite perceptible in what
He has made. That is to say, the created universe offers
sufficient evidence of its ' divine Original.' ' I had rather,'
wrote Francis Bacon, ' believe all the fables in the Legend, and
the Talmud, and the Alcoran, than that this universal frame is
without a mind. And therefore God never wrought miracles to
convince atheism, because His ordinary works convince it.' And
the natural philosophy of the present age, if we may believe
some of its most eminent exponents, does not discourage us
from seeing in the universe something like a ' great thought ' of
a mind beyond our own.

Paganism, therefore, in Paul's judgment, has not the excuse
of ignorance. The truth is there, but the impiety and wickedness of men hinder it. It is not a case of intellectual error at
bottom, but of moral obliquity. **Though they knew God,**
they have not glorified Him as God, nor given thanks to 21
Him. That is, their attitude to life and the world is an irreligious one, though the impulse to religion was present in the
very *data* of life and the world.

They have turned to futile speculations till their ignor-
ant minds grew dark. This must not be taken as a deliberate
judgment on the teaching of Greek philosophy in its higher
forms. With this, Paul had no direct acquaintance. What he
saw plainly was that, in practice, philosophy (as popularly understood) easily came to terms with the grossest forms of superstition and immorality; and so it did: just as it is a grave count
against the lofty philosophy of Hinduism that it utters no
effective protest against the most degrading practices of popular
religion in India to-day. Platonists and Stoics, and even
Epicureans, might in their esoteric circles cultivate the most
sublime speculations about the nature of the Divine, but at
every turn the traveller in the Graeco-Roman world met with
frank idolatry and its moral accompaniments. This was what 22
Paul saw. The pagans, heirs of all the achievements of Greek
thought, **claimed to be wise, but they have become fools:**
they have exchanged the glory of the immortal God for

the semblance of the likeness of mortal man, of quad-rupeds, and of reptiles. That is the head and front of their offending. To the stern monotheism of the Jew, idolatry is the root of all evil. It is the characteristic manifestation of the **impiety and wickedness** by which men **hinder the Truth.** As a matter of fact, Paul would have found support in principle for his condemnation of idolatry from many of the best minds in paganism itself. There was a good deal of propaganda for monotheism at the time, quite apart from Christianity and Judaism (see, for example, E. Norden's *Agnostos Theos*). But the fact remains that this was not effective in pagan society, either in Paul's time or down to the extinction of paganism in the Roman Empire. The subtle Greek mind found a place in practice for that which it condemned in principle. Nevertheless, there was a sufficiently widespread sense of the religious in-adequacy of idolatry for a rigid monotheist to awake a response in the minds of his hearers when he stigmatized idolatry as **impiety and wickedness,** and that gave a strength to Paul's position.

It is disputed among authorities on the comparative history of religions whether or not, in point of fact, idolatrous poly-theism is a degeneration from an original monotheism of some kind; but at least there is a surprising amount of evidence that among very many peoples, not only in the higher civiliza-tions of India and China, but in the barbarisms of Central Africa and Australia, a belief in some kind of Creator-Spirit (the *Urheber-Gott*) subsists along with the superstitious cults of gods or demons, and often with a more or less obscure sense that this belief belongs to a superior, or a more ancient, order.[1]

24-32 We now come to the main point, that this **impiety** and **wickedness** brings with it its own retribution; and this retri-bution is here and now being revealed. Paul does not approach the matter, in the manner of an Old Testament prophet, by threatening the prosperous, godless Empire (like Assyria and Babylon) with coming disasters. As we shall presently see, he does hold in reserve the terrors of an actual Day of Judgment. But, in essence, the retribution of sin is already at work, in the moral rottenness of pagan society. The vices of paganism, with their natural and inevitable concomitants, are themselves the Nemesis of the fundamental error of taking up an irreligious attitude to life, in spite of the knowledge of God which is native

[1] See, for example, the evidence given in N. Söderblom, *Das Werden des Gottes-glaubens*.

to the human mind. To enforce his point he paints a picture of pagan society which is unrelieved darkness. To obtain a complete picture, in its proper *chiaroscuro*, we must correct the present description from what is said in ii. 14-15. But the facts to which he here calls attention are sufficiently attested by the satirists of the imperial period.

The opinion that the vices of paganism are the consequence of idolatry is a commonplace of Jewish propaganda of the time. We find it, not only in rabbinical teaching, but notably in the Book of Wisdom, written in Greek by a Jew of Egypt, probably not very long before the date of this epistle. There is a long passage, chaps. xiii.-xiv., dealing with this subject. Paul follows its line of thought so closely that our present passage might be taken for a brief summary of it.

When Paul is writing as a moralist, and has occasion to deal with the vices, he ordinarily follows a classification which is usual in popular moralists of the time. They were accustomed to group vices as (*a*) sensual, and (*b*) anti-social. That Paul was familiar with this classification is clear from his lists of vices in 1 Cor. v. 10-11; 2 Cor. xii. 20-21; Gal. v. 19-21; Eph. v. 3-5; Col. iii. 5, 8. It is echoed in brief in Rom. xiii. 13. It is probable that he is following it here, though a measure of uncertainty about the precise translation of one or two of his terms leaves it not quite clear. In particular, the term which Moffatt has rendered **lust** occurs among the anti-social group. This word, *pleonexia*, has a long history in Greek ethical writing. Its general connotation is that of ruthless, aggressive self-assertion. In Plato, for example, it is the characteristic vice of the tyrant; and all through Greek literature it describes the man who will pursue his own interests with complete disregard for the rights of others and for all considerations of humanity. Such ruthless self-assertion may show itself in the sphere of sexual relations, and so the term *pleonexia* is found in association with the sexual vices. But it is never simply **lust,** which is the proper equivalent for a different Greek word (*epithymia*) which occurs in verse 24 above. On the other hand, in the Greek moralists it constantly stands at the head of the class of anti-social sins. Probably Paul here uses it in this sense. I should render the first four terms in verse 29 (in accordance with their usage in the Greek moralists): 'injustice, criminality, ruthless self-assertion, malice.'

We have then before us the usual two classes: sensual vices

in 24-27, anti-social vices in 29-31. The general heading of
the second class, **that which is improper,** is the technical
term employed by Stoic moralists. The emphasis, for Paul's
present purpose, falls upon the first class. He sees the most
signal proof of the moral rottenness of pagan civilization in the
27 prevalence of homo-sexual perversion, with its disastrous consequences—for those who practise it are **getting in their own
persons the due recompense of their perversity.** Ancient
literature is full of evidence to corroborate Paul's statements.
This is for him the outstanding manifestation of the retribution
for the **impiety and wickedness of those who hinder the
Truth.**

It is, however, all of a piece with the phenomena of social
disintegration described in verses 29-31. The memories of
civil strife were only a generation old when Paul was a boy at
Tarsus. A fresh outbreak of **envy, murder, quarrels, intrigues, and malignity** came within a decade of Paul's
writing, with the War of the Four Emperors, and widespread
provincial revolt. Good citizens had reason to fear the forces
of disruption working beneath the surface of the Roman order.
The secret force of lawlessness, as Paul had written a few
years earlier (2 Thess. ii. 7), **is at work already.** All this he
saw as the necessary consequence, and therefore the just retribution, for the apostasy of the human heart from God. What
would he have said of the world-wide peril of social disruption
which confronts us to-day?

The count against pagan society is brought to a sharp point
32 in the closing verse: **though they know God's decree** [cf. ii.
14-15] **that people who practise such vice** [he still has his
mind mainly upon the unnatural vices of 24-27] **deserve
death, they not only do it themselves, but applaud those
who practise it.** This precisely hits off the fatal ambiguity of
the moral judgment of Graeco-Roman civilization. That the
ordinary man of the time had a bad conscience about such
practices is hardly doubtful, and the maxim of Stoicism, that
what is ' contrary to nature ' is evil, was widely accepted. But
public opinion acquiesced in, condoned, or even, as Paul says,
applauded practices which it often surrounded with an un-
wholesome sentimentality. This is the sign, says Paul, of a
' reprobate reason ' (for the rendering instinct is uncalled for:
the Greek word is the one regularly used by philosophers as
well as by ordinary writers for the rational element in personality). The reason, which is ' the candle of the Lord in the

'soul of man,' has lost its power of judgment. This is the Nemesis of sin: the revelation of ' the Wrath.'

All through this passage the disastrous progress of evil in society is presented as a natural process of cause and effect, and not as the direct act of God. God gave men at the first a revelation of His **everlasting power and divine being,** through His works in creation. It was by men's own act that they refused to worship Him and so fell under the power of evil; that their instincts became perverted and their reason reprobate. It is a wholly natural consequence that they are **getting in their own persons the due recompense of their perversity;** for such practices inherently **deserve death.** The act of God is no more than an abstention from interference with their free choice and its consequences. **God has given them** 28 **up in their heart's lust to sexual vice. . . . God has given** 26 **them up to vile passions. . . . God has given them up to** 28 **a reprobate** reason. **It is an awful thing,** says the Epistle to the Hebrews (x. 31) **to fall into the hands of the living God.** Paul, with a finer instinct, sees that the really awful thing is to fall out of His hands, and to be left to oneself in a world where the choice of evil brings its own moral retribution. He has therefore succeeded in dissociating the fact of retribution from any idea of an angry God visiting His displeasure upon sinful men, even though he retains the old expression ' the Wrath of God.' The whole process is a part of the divine government of the universe, and in this sense it is God who ' brings the Wrath upon men ' (as in iii. 5), but it is not thought of as the direct expression of God's attitude to men. Thus the way is left clear for maintaining without paradox, not only that His attitude to ' vessels of wrath ' is one of ' longsuffering ' (ix. 22), but that He actually loves men in their sins, and through Christ saves them from the Wrath (v. 8-10. Note that, in this passage, Moffatt translates, not ' His anger,' but **' the Wrath,'** though the Greek word is the same, feeling, no doubt, that it is too paradoxical to say that God loves sinners and saves them from His own anger).

ii. 1–iii. 20: SIN AND RETRIBUTION
IN THE JEWISH WORLD

So far, Paul has been castigating the vices of paganism. We seem to overhear the tones of his preaching style, when he **argued about morality, self-mastery, and the future judgment** (Acts xxiv. 25). He must have delivered many such sermons to mixed audiences up and down Greece and Asia Minor; and down to this point he no doubt won the enthusiastic applause of his Jewish hearers. Now he turns upon them—' Yes; you agree with all that I say about the pagans; but—are you any better?' It reminds us of Amos. He began, ' **After crime upon crime of Damascus . . . of Gaza . . . of the Ammonites . . . of Moab, I will not relent** ' (loud applause)—and then, ' **After crime upon crime of Israel, I will not relent. . . . You alone of all men have I cared for; therefore I will punish you for your misdeeds . . . . What are you more than Ethiopians, O Israelites? the Eternal asks** ' (Amos i. 3–ii. 16, iii. 2, ix. 7). Long experience had taught Paul what an effective approach this was to the conclusion he wished to drive home: **No distinctions are drawn: all have sinned** (Rom. iii. 22–23).

From this point the sermon takes the form of a dialogue with an imaginary Jewish hearer, in which Paul follows the practice of contemporary popular preachers of Stoicism, whom he had doubtless heard in the market-place of Tarsus or other towns (see introductory note to chaps. ix.–xi.). It is important to bear in mind that, all through this passage, Paul is speaking as a good Jew, and meeting his Jewish hearers on their own ground. What he says about the Law and its observance, and about judgment on the basis of the Law, applies to men outside the sphere of the Gospel. It leads up to the conclusion that on Jewish presuppositions there is no more hope of salvation for the Jew than for the Gentile whom he condemns. At that point the Gospel comes in (see iii. 23–30).

ii. 1–16: *The Impartiality of the Law of Retribution*

ii.
1 **Therefore you are inexcusable, whoever you are, if you pose as a judge, for in judging another you condemn yourself; you, the judge, do the very same things**

yourself. 'We know the doom of God falls justly 2
upon those who practise such vices.' Very well;
and do you imagine you will escape God's doom, 3
O man, you who judge those who practise such vices
and do the same yourself ? Or are you slighting all 4
His wealth of kindness, forbearance, and patience ?
Do you not know His kindness is meant to make
you repent ? In your stubbornness and impenitence 5
of heart you are simply storing up anger for yourself
on the Day of anger, when the just doom of God is
revealed. For *He will render to everyone according to what he
has done,* eternal life to those who by patiently doing 6
good aim at glory, honour, and immortality, but 7
anger and wrath to those who are wilful, who disobey 8
the Truth and obey wickedness—anguish and calamity for every human soul that perpetrates evil, for 9
the Jew first and for the Greek as well, but glory,
honour, and peace for everyone who does good, for 10
the Jew first and for the Greek as well. There is no 11
partiality about God.

All who sin outside the Law will perish outside
the Law, and all who sin under the Law will be 12
condemned by the Law.
For it is not the hearers of the Law who are just in
the eyes of God, it is those who obey the Law who 13
will be acquitted, on the day when God judges the
secret things of men, as my Gospel holds, by Jesus 16
Christ. When Gentiles who have no law obey 14
instinctively the Law's requirements, they are a law
to themselves, even though they have no law they
exhibit the effect of the Law written on their hearts, 15
their conscience bears them witness, as their moral
convictions accuse or it may be defend them.)*

The person who **poses as a judge** is of course the Jew who 1
is scandalized by the sinfulness of idolatry, as becomes clear
in the development of the argument. His judgment on the
pagan world recoils on himself. The root of all the evil that
he condemns among pagans is unfaithfulness to the knowledge
of truth that they possess. But unfaithfulness to one's know-

* Verse 16 is the sequel to the first clause of verse 14. The rest of verse 14 and
the whole of verse 15 form a short paragraph which is either a marginal note or an
awkward insertion. To preserve the sequence of thought I have re-arranged the
verses as above.

ledge of the truth is sin, alike whether that knowledge rests on the common instinct of mankind or on a special revelation. 2 'We know,' says the Jew complacently, 'the doom of God 3 falls justly upon those who practise such vices.' 'Very well,' Paul retorts, 'and do you imagine you will escape God's doom, O man, you who judge those who practise such vices and do the same yourself?' In what sense Paul made such a charge, we must learn from verses 17 sqq. His object is to awaken the conscience of his Jewish hearers to 4 self-criticism. God has shown to the Jewish people a wealth of kindness, forbearance, and patience. Their tendency was to accept all this as a proof of the divine partiality to the Chosen People. We may turn back to the Book of Wisdom (which, as we have seen, Paul has been following closely). 'But Thou our God,' says the author, 'art gracious and true, longsuffering and in mercy ordering all things. For even if we sin we are Thine, knowing Thy dominion: but we shall not sin, knowing that we have been accounted Thine' (Wis. xv. 1–2). Too many Jews, doubtless, stopped short of the last clause, and reflected with much self-satisfaction, 'While therefore Thou dost chasten us, Thou scourgest our enemies ten thousand times more' (Wis. xii. 22). This, says Paul, is slighting all His wealth of kindness, forbearance, and patience. The kindness of God is not an expression of His approval and favour towards a chosen race: it is meant to make you repent. This thought was not strange to Judaism—cf. Wis. xi. 23–24: 'But Thou hast mercy on all men, because Thou hast power to do all things, and Thou overlookest the sins of men to the end that they may repent. For Thou lovest all things that are, and abhorrest none of the things which Thou didst make.' In Paul's Christian thought it takes a more positive and effective form, agreeably to the teachings of the Gospel about the Father who is 'kind toward the unthankful and evil,' the Shepherd who will 'go after that which is lost until He find it.'

5   The Jew, then, knows God as kind and merciful: stubbornness and impenitence of heart in the face of such kindness removes him out of the sphere of divine grace, as surely as does the sin of idolatry among the pagans. In each case the Wrath falls upon those who are wilful, who disobey the Truth 8 and obey wickedness. Thus the impenitent Jew is simply 5 storing up wrath for himself on the Day of Wrath, when 6-10 the just doom of God is revealed. The description of rewards and punishments which follows shows that Paul here has in

view the traditional Day of Judgment, when the revelation of the Wrath will be complete. This is in accord with the eschatology which primitive Christianity inherited from Judaism, and his Jewish hearers would recognize it at once. But, for Paul the Christian, there was no sharp line between this future consummation and the experience of the present. In the whole thought of primitive Christianity, and not least in Paul, it is assumed that the 'Age to Come' (of Jewish hopes and fears) has already dawned. In the Christian Church, the 'powers of the Age to Come' are already part of experience; in the world without, the Judgment has already begun. It was only as time grew long that the Day of Judgment receded altogether into an imaginary future. In Paul's time it could still be thought of simply as completing a process already far advanced. Thus the difference between the revelation of Wrath in chap. i., where it is a process observable in the facts of pagan civilization, and the Day of Wrath here, which is an 'eschatological' event in the future, is smaller than it appears to us. They are only two ways of looking at one fact. The main point that Paul wishes to urge is that, however the Wrath is revealed, there is no substantial difference between Jew and pagan when it is revealed. The moral order is one; its laws operate consistently: **anguish and calamity for every human soul that** 9 **perpetrates evil; . . . glory, honour, and peace for everyone who does good. . . . There is no partiality about God.** 10-11

The only difference between Jew and Greek is that, since the Jew received a more direct and specific revelation of God in the Law, he is in a sense more immediately exposed to the operation of the moral order, for good or ill: the rewards of virtue and the penalties of vice alike are **for the Jew first, and** 9-10 **for the Greek as well.** This is exactly the position of Amos and the prophets in his tradition. In the thought of Paul it is little more than a survival of his inherited and deeply ingrained feeling that somehow his own people must receive special treatment. But when that feeling takes the form, not of a claim to special privilege, but rather of an admission of special responsibility, it is comparatively harmless. (It is not altogether unlike Paul's strong sense of a personal vocation, which leads him to refuse privileges which he allows to other apostles—1 Cor. ix.—and lays upon him uncommon burdens of responsibility.) In the present context we observe that the priority assigned to the Jew in the Judgment corresponds to the priority of the Jew in hearing the Gospel (i. 16), which, of course, was a simple matter of historical fact.

For the purpose of the argument, however, it is hardly relevant, for the qualification it introduces is apparent rather than real. Jew and Gentile are judged each by the standard of his own knowledge of the truth. The mere possession of the Law gives the Jew no position of advantage; it only deter-13 mines the standard by which he shall be judged. **For it is not the hearers of the Law who are just in the eyes of God, it is those who obey the Law who will be acquitted.** That is not quite the moral truism it might appear, for there was certainly a tendency in popular Judaism to rest content with the immense privilege of knowing the Law. There are expressions in rabbinic traditions, as well as in books like the Wisdom of Solomon, which might well be turned to support such an attitude. The rabbis discussed whether the ' hearing ' or the ' doing ' of the Law were more important. One rabbi is quoted as saying, ' **If thou wilt hear** [Exod. xv. 26] is the most universal rule, in which the whole Law is contained ' (Rabbi Eleazar of Modi'im. quoted by Strack-Billerbeck on this passage). But orthodox Pharisaism unhesitatingly gave Paul's answer to the question: ' Not learning is the Leader [into eternal life], but doing is the Leader ' (rabbinic commentary on Lev. xviii. 4, quoted by Strack-Billerbeck). Paul speaks as a good Pharisee.

Verse 16 has been transposed by Dr. Moffatt. This is perhaps the best way of restoring the order, which has somehow or other become disturbed. Verse 16 is not very naturally connected with verse 15: if we read it where the MSS. give it, then either we must regard it as an afterthought added by Paul in the course of dictation or we must treat verses 14-15 as a parenthesis. If, as is antecedently probable, the bulk of this chapter represents an address to Jews which Paul had already given substantially in this form, perhaps many times, before he wrote this epistle, then it is likely enough that Paul had a written copy of it by him, and inserted verses 14-15 parenthetically when he adapted it to an epistle meant for Gentile as well as Jewish readers. That they are an interpolation by someone other than Paul is a supposition which has no probability: they are quite in accord with i. 19-20, 32a. It is to be observed that verse 16 contains the only definitely Christian (as opposed to Jewish) statement in the chapter:

God judges the secret things of men, as my Gospel holds, by Jesus Christ. For his teaching on this subject see 1 Cor. iv. 4–5; 2 Cor. v. 10; Rom. xiv. 10–12. It is only the words following **men,** of course, that are non-Jewish, and, if we have before us an original address of Paul to Jews, we can understand why he felt it necessary to insert the words **as my Gospel holds.** If the chapter was originally composed for Christian readers, it is hard to see why he should have put them in.

Verses 14–15 are conceived in the same spirit as i. 19–20. Pagans have in ' natural religion ' both a knowledge of God through His work in creation, and also a knowledge of the eternal principles of right and wrong, **a law written on their 15 hearts;** and so, although they **have no law** (in the sense of a special revelation) yet **they are a law to themselves. 14** Here Paul comes very near to the Greek moralists. Thus Plutarch (quoted by Wettstein on this passage) asks, ' Who shall govern the governor ? ' and replies, ' Law, the king of all mortals and immortals, as Pindar called it; which is not written on papyrus rolls or wooden tablets, but is his own reason within the soul, which perpetually dwells with him and guards him, and never leaves the soul bereft of leadership.' Similarly, Aristotle says, ' The cultivated and free-minded man will so behave as being a law to himself ' (*Eth. Nic.*, 1128 A). This inner law, according to the Stoics, is the ' law of nature.' Their teaching was that, as the whole universe is rational, each member of it has an immanent law of its being which is consonant with its function in the whole. Thus, for man, right and wrong are determined by the immanent law of human nature as such; and man, being himself rational, is capable of discerning this law and living by it. What is in this sense ' natural ' is right; what is ' contrary to nature ' is wrong. A man's ' conscience '—that is, his consciousness of himself as a rational and moral being—recognizes the immanent law of his nature, and judges his own actions by its standard. This doctrine of the law of nature and the judgment of conscience is perhaps the most important permanent contribution of Stoicism to ethics. The Stoics invented the term ' conscience,' and Paul is speaking exactly like a Stoic 15 when he says, ' **Their conscience bears them witness, as their moral convictions accuse or it may be defend them.**' Neither for Paul nor for the Stoics is conscience a legislative faculty: it does not make the law; it recognizes it and judges conduct by it. The law is for the Stoic the law of nature, for the Jew the Law of Moses, for the Christian the Law of Christ (Gal. vi. 2) or, which comes to the same thing, the Law of the Spirit (Rom. viii. 2). This saves the Stoic and the Pauline doctrine of conscience from the anarchic individualism which is the danger of some modern forms of the doctrine. Now for Paul the Mosaic Law is the most complete revelation of the will of God there is, in terms of precepts and prohibitions; but the 'law of nature' is not a different law, but only a less precise and complete revelation of the same eternal law of right and wrong. Thus the pagan's obedience or disobedience to the law of nature is on all fours with the Jew's obedience or disobedience to the Law of Moses.

In spite of his pessimistic judgment on pagan society, Paul here admits at least the possibility that **Gentiles who have no law obey instinctively** [literally, 'by nature,' in accordance with Stoic teaching] **the Law's requirements.** Nor is this a merely formal admission in passing: he makes use of it in his argument that a good pagan is better than a bad Jew (ii. 25). For the purposes of his general argument, he takes the extreme view that no one, whether Jew or pagan, does or can obey the law; but in concrete cases he allows that in some measure at least the good pagan (and of course the good Jew, as he implies in ii. 28) can do the right thing. We note this as against the doctrines of 'total depravity,' and the complete impotence of the human will, which have been attributed to Paul. He would no doubt have agreed with the pessimistic author of 2 Esdras, with whom he has so much in common: ' Thou shalt find that men who may be reckoned by name have kept Thy precepts; but nations Thou shalt not find ' (2 Esd. iii. 36). His immediate point, however, is to maintain against his supposed Jewish interlocutor that the pagan has just as good a chance of being **acquitted on the day when God judges the secret things of men**, as any Jew, just as the Jew who sins **under the Law** is as certain of condemnation as those **who sin outside the Law.**

CIRCUMCISION

ii. 17–29: *The Moral Failure of Judaism*

17 If you bear the name of ' Jew,' relying on the Law, priding yourself on God, understanding His will, and with
18   a sense of what is vital in religion; if you are in-

structed by the Law and are persuaded that you are
a guide to the blind, a light to darkened souls, a 19
tutor for the foolish, a teacher of the simple, because 20
in the Law you have the embodiment of knowledge
and truth—well then, do you ever teach yourself, 21
you teacher of other people? You preach against
stealing; do you steal ? You forbid adultery; do 22
you commit adultery ? You detest idols; do you
rob temples ? You pride yourself on the Law: do 23
you dishonour God by your breaches of the Law ? 24
Why, it is *owing to you* that *the name of God is maligned among
the Gentiles*, as scripture says ! Circumcision is 25
certainly of use, provided you keep the Law: but
if you are a breaker of the Law, then your circumcision is turned into uncircumcision. (If then the 26
uncircumcised observe the requirements of the Law,
shall not their uncircumcision be reckoned equiva- 27
lent to circumcision ? And shall not those who are
physically uncircumcised and who fulfil the Law,
judge you who are a breaker of the Law for all your
written code and circumcision?)

He is no Jew who is merely a Jew outwardly,   28
   nor is circumcision something outward in the
   flesh;
he is a Jew who is one inwardly,   29
   and circumcision is a matter of the heart,
   spiritual not literal—
   praised by God, not by man.

Paul now turns directly to the Jew, with a fiercely satirical
attack upon his complacent self-satisfaction, which elaborates
the charge made in verse 3. The Jew is convinced that in the 20
Law he has **the embodiment of knowledge and truth,** and
that conviction produces an overweening pride in his religious
privileges, and a contempt for 'lesser breeds without the Law.'
That this was so, Jewish literature in general bears witness.
Further, the Jew living abroad, among pagans, felt himself 19
called to be **a guide to the blind, a light to darkened souls.**
Expressions of this kind are common enough in Jewish writers.
There is doubtless an allusion to them in the Gospel sayings
about ' blind leaders of the blind ' (Matt. xv. 14; cf. xxiii. 24;
Luke vi. 39); and, as in the Gospels the charge against the
Pharisees is that ' they say, and do not ' (Matt. xxiii. 3), so 21

Paul asks, **'Do you ever teach yourself, you teacher of other people?'** Almost the same words are used of certain teachers of the Law by the early Rabbi Saul ben Nannos: ' Thou hast some men . . . who teach others and do not teach themselves ' (quoted by Strack-Billerbeck on this passage). By

21–   way of example, Paul accuses Jews of stealing, adultery, and
23   temple-robbing, contrary to the provisions of the Law which they taught to Gentiles. The charges are startling, but Paul would have stultified himself by making them if they had no ground. As a matter of fact, there is evidence enough of the terrible degradation of Jewish morals in the period preceding the Destruction of the Temple. Thus we have a discourse from Paul's younger contemporary, Jochanan ben Zakkai,[1] delivered probably not much more than ten years after the date of this letter, in which he bewails the increase of murder, adultery, sexual vice, commercial and judicial corruption, bitter sectarian strife, and other evils. There is in Paul's words an added tone of bitter indignation—the indignation of the highminded Jew who moved about among the great cities of the pagan world and found the very name of Jew made a byword by the evil

23   ways of its bearers. The dishonour of the Jew reflected upon his religion. It was as the prophets had said of their own times:

24   **it is owing to you that the name of God is maligned among the Gentiles, as scripture says** (Isa. lii. 5). Similarly, a later rabbi says: ' When anyone studies the Scriptures and the Mishna and waits upon the Wise, and does not order his conduct honestly . . . what do people say of him? . . . " So-and-so, who has learned the Law, how depraved are his works, how ugly his ways! " He it is of whom the Scripture says, " They profaned my holy Name " ' (Ezek. xxxvi. 20). Thus, whether as apostle or as rabbi, Paul would have pressed

23   upon his Jewish hearers the challenge, **You pride yourself on the Law: do you dishonour God by your breaches of the Law?**

Paul has now made more precise his arraignment of the Jews **who judge those who practise such vices and do the same** themselves; and by implication he presses again the question, **Do you imagine you will escape God's doom?** The Jew, however, had something yet to fall back upon. It was orthodox doctrine that all who were by circumcision included in the covenant made with Abraham were sure of eternal life. We

25   must imagine at this point a Jewish objector making this plea.

[1] Quoted by Strack-Billerbeck *ad loc.*

Paul replies: ' **Circumcision is certainly of use, provided you keep the Law; but if you are a breaker of the Law, then your circumcision is turned into uncircumcision.**' He is still speaking, of course, as a Jew, within the sphere of the Law, and not in terms of the Gospel. In an absolute sense, when once Christ is known, **what counts is neither circumcision nor uncircumcision, but a new creation** (Gal. vi. 15). But he is willing to argue with Jews on their own presuppositions, and to grant that circumcision has value. But this value is contingent on the keeping of the covenant of which circumcision is the sign, i.e. upon the full observance of the Law; for, as he says to the Galatians (v. 3) '**I insist again to everyone who gets circumcised, that he is obliged to carry out the whole of the Law.**' This does not seem to be normal rabbinic doctrine. Yet there is evidence enough that serious thinkers were ill-content with the assumption that bad Jews would be saved solely by virtue of their circumcision. Not only did John the Baptist pronounce the Pharisees in danger of the **coming Wrath,** and rebut their plea that as Abraham's children they were safe from it (Matt. iii. 7-9), but the author of 2 Esdras, as we have seen, doubts gravely whether more than an insignificant remnant of the Chosen People could be saved. Even more orthodox rabbis taught that gross sinners and apostates from Israel would be miraculously deprived of their circumcision after death, in order that they might be eligible for Gehenna; in Paul's words, **their circumcision is turned into uncircumcision.** Where Paul differed from them, apparently, is that he counted *any* infraction of the Law as meriting the forfeiture of Jewish privileges. This is not the teaching of the Talmud at any rate. Whether there was a more rigorist school of rabbinic thought in Paul's time, we cannot say. It is not unlikely, for we know that, after the disasters of A.D. 70 and 135, rabbinic teaching did tend to become in some respects milder and more considerate of human weakness.[1]

Paul now turns his proposition round—if the bad Jew is no better than a pagan, then also the good pagan is equal to a Jew: **If then the uncircumcised observe the requirements of the Law, shall not their uncircumcision be reckoned as circumcision?** The vast majority of Jewish teachers would have answered unhesitatingly, ' No.' The saying of Rabbi Meir (about A.D. 150) stands almost alone in the Talmud:

26

---

[1] On this see Easton, *Christ in the Gospels*, chap. iv.

' The Scripture says, " The man that doeth them shall live by
them " [Lev. xviii. 5]. It does not say " the priest," or " the
Levite," or " the Israelite," but " the man." That teaches that
even a Gentile, who concerns himself with the Law, is as the
High Priest.' But Meir, of course, was thinking of proselytes.
Paul probably has in mind those Gentiles who though they
have no Law obey instinctively the Law's requirements,
and **exhibit the effect of the law written on their hearts**
(verses 14-15). This is certainly not orthodox rabbinism,
though probably many of the more liberal Jews living in the
Greek world would have been prepared to accept it.

27   Paul then goes further still; not only does a good pagan
stand as good a chance in the Judgment as any Jew, but a good
pagan has actually a better standing than a bad Jew; **he will
judge** the Jew who is **a breaker of the Law, for all his
written code and circumcision.** We recall the saying in
the Gospels: **The men of Nineve will rise at the judgment
with this generation and condemn it; for when Jonah
preached they did repent** (Luke xi. 32; Matt. xii. 41). This
of course is the conclusion Paul wishes to drive home: his
main point is not that the pagan, if he does right, will escape
the Wrath, but that the Jew, unless he does right, will certainly
not escape it. It *may* be that some pagans do right, but it is
certain that Jews as a whole do not keep their Law; and, that
being so, they have not a shadow of hope on the ground of
their position of national privilege.

The Jew has still one possible reply. He might urge that
Paul has drawn up an indictment against a whole nation, but
that many of that nation do not fall under its terms: it is not
true that all Jews are thieves, adulterers, or temple-robbers.
Therefore (the Jew might plead), even granting the extremely
rigorous position that Paul has taken up, there are, after all,
some Jews who keep the Law and therefore may hope to escape
the Wrath. Paul's reply to such a plea would be that to observe
the precepts and prohibitions of the Law outwardly is not
enough; the inner life of thought, desire, motive, and affection
must be in accordance with the will of God; and this, he
contended, was not possible under the Law (see vii. 7-25).
28 **He is no Jew who is merely a Jew outwardly ... he is
29 a Jew who is one inwardly.** For the true circumcision **is a
matter of the heart, spiritual not literal.** This is an echo
of prophetic teaching (Jer. iv. 4; Deut. x. 16, xxx. 6), very little

emphasized in rabbinic Judaism, so far as our evidence goes; but familiar in the writings of the liberal Jew, Philo of Alexandria. Doubtless Paul would have found general agreement that it was desirable that outward observance should be accompanied by purity of heart, but it was not the way of rabbinic Judaism to emphasize this. He himself as a Jew certainly strove after such inward purity; but this absolute insistence upon it we can hardly avoid tracing back to the influence of Gospel teaching like that of the Sermon on the Mount, in whatever form it reached him. Formally, the whole argument of the chapter is addressed by a Jew to Jews; and it proceeds from assumptions which might at least be taken to be implied in Jewish belief; but it touches the teaching of the Gospels at so many points that we cannot but conclude that Paul had that teaching in mind. The Gospel teaching on these matters may be broadly described as anti-Pharisaic. What effect it had upon the Pharisees who heard it we do not know, except that it exasperated many of them beyond bearing. It is all the more interesting to see how a Pharisee who had overcome his initial prejudice against it, and accepted its authority, brought it to bear upon his Pharisaic assumptions.

Cm̄t: see p. 71 at *

iii. 1–8: *Some Objections from the Jewish Side*   iii

Then what is the Jew's superiority? What is the good of 1
circumcision? Much in every way. This to begin 2
with—Jews were entrusted with the scriptures of 3
God. Even supposing some of them have proved
untrustworthy, is their faithlessness to cancel the
faithfulness of God? Never! Let God be true to His
word, though *every man be perfidious*—**as it is written,** 4
That thou mayest be vindicated in thy pleadings,
and triumph in thy trial.

But if our iniquity thus serves to bring out the justice
of God, what are we to infer? That it is unfair of 5
God to inflict His anger on us? (I speak in a merely
human way.) Never! In that case, how could He
judge the world? You say, ' If my perfidy serves to 6
make the truthfulness of God redound to His glory, 7
why am I to be judged as a sinner? Why should we
not do evil that good may come out of it?' (which 8
is the calumny attributed to me—the very thing

some people declare I say). Such arguments are rightly condemned.

The Jewish objector is thus driven from his last ditch. '**Then what is the Jew's superiority?**' he exclaims; '**what is the good of circumcision?**' The logical answer on the basis of Paul's argument is, ' None whatever! ' But the trouble is that the ' Jewish objector ' is in Paul's own mind. His Pharisaism—or shall we say, his patriotism?—was too deeply engrained for him to put right out of his mind the idea that somehow the divine covenant with mankind had a ' most favoured nation clause.' And so he surprisingly answers his own question: '**Much in every way.**' Then he embarks on 2 what should have been a list of the various ways in which the Jews had such superiority, but actually gets no further than the first item: **this to begin with—Jews were entrusted with the scriptures of God.** [We might complete his list for him out of Rom. ix. 4–5: **Theirs is the Sonship, the Glory, the covenants, the divine legislation, the Worship, and the promises; the patriarchs are theirs; and theirs too (so far as natural descent goes) is the Christ.**] But immediately he falls into a difficulty. What advantage is there in possessing the Scriptures if, as he has already said, **It is not the hearers of the Law who are just in the eyes of God, it is those who obey the Law who will be acquitted. . . . If you are a breaker of the Law, then your circumcision is turned into uncircumcision?** His answer is obscure (as 3 indeed it almost had to be if he was to circumvent his own logic): '**Even if some of them have proved untrustworthy, is their faithlessness to cancel the faithfulness of God?**' Note, it is **some of them.** But the implication of the argument of these chapters, indeed its express conclusion (iii. 9–20), is that *all* Jews, as well as *all* pagans, are **under sin.** The concession implied in this verse must be set alongside the admission that some Gentiles may **obey instinctively the Law's requirements.**

But in order to understand the very compressed argument of the verse we must have recourse to what we can learn from the extended treatment of the same problem in ix.–xi. Briefly, Paul's position is this: the covenant made with Abraham (the background of **the scriptures of God** which were entrusted to the Jews) involved a promise of blessing for Israel. Israel as a whole broke covenant with God, and forfeited the blessing.

That looks like a frustration of the promise; but God has not really gone back on His word, because (a) God was justified in refusing the blessing, because Israel rejected His will; (b) a faithful remnant of Israel did receive the blessing, by becoming incorporated in the Church of Christ; (c) as regards the rest, their rejection was God's way of bringing in the Gentiles, and, through the bringing in of the Gentiles, somehow all Israel will be saved in the end. Whether this multiplication of pleas in justification of God's ways strengthens the case may be questioned; but if we assent to Paul's presentation of the case, it does supply some sort of answer to the question posed here: What advantage does the Jew get from possessing the Scriptures, if they pronounce his own condemnation for disobeying them? The ultimate answer is that, in spite of all, the promises which they contained will be fulfilled at long last for those to whom they were entrusted. This point, however—which is point (c)— Paul does not here make. He confines himself to (a): that God's **faithfulness** is shown by His rejection of the Jews for their **unfaithfulness.** That is intelligible; but it does not show how there is advantage to the Jew in possessing the Scriptures; nor does it justify the assertion that the **Jew's superiority** is **much in every way.** It may be that Paul was intending to pass on to points (b) and (c); but, if so, he was diverted by a secondary problem raised by his solution of the first.

The question in verse 3 is, in effect: Is God to be expected to be false to His word by letting Israel off lightly for their disobedience? The answer is: ' **Never! Let God be true to His word, though every man be perfidious.**' Then 4 comes the further problem: **if our iniquity thus serves to bring out the justice of God** [namely, in denying the blessing 5 to unfaithful Israel], **what are we to infer? That it is unfair of God to** bring retribution upon us? (for so I should prefer to translate, as I have shown above). ' **I speak in a merely human way,**' Paul adds, apologizing for the mere suggestion that God could be **unfair**: even to use the term is a bold anthropomorphism, he means to say. Of course he cannot contemplate the idea: God unfair?—**Never ! In that case, how could He judge the world?** That is simply a reiteration of Abraham's 6 plea in Gen. xviii. 25: ' Shall not the Judge of all the earth do right? ' It is not, of course, an argument, but an appeal to the deeply rooted feeling that the world is a moral order and that a principle of justice lies at its heart. It may be that in the end no theodicy can do much more than make this appeal. But as a step in Paul's debate with the Jewish objector it will not do; for his objection is that Paul's doctrine of the rejection of Israel impugns the ultimate justice, and therefore must be wrong. At best, all that Paul says is, ' You and I both agree that it is inconceivable that God should be unjust, and you must understand all that I say in that sense.' But, as Paul sees, the objector will not be satisfied with that.

7   He presses his point: **' If my perfidy serves to make the truthfulness of God redound to His glory, why am I to be judged as a sinner?'** One sees how this objection arises in the Jewish mind. The Jew had been taught that the glory of God was the supreme end of human existence, to be realized particularly through His people Israel; that He had given the Law to His people as a pledge of His favour, that His favour would be manifested in the prosperity and ultimate salvation of Israel and that this would redound to the glory of God before all nations. Paul now says that, on the contrary, the **perfidy** of Israel would give proof of the **truthfulness of God,** and *this* would **redound to His glory.** But, the Jew argues, if the glory of God is manifested by the rejection of Israel (a monstrous idea), then Israel is promoting the glory of God by its unfaithfulness: but that which promotes the glory of God should not

8 be condemned as sin. Hence Paul's teaching leads to a complete moral chaos. If what he says is true, **why should we not do evil that good may come out of it?**

This was the kind of charge to which Paul was particularly sensitive. It arose in a more dangerous form when his doctrine of free grace was misunderstood in an antinomian sense, as we learn from vi. 1. There he takes it with full seriousness, and devotes a whole long section of the epistle to confuting it. Here it comes in much less forcibly, as the result of a rather scholastic kind of debate. Paul brushes it aside with the words, **Such arguments are rightly condemned.** So they may be, but Paul had no right, having challenged the debate, to close it in this cavalier fashion.

The fact is that the whole argument of iii. 1–8 is obscure and feeble. When Paul, who is normally a clear as well as a forcible thinker, becomes feeble and obscure, it usually means that he is defending a poor case. His case here is inevitably a poor one, since he is trying to show that, although **there is no partiality about God,** yet **the Jew's superiority** is, somehow, **much in every way.** It is no wonder that he becomes embarrassed, and in the end dismisses the subject awkwardly. The argument of the epistle would go much better if this whole section were omitted. So far as its problem is a real one, it is dealt with far more seriously and persuasively in chaps. ix.–xi.

iii. 9–20: *The Condemnation of the Jews*

Well now, are we Jews in a better position? Not at all. 9
**I have already charged all, Jews as well as Greeks,
with being under sin—as it is written,**   10

> *None is righteous, no, not one;*
>> *no one understands, no one seeks for God.*   11
> *All have swerved, one and all have gone wrong,*   12
>> *no one does good, not a single one.*
> *Their throat is an open grave,*   13
>> *they are treacherous with their tongues,*
> *the venom of an asp lies under their lips.*
> *Their mouth is full of cursing and bitterness,*   14
>> *their feet are swift for bloodshed,*   15
> *their ways bring destruction and calamity,*   16
>> *they know nothing of the way of peace;*   17
>> *there is no reverence for God before their eyes.*   18

**Whatever the Law says, we know, it says to those who
are inside the Law, that every mouth may be shut** 19
and all the world made answerable to God; *for no person
will be acquitted in His sight* **on the score of obedience to** 20
**law.   What the Law imparts is the consciousness
of sin.**

Paul now, feeling no doubt that his argument in the preceding section has got nowhere, repeats the question of iii. 1 in other words: ' **Well now, are we Jews in a better position** 9 [than pagans]? ' The answer, if Moffatt's translation is right, is the direct opposite of the answer given in iii. 2: ' **Not at all.**' But it must be confessed that neither the reading nor the meaning of the Greek is quite certain here. The text and the interpretation of the question are doubtful, but Moffatt's rendering is probably to be accepted. The Greek wording of the answer might be read either as ' Absolutely not,' or as ' Not absolutely.' In the only other passage where Paul uses the expression it is similarly ambiguous (1 Cor. v. 10), and there Moffatt's paraphrase suggests that he took it to mean ' Not absolutely ' ('**Not**

. . . literally' is his actual rendering). Here, however, he takes it to mean 'Absolutely not'; and this seems to be more in accord with normal usage. But one would like to save Paul from such a direct self-contradiction within a few verses, and the words do admit of the sense that, though temporarily and relatively the Jews have a certain advantage, yet in an absolute view of the matter that advantage vanishes. This is very near to his conclusions in chaps. ix.–xi., and it is at least a possible interpretation of the Greek here. In any case, the Jew has no such advantage as would give him exemption from the in-

10– evitable working of the principle of retribution as expounded

18 in i. 18–ii. 29: **I have already charged all, Jews as well as Greeks, with being under sin.** This position Paul now buttresses, in his rabbinic manner, with a string of quotations from the Old Testament (Ps. xiv. 1, liii. 2–4, v. 9, cxl. 3, x. 7; Isa. lix. 7–8; Ps. xxxvi. 1). He quotes apparently from memory sometimes reproducing the exact words of the Septuagint, some-times giving a more or less free rendering. The purport of the passages is the unrelieved sinfulness of men, and Paul takes

19 this to mean primarily the sinfulness of the Jews, on the ground that **whatever the Law says, it says to those who are inside the Law.** The word **Law** is here used in its wider

20 sense of the entire Hebrew Canon (as in 1 Cor. xiv. 21). Thus the authority of Scripture is invoked to confirm the demonstra-tion of chap. ii. that Jews no less than pagans are **answerable to God** for their sins, and that **no person will be acquitted in His sight on the score of obedience to law,** whether it be the law of nature or of Moses. (The possible exceptions of ii. 10, 14–15, 26 are left out of sight.) In either case, **what the Law imparts is the consciousness of sin.** This maxim, which expresses a deep psychological insight, receives its full exposition in vii. 7–25.

II. THE RIGHTEOUSNESS OF GOD IN
JUSTIFICATION

(iii. 21–iv. 25)

The preliminary stage of the argument is now concluded. Paul has shown that, apart from the Gospel, there is nothing to be found in the world but sin and its retribution: the Wrath is revealed, but not yet the righteousness of God. For, as we have seen, the righteousness of God must be revealed in the deliverance of man from sin and wrath. Thus the study of the Gentile world enlightened by the law of nature, but breaking that law, and of the Jewish world enlightened by the Law of Moses, but equally breaking that Law, has laid bare the need for some further revelation. Paul can now return to his original thesis: **God's righteousness is revealed by faith and for faith** (i. 17), and he sets out to show how this is so. In a world given over to sin and retribution, the righteousness of God is revealed first in justifying sinful men on the ground of faith (iii. 21–iv. 25), and secondly by saving them out of the sinful order of the world into a new order of life and righteousness (v.–viii.).

iii. 21–26: STATEMENT OF THE DOCTRINE
OF JUSTIFICATION

But now we have a righteousness of God disclosed apart from law altogether; it is attested by the Law and 21 **the prophets, but it is a righteousness of God which comes by believing in Jesus Christ. And it is meant** 22 **for all who have faith. No distinctions are drawn. All have sinned, all come short of the glory of God,** 23 **but they are justified for nothing by His grace** 24 **through the ransom provided in Christ Jesus, whom God put forward as the means of propitiation by His blood, to be received by faith. This** 25 **was to demonstrate the justice of God in view of the fact that sins previously committed during the time of God's forbearance had been passed**

26   **over; it was to demonstrate His justice at the present epoch, showing that God is just Himself and that He justifies man on the score of faith in Jesus.**

In verses 21–22 we have a full and careful re-statement of the thesis of i. 17. **God's righteousness,** he said there, **is revealed** in the Gospel **by faith and for faith.** More precisely, he now says, **we have a righteousness of God dis-**
21 **closed apart from law altogether: it is a righteousness**
22 **of God which comes by believing in Jesus Christ; and it is meant for all who have faith.** The new revelation of God's righteousness is **apart from law,** in so far as the Law is **a code of commands** (Eph. ii. 15)—that is, it is in no sense a mere development of the legalistic Judaism in which Paul had been brought up. But, on the other hand, it was not unrelated to the Law in its wider sense, as God's self-revelation of Himself in the Old Testament; for **it is attested by the Law and the prophets.** It is because Paul believed this that he so constantly appeals to the Old Testament for confirmation of his teaching.

This has been thought to be inconsistent with his position that **Christ is an end to law** (Rom. x. 4). But Paul divined, what modern criticism of the Old Testament has clearly proved, that legalistic Judaism was after all a one-sided development of the religion of the Old Testament. In the prophets, in the Psalms, and even embedded in the Pentateuch itself, there is a conception of God in His relation to men which goes far beyond the merely legal conceptions of orthodox Judaism in Paul's time, and is in the most real sense the direct antecedent of Christianity. Paul's citation of Old Testament passages often strikes us as arbitrary, and his interpretation of them as fanciful, but at bottom what he is doing is to appeal to the prophetic strain in biblical religion against the legal strain which prevailed in the Judaism of his own time. Jesus Himself had insisted on the continuity of His own work with that of the prophets, and had deliberately set the prophetic conception of religion over against the Pharisaic, and in this Paul followed him.[1] In the second century, Marcion, believing himself to be interpreting Paul, called upon the Church to abandon the Old Testament, and he has many followers to-day. But the Church rightly

[1] See my article, 'Jesus as Teacher and Prophet,' in *Mysterium Christi*.

refused Marcion's way, in spite of his religious fervour and moral earnestness.

DEFINITION OF SIN

We proceed, then, with Paul's carefully considered statement. **22** The righteousness of God **is meant for all who have faith; no distinctions are drawn.** He has risen above the level of the questions that embarrassed him in iii. 1–8, and takes his stand on a clear principle. With the discussions of i. 18–ii. 29 in view, he can sum up the condition of mankind in the words, **23** **All have sinned; all come short of the glory of God.** The latter clause may be taken as a definition of sin. Man was created to bear the likeness of God; ideally he is ' the image and glory of God ' (1 Cor. xi. 7. I do not understand Moffatt's translation there). This gives us the clue to the meaning of the present passage. **The glory of God** is the divine likeness which man is intended to bear. In so far as man departs from the likeness of God he is sinful. To **come short of the glory of God** is to sin. This definition, simple, broad, and profound, should be borne in mind whenever Paul has occasion to speak about sin. (See, further, notes on v. 12–14.)

The following clauses describe what God does for men who **24-** are in this sinful condition. They are so important, and so **25** precisely formulated, that it will be well to supply something like a glossary of the terms used.

JUSTIFICATION

First, the terms **righteous, just; righteousness, justice; justify;** all represent Greek words from one single root. In rendering them into English we are embarrassed by the fact that there is no English verb corresponding to the adjective **righteous,** while, on the other hand, the adjective **just,** corresponding to the verb **justify,** is a much less adequate translation of the Greek adjective than **righteous.** The Greek word translated **justify** means in Greek writers ' to account or pronounce right,' or ' to treat justly.' (It does not mean, ' to make righteous.') In the former sense it may be rendered, ' to acquit,' and Dr. Moffatt has, in fact, rendered it so in iii. 20. That is the surface meaning, so to speak, of the word as used by Paul. Sinful men before the divine tribunal are acquitted, **for nothing,** by God's decree as Judge. They need do nothing to secure their acquittal, for it is not on the ground of any merit, but **by His grace;** grace being the free, even arbitrary, favour of a sovereign.

But, to get the flavour of the word **justify** as used by Paul,

The dealing of God with sinful men.

we must have in mind the language of the Hebrew Bible with which he was familiar. I have dealt above with the meaning of ' righteousness ' for the Hebrews (note on i. 17). **Justification** is for them an act by which a wronged person is given his rights, is vindicated, delivered from oppression. *and then in a position just-as if he were freed it had never happened* When the Second Isaiah looks forward to the coming of the righteousness of Jehovah, he thinks of it in terms of the ' justification ' of His people, i.e. their deliverance from the power of evil under which they are oppressed. This Hebrew background colours the Greek terms. Paul uses them in a way which hovers between their wider Hebrew and their narrower Greek connotation. When he says, **they are justified for nothing by His grace**, the idea uppermost in his mind is that of deliverance. But as he is stating it in legal, forensic terms, deliverance takes the form of an acquittal in court.

(a) To say that guilty men are acquitted before the divine tribunal is sheer paradox. Paul meant it to be so. If the dealing of God with sinful men is to be described in legal terms at all (as Paul and his fellow-Pharisees were accustomed to describe it), then it can be described only in terms of paradox. For the fact is that, though men have deserved ill of God, He does not give them their deserts; though they have merited His hatred, He gives them His love; He is ' kind toward the unthankful and evil.' Jesus could describe it in these purely personal terms; He was living it out in His own personal relationships, as the ' friend of publicans and sinners.' But if it has to be put in terms of the law-court, how *can* you put it except by saying that God acquits the guilty—a thing monstrous at law? We may note that in the Old Testament the very phrase, ' to justify the wicked,' is constantly used of unjust judges (e.g. Isa. v. 23; Prov. xvii. 15; Exod. xxiii. 7). Paul therefore was fully aware what a daring thing he was doing in attributing such a thing to God. The real moral is that the personal relations of God to men cannot be described in legal terms at all. The revelation of His righteousness is **apart from law altogether.**

But meanwhile there is a value in the paradox. Paul is addressing people to whom, as to himself, it came natural to think of religion in terms of law, and a challenging paradox was the best way of making his point. Further, the metaphor of the law-court gave him the opportunity of emphasizing the sovereignty of God. When the prisoner at the bar has no case, all he can do is to throw himself on the mercy of the court.

In this court the Judge is one whose will is law: if He acquits the prisoner, then he leaves the court without a stain on his character. **It is all the doing of the God who has reconciled me to Himself . . . for in Christ God reconciled the world to Himself instead of counting men's trespasses against them** (2 Cor. v. 18-19). But again, this forensic way of thinking in religion is not the arbitrary invention of the Pharisees; it is natural to all whose religion is strongly ethical. Conscience itself is a tribunal (cf. ii. 16) and we naturally speak of conscience 'accusing' and 'condemning' us. Now when, as in all ethical religions, the awed feeling of reverence which is the typically religious feeling is directed towards God as the supreme Right personified, the condemnation of conscience inevitably produces the sense of guilt before God, which hinders communion with Him. Paul meets this universally familiar experience with the startling statement that God acquits the guilty. If we can accept this, we are able to confront our moral task free of the crippling disability of a guilty conscience. It is a matter of common experience among men that a wrongdoer can best be helped to better ways if someone can be found for whose opinion he has the highest respect, and who will treat him, not as the hopeless wastrel he may have been, but as the decent citizen he has it in him to become. This was how Jesus treated the publicans and sinners (see especially Luke xix. 1-10). If a sinner can believe that God treats him in that way, his battle against sin is half won. This is the psychological value of Paul's doctrine of justification.

The next of Paul's leading terms which needs definition is ransom. The Greek word used here is commonly used in writers and inscriptions of the period with reference to the liberation of slaves or prisoners of war. This was frequently effected by the payment of a sum of money as ransom. But Paul's term (*apolytrosis*) is not concrete, as the English word **ransom** suggests, but abstract (=the act of redeeming). Further, it can be used without any explicit reference to the payment of money, as a simple equivalent of 'emancipation' (*apeleutherosis*—as, for instance, in an inscription published in Hicks and Hill's *Inscriptions of Cos.*, No. 29). This is the basis of Paul's usage. But once again the particular colour is given by the Old Testament associations of the word. When the children of Israel were liberated from bondage in Egypt, they were regarded as slaves 'redeemed' by Jehovah (e.g. Deut. vii. 8);

and the later prophets similarly spoke of the liberation from captivity in Babylon as ' redemption ' (e.g. Isa. li. 11). We learn from Gal. iii. 23–iv. 5 that Paul could conceive the work of Christ as being the emancipation of the people of God from bondage—a parallel on a higher level to the redemption of Israel from Egypt and from Babylon. This is the thought in the present passage. Our justification depends upon the fact that God has intervened to emancipate His people from bondage to sin. Those who by faith in Him through Christ accept a place among His people are justified.

Thirdly, we have the term **propitiation.** The Greek word (*hilasterion*) is derived from a verb which in pagan writers and inscriptions has two meanings: (*a*) ' to placate ' a man or a god; (*b*) ' to expiate ' a sin, i.e. to perform an act (such as the payment of a fine or the offering of a sacrifice) by which its guilt is annulled. The former meaning is overwhelmingly the more common. In the Septuagint, on the other hand, the meaning (*a*) is practically unknown where God is the object, and the meaning (*b*) is found in scores of passages. Thus the biblical sense of the verb is ' to perform an act whereby guilt or defilement is removed.' The idea underlying it is characteristic of primitive religion. The ancients felt that if a *taboo* was infringed, the person or thing involved became unclean, defiled or profane. The condition of defilement might be removed by the performance of the appropriate act: it might be washing with water, or sprinkling with blood, or simply the forfeiture of some valuable object to the deity concerned with the *taboo*. Such acts were felt to have the value, so to speak, of a disinfectant. Thus in the Old Testament a whole range of ritual actions are prescribed for disinfecting the priest, the altar, or the people from various forms of defilement, ritual or moral. Our versions in such cases use the phrase ' to make propitiation '; but the more proper translation would be ' to make expiation.' This meaning holds good wherever the subject of the verb is a man. But, as religious thought advanced, it came to be felt that, where the defilement was moral, God alone could annul it; and so the same verb is used with God as subject in the sense ' to forgive.' [1]

In accordance with biblical usage, therefore, the substantive (*hilasterion*) would mean, not **propitiation,** but ' a means by

Incense

---

[1] The full evidence for all this is given in my book, *The Bible and the Greeks*, pp. 82–95, where I have examined, I believe, every occurrence of the verb in the Septuagint.

which guilt is annulled ': if a man is the agent, the meaning would be ' a means of expiation '; if God, ' a means by which sin is forgiven.' Biblical usage is determinative for Paul. The rendering **propitiation** is therefore misleading, for it suggests the placating of an angry God, and although this would be in accord with pagan usage, it is foreign to biblical usage. In the present passage it is God who **puts forward the means** whereby the guilt of sin is removed, by sending Christ. The sending of Christ, therefore, is the divine method of forgiveness. This brings the teaching of the present passage into exact harmony with that of v. 8–9.

Fourthly, something must be said here about the use of the word **blood**, and what is said will apply also to its use in v. 9 and other similar passages. As we have seen, one method for annulling the defilement of sin was the offering of a sacrifice, and particularly the shedding of the blood of a victim. There can be little doubt that when Paul uses the word **blood** in conjunction with the word for expiation he is thinking in sacrificial terms. The divine method for the forgiveness of sins takes effect through the sacrifice of Christ. But we have still to ask why was value attached to blood in ancient religion? The answer is given in Gen. ix. 4; Lev. xvii. 11; Deut. xii. 23: **the blood is the life.** Thus, when Paul speaks of the blood of Christ, he is thinking of His life as laid down in self-dedication to God. Thus he can say elsewhere that it is Christ's **obedience** that effects our salvation (v. 19): His death is the crown and seal of that obedience, for **He humbly stooped in His obedience even to die, and to die on the cross** (Phil. ii. 8). The language of sacrifice expresses figuratively a reality which is personal and ethical. Similarly, in speaking of the Sacrament of the Lord's Supper (1 Cor. x. 16), Paul can say, **The cup of blessing which we bless, is that not participating in the blood of Christ?**—i.e. participating in His life as dedicated to God (see also Rom. vi. 1–11 and notes there). The sacrificial language is not natural to us,[1] but to Paul's readers, Jewish and Gentile alike, it was deeply impressive, because associated with some of their most sacred thoughts and experiences. (See p. 199)

Finally there is the word **faith.** This has already been discussed and defined in the notes on i. 17. It describes the attitude of pure receptivity in which the soul appropriates what

---

[1] But see xii. 1, xv. 16, and notes there.

God has done. Observe that Moffatt's translation removes the ambiguity of our current versions, which makes it possible for the clause ' in His blood ' to be connected with ' faith.' But ' faith in His blood ' would be an impossible expression for Paul to use. Faith is for him always faith in God through Christ. So here the divine forgiveness, working through the **blood,** i.e. the consecrated life, of Christ, is **to be received by faith,** i.e. by an act of sheer trust in God the All-sufficient.

Having now defined our terms, we may proceed to the interpretation of Paul's comprehensive statement. We find that he is combining three metaphors: the first taken from the law-court—the metaphor of justification; the second taken from the institution of slavery—that of emancipation; the third taken from the sacrificial ritual of ancient religion—that of expiation by blood. Under all three metaphors he describes an act of God for men. In the first, God takes the part of the judge who acquits the prisoner; in the second, that of the benefactor who secures freedom for the slave; in the third, that of the priest who makes expiation. But in Paul's biblical background all these metaphors had already moved part of the way into reality. The deliverance of Israel from bondage had been described by the prophets both as ' justification ' and as ' emancipation '; and the language of the Septuagint shows that there was already a sense that the only final expiation of sin was the forgiveness granted by God Himself. Thus his own thought was less at the mercy of his metaphors than that of his Greek readers might be, lacking his biblical background. But the metaphors serve in each case to emphasize the pure objectivity of that which God has done for men. Paul is not here concerned, as he will be in the next section (v.–vii.), with the inward effect of all this in the lives of men. He is concerned with their status before God, which is altered by an act of God Himself—from condemnation to acquittal, from bondage to freedom, from guilt to innocence. The change of status described in this threefold way is, as he presently shows, accompanied by an inward change from sinfulness to right living, from moral impotence to moral competence. But what he is here concerned to make clear is that by no possible effort of his own could man alter his status before God any more than a guilty prisoner could acquit himself, or a slave free himself, or an ' unclean ' person become ' clean ' without supernatural means; but that God, by a sheer act of grace, has made this change of status possible.

None of the three metaphors can make the same direct appeal
to us that they did to Paul; but perhaps we can arrive through
them at the substance of what he is saying. All men, he says,
are sinful, for they do not live in that likeness to God for which
man is designed. This sets a barrier between us and God. No
efforts of ours at self-improvement can make us fit to associate
with God, for they cannot get rid of the guilt of our past. Shake-
speare has given us a study of a guilty conscience in Lady
Macbeth (see Act V., scene i.), and the outstanding feature of
it is the sense that evil once committed remains as a permanent
element in the personality. ' What, will these hands ne'er be
clean? There's knocking at the gate. What's done cannot be
undone. To bed, to bed, to bed! ' For anyone who believes
in God as holy and righteous that permanence of guilt means a
permanent separation from Him. And yet, on the other hand,
our only hope of being better is to come into touch with God,
who is the sole source of all goodness. There is therefore an
impasse. Only if a man can come to believe that God Himself
has passed the barrier of guilt and come to him, can religion
help him to become better. Now, what Paul declares as ' the
Gospel of God ' is that God has, in fact, not only passed the
barrier, but removed it.

The assurance that He has done so he finds in the fact of
Christ. He had the story of Jesus before him, even though
our Gospels were not yet written, and the facts on which Paul
went are there accessible to us. We read there how Jesus dealt
with the paralytic (Mark ii. 1–12), the sinful woman (Luke
vii. 36–50), the publicans and sinners who crop up all through
the Gospels; we read His own parables by which He interpreted
and defended His action, especially that of the Prodigal Son
(Luke xv. 11–32); and we read the Gospel story as a whole,
observing how the attack He made upon the barriers which
had been set up by the religious against the sinful led directly
to His death, so that in this sense (as well as in others) He died
for other people's sins. These are the *data* for Paul's conclusion
that God provided for the justification of sinners by means of
the self-sacrifice of Christ in life and death. With the Gospels
before us, we must either agree with the enemies of Jesus that
He suffered justly for an attitude to sin which undermined the
foundations of morality; or we must concede that this way of
dealing with sinful men is inherently divine, and an index to
God's unchanging attitude to sinners. When a man comes to
believe that, and accordingly trusts himself to God as thus

conceived, he knows that the sense of guilt with which he has been oppressed does not separate him from God, and he can make a fresh start with divine assistance. This is not to make justification a merely subjective matter, for everything depends on the concrete fact of the life of Christ, which is objective as any fact of history is objective. It is an act of God in history. Not that anything that Christ did altered the attitude of God towards men. His coming represents the crucial phase of God's self-revealing activity in all history (which Paul traces from the call of Abraham downwards); but God always was and always is that which Christ showed Him to be.

25*b*- The following clauses indicate how this act of justification is
26 related to the righteousness of God. In reading them we must bear in mind that **righteous** and **just** are only different English renderings of the same Greek word; and so are **righteousness** and **justice.** Dr. Moffatt has chosen here to use **just** and **justice,** although in verses 21 and 22 he had used **righteousness,** presumably because only so could the connection of these words with **justify** be made clear. But the **justice** of God in verse 26 is the same thing as the **righteousness of God** in verses 21-22. Now, we have seen that, according to the prophets who supply the background of Paul's religious thinking, the righteousness of God is shown in the deliverance of His people from the power of evil, in the victory of the good cause in them and through them in the world. Thus in order that God may be revealed as righteous it is necessary that He should be revealed as delivering men from the power of evil, as ' justifying ' them in the Old Testament sense of the word. This was, Paul asserts, the purpose and the result of the life and death of Christ, with all that ensued: **it was to demonstrate His justice** [righteousness] **at the present epoch, showing that God is just** [righteous] **Himself, and that He justifies** [vindicates or delivers] **man.** There is no suggestion that a device has been found by which the justice of God can be satisfied (by the vicarious punishment of sin, for example), while at the same time His mercy is exerted to save the sinner. No such antithesis between justice and mercy was in Paul's mind. The justification of the sinner—his deliverance from the guilt of sin —is the conclusive proof of the righteousness of God. Paul emphasizes the point that this proof has been given **at the present epoch.** This is a reference to the idea (which I have

dealt with on i. 17–18) that with Christ the 'Age to Come' begins—

Magnus ab integro saeclorum nascitur ordo.

In the past age there was no such radical dealing with the problem set by the sin of man. **Sins previously committed ... had been passed over.** This could be understood as a mere matter of **forbearance** on God's part. The danger of such a conception of God, as forbearing, lenient, indulgent to the sin of His people, has been already touched upon (see ii. 3–4 and notes there). The mere passing-over of sins was, so to speak, a provisional measure, suitable to the age in which God's decisive action was still awaited. Such forbearance could not make any difference to the fact that in due time sin would by the law of cause and effect bring its own retribution—the Wrath. It was no revelation of the 'righteous acts of the Lord.' God's righteousness is revealed if, over against the terrible spectacle of the Wrath at work (as Paul has described it in chap. i.), there is a divine intervention by which man is delivered from sin and wrath. And now that the New Age has dawned, such an intervention has taken place, and it proves finally that **God is just,** in that **He justifies man.**

The above exposition of the thought of this passage—a key-passage in Paul's teaching—runs very differently, it must be confessed, from the traditional doctrines based upon it; the ransom paid to the devil, the propitiation of the wrath of God, the satisfaction demanded by His justice and afforded by Christ's vicarious endurance of the penalty of sin, and so forth. I have tried to show, by close examination (at some risk of tedium to the reader) of the actual language used by Paul, that no such ideas can be supposed to have been in his mind. Why, then, have they been attributed to him? There are strong historical reasons why he was misunderstood. To begin with, the classical theologians of the Christian Church, from Origen onwards, were Greeks, with little inward sense for the Hebrew and biblical ideas which formed the atmosphere of Paul's thinking. Later, ideas derived from Roman law prevailed, and gave a false colouring to his language. Further, in the Middle Ages and at the Reformation, when a supposedly Pauline theology was re-framed, ancient ideas of sacrifice were no longer alive, and the language which derived from them was not understood. For these and similar reasons a passage like the present became unintelligible, and current or traditional

theological ideas were read into it. In our own day the fresh
study of ancient thought and language, both Hebrew and
Greek, has placed new instruments in the hands of the interpreter of Paul, and we can approach him with some better
prospect of coming in touch with his mind. But while we reject
some of the historic statements of Pauline theology, we must
admit that they were not untrue to his intention, in so far as
they enabled men to believe reasonably, in terms of the thought
of their time, that God in Christ has done whatever needed to
be done in order that men might be freed from the guilt of their
sin, and start upon a new life in the strength of divine grace.
That is the essence of the matter, and many theological doctrines
which we must think alien in their detail from Paul's thought
have nevertheless safeguarded for their time the Gospel which
he preached.

iii. 27–31: COROLLARIES OF THE DOCTRINE
OF JUSTIFICATION

27 **Then what becomes of our boasting? It is ruled out
absolutely. On what principle? On the principle
of doing deeds? No, on the principle of faith. We**
28 **hold a man is justified by faith apart from deeds of
the Law altogether. Or is God only the God of Jews?**
29 **Is He not the God of the Gentiles as well? Surely He**
30 **is. Well then, there is one God, a God who will
justify the circumcised as they believe and the un-**
31 **circumcised on the score of faith. Then ' by this
faith ' we ' cancel the Law '? Not for one moment !
We uphold the Law.**

This passage begins by affirming an important corollary of
the doctrine of justification by grace through faith. It is that
27 **boasting** before God (cf. iv. 2) is **absolutely ruled out.**
Boasting represents the same verb which is used in ii. 17,
priding yourself in God; the corresponding noun is used in
iv. 2, **something to be proud of.** It is to Paul's mind a
fundamentally irreligious attitude. It finds crude expression in
the prayer of the Pharisee in the parable of Luke xviii. 10–14,
and the Gospels and Paul agree in representing it as the great
danger to which the devout and law-abiding Pharisee was
exposed.

Paul himself seems to have been particularly tempted to it. He had an innate pride, fostered no doubt by his peculiar situation as a Roman citizen and at the same time a Jew of the Dispersion; possessing an assured social position, and yet a member of a despised minority in the society in which he moved. Galled by the sense of inferiority he was made to feel as a Jew, he found compensation in the religious superiority of his race— **bearing the name of Jew, relying on the Law, priding himself on God, understanding His will, a guide to the blind, a light to darkened souls, a tutor for the foolish, a teacher of the ignorant, because in the Law he had the embodiment of knowledge and truth**—like the Jew whom he satirizes in ii. 17 sqq. But, unlike him, he strove to be an exceptionally good Jew, **immaculate by the standard of legal righteousness** (Phil. iii. 6). He was not satisfied with any normal and ordinary achievement; he must excel: **I out-stripped,** he says, **many of my own age and race in my special ardour for the ancestral traditions** (Gal. i. 14). This temptation to satisfy an innate pride by striving after superiority to others did not altogether leave him when he became a Christian. Other apostles might take pay for their work; he would not: **I would die sooner than let anyone deprive me of this, my source of pride** (1 Cor. ix. 15). [Read the whole context, and read also the tirade of 2 Cor. xi.: **(I am mad,** he adds, **to talk like this. . . . There is nothing to be gained by this sort of thing.)**] It is no wonder that, looking back on his pre-Christian days, he realized that his Pharisaic training, with its insistence on the attainment of righteousness before God by scrupulous observance of the Law, had stimulated this tendency in its worst form. The very ideal of his religious life, he now saw, had been an utterly irreligious attitude of boastful self-confidence. His conversion meant letting go everything which had fostered this self-confidence: **For Christ's sake I have learned to count my former gains a loss; indeed I count anything a loss, compared to the supreme value of knowing Christ Jesus my Lord . . . possessing no legal righteousness of my own, but the righteousness of faith in Christ, the divine righteousness that rests on faith** (Phil. iii. 7–9; read the whole context.) And so, **No boasting for me, none except in the cross of our Lord Jesus Christ, by which the world has been crucified to me and I to the world** (Gal. vi. 14).

This is the experience that lies behind his present insistence

that in any really religious life **boasting is ruled out absolutely.** It never can be excluded where the basal principle of religion is **the principle of doing deeds,** but only **on the principle of faith.** Christianity therefore (is the implied argument) is true religion, because **we hold that a man is**
28 **justified by faith apart from deeds of the Law altogether.**

And now comes a further point. It is true religion also,
30 because it is the only consistent monotheism. If **there is one God** (which is the fundamental creed of Judaism) then He must be not **only the God of the Jews,** but **the God of the Gentiles as well,** and therefore must treat Jews and Gentiles on the same footing. We see here why, for Paul, justification by grace through faith, and the universality of the Christian religion, go together, and why the *apologia* for his Gentile mission always has to be based on his theology of grace. He shows here profound insight. In Judaism, as it developed after the Exile, the prophetic assertion of the unity and universality of God, and the belief that Israel was His chosen People, lay in uneasy juxtaposition (see my book *The Authority of the Bible*, chaps. viii. and x.). Only along Christian lines was the antinomy solved, and the principle of monotheism carried to its logical conclusion.

31   The natural conclusion from all this is that **by this faith we cancel the Law**—a conclusion most distasteful to Paul's Jewish or Jewish-Christian readers. He hesitates to draw the conclusion. It would have made things clearer if he had boldly done so. But the word ' Law '—or, rather, the Hebrew *Torah* which it represents—as we have already seen (notes on iii. 21), had a double meaning: it meant the **code of commands** (Eph. ii. 15—the *halakha*, as the rabbis called it); but it meant also the total revelation of God in the Old Testament. This wider meaning would always be in the background of Paul's thought; and he could not admit that, in this sense, faith cancelled the Law. For the Old Testament revelation held within it the principles of a religion of faith, over and above the **code of commands,** so that the ' righteousness of God by faith ' is **attested by the Law and the prophets,** and, in this sense, Paul could say, **We uphold the Law.** His Greek readers, however, could not be expected to bear in mind that ' Law ' meant *Torah*, and that *Torah* had a wider sense; and in the sense which ' Law ' has borne in most of this discussion it is confusing and misleading to say that **we uphold the Law,** unless by that is meant that the moral principles which underlie

the precepts of the Law are, in fact, fulfilled by those who rely on divine grace. That Paul believed (as we shall presently see), but it is not relevant here.

iv. 1–25: THE FAITH OF ABRAHAM

We are now to have a long digression or excursus, in which Paul illustrates and confirms his doctrine of justification **apart from Law** by a reference to Abraham, who as the founder of the Chosen Race had a large place in the religious thought of Judaism. His argument here becomes scholastic and rabbinic in method, depending on the exegesis of scriptural passages, and it clearly has in view discussions within the rabbinical schools which are only partially known to us. But the general bearing of the argument is clear enough. Paul has just said that by the doctrine of justification by grace through faith **we uphold the Law.** As we have seen, this is best taken to mean that the *Torah* in the wider sense, the Old Testament revelation as a whole, contains within it a conception of religion as personal trust in God, more fundamental than the legal strain in it which received one-sided emphasis in Pharisaic Judaism. From this point of view, Abraham is an example of an outstanding religious personality, recognized as such by the strictest Pharisee, who nevertheless lived by faith rather than by Law. In Gal. iii. 15–18, Paul argues that the promise made to Abraham is wholly independent of the Law, and could not be affected by it: **once a man's will is ratified, no one else annuls it or adds a codicil to it. Now the Promises were made to Abraham and to his offspring. . . . The Law which arose 430 years later does not repeal a will previously ratified by God.** There also the argument is thoroughly scholastic in form, but it directs our attention to a type of Old Testament religion which is not legalist, which is prior to the Law, and which persists all through, along with the growing legalism of the Jewish system.

As a matter of fact, most of the stories of Abraham are recognized by modern critics as belonging to that *stratum* of the Pentateuch which took form under the influence of the earlier prophets, before the intense legal development of the period of the Exile and later. Without, therefore, deciding the question of the historical character of these narratives, we can quite honestly use them as representing an earlier and simpler form of religion than the Law as a code of commandments. (We should say, not that Abraham lived 430 years before the Law was given by Moses, but that the most characteristic stories of Abraham were written some four centuries before the Pentateuch was completed and became the exclusive basis of Jewish religion.) The conception of Abraham the Friend of God (Isa. xli. 8), who set out on perilous adventures in obedience to a divine leading, trusted to the Higher Power through many trials, lived in a hope which had no visible foundation, prayed for sinful Sodom with great humility before the Judge of all the earth (' Behold now, I have taken upon me to speak unto the Lord, which am but dust and ashes '), and was willing to make sacrifice of his dearest treasure at the divine bidding—this conception of the religious man has a real inward affinity with Paul's.

iv.

1 But if so, what can we say about Abraham* our fore-father by natural descent? This, that if ' Abraham

2 was justified on the score of what he did,' he has

3 something to be proud of. But not to be proud of before God. For what does scripture say? *Abraham*

4 *believed God and this was counted to him as righteousness.* Now

5 a worker has his wage counted to him as a due, not as a favour; but a man who instead of ' working '

6 believes in Him who justifies the ungodly, has his faith counted as righteousness. Just as David himself describes the bliss of the man who has righteousness counted to him by God apart from what he does—

7 *Blessed are they whose breaches of the Law are forgiven, whose sins are covered!*

8 *Blessed is the man whose sin the Lord will not count to him.*

9 Now is that description of bliss meant for the circum-cised, or for the uncircumcised as well? *Abraham's*

10 *faith, I repeat, was counted to him as righteousness.* In what way? When he was a circumcised man or an un-circumcised man? Not when he was circumcised,

11 but when he was uncircumcised. He only got cir-cumcision as a sign or seal of the righteousness which belonged to his faith as an uncircumcised man. The object of this was to make him the father

12 of all who believe as uncircumcised persons and

* Omitting, with B, 1908* and Origen, εὑρηκέναι.

thus have righteousness counted to them, as well as
a father of those circumcised persons who not only
share circumcision but walk in the steps of the faith
which our father Abraham had as an uncircumcised
man.

The promise made to Abraham and his offspring that 13
he should inherit the world, did not reach him
through the Law, but through the righteousness of 14
faith. For if it is adherents of the Law who are
heirs, then faith is empty of all meaning and the 15
promise is void. (What the Law produces is the
Wrath, not the promise of God; where there is no 16
law, there is no transgression either.) That is why
all turns upon faith; it is to make the promise a
matter of favour, to make it secure for all the offspring, not simply for those who are adherents of
the Law but also for those who share the faith of
Abraham—of Abraham who is the father of us all
(as it is written, *I have made you a father of many nations*). 17
Such a faith implies the presence of the God in
whom he believed, a God who makes the dead live
and calls into being what does not exist. For
Abraham, when hope was gone, hoped on in faith, 18
and thus became *the father of many nations*—even as he
was told, *So numberless shall your offspring be.* His faith 19
never quailed, even when he noted the utter impotence of his own body (for he was about a hundred
years old) or the impotence of Sara's womb; no
unbelief made him waver about God's promise; 20
his faith won strength as he gave glory to God and
felt convinced that He was able to do what he had 21
promised. Hence his faith *was counted to him as righteousness*. And these words *counted to him* have not been 22
written for him alone but for our sakes as well; 23
faith will be *counted to* us as we believe in Him who 24
raised Jesus our Lord from the dead, Jesus who was
delivered up for our trespasses and raised that we might 25
by justified.

It was the common assumption of all schools of Jewish
thought that 'Abraham was perfect in all his deeds with the
Lord, and well-pleasing in righteousness all the days of his
life' (Jubilees xxiii. 10—written at the end of the second century

B.C.), in other words, that he 'kept the law of the Most High' (Ecclus. xliv. 20). At the same time, the Old Testament laid stress on his 'faith.' This emphasis was congenial to the freer type of Jewish thought represented, for example, by Philo, but much less sympathetic to thinkers of the Pharisaic or rabbinic type. While they recognized the place of 'faith' in religion, as belief in the One God and fidelity to Him, they were at pains to make it clear that such fidelity could only be expressed in the keeping of the Commandments. But how could Abraham be said to keep the Law, if the Law was identified with the Code of Commandments supposed to have been delivered by Moses? The answer given was that he kept the whole Law by anticipation. The numerous statements to this effect in the Talmud show that it was orthodox rabbinic doctrine. Its earliest appearance seems to be in the Apocalypse of Baruch (lvii. 2): 'At that time [the time of the patriarchs] the unwritten law was named among them, and the works of the commandment were then fulfilled.' This apocalypse is but little later than Paul's time, and he may well have been acquainted with the doctrine. Thus he introduces his Jewish objector averring that **Abraham was justified on the score of what he did.** This was in substance the doctrine of Jesus ben Sirach: 'He kept the law of the Most High, and was taken into covenant with Him. . . . *Therefore* He assured him by an oath that the nations should be blessed in his seed.' (Ecclus. xliv. 20–21.) But, Paul urges, this

3-5 goes against the letter of Scripture, which says **Abraham believed God, and this was counted to him as righteousness.** These words, he argues, ' counted as righteousness,' imply that he had no actual righteousness, but was credited with that which he did not in himself possess.

6-8   This sense of the words, he goes on, may be illustrated from Ps. xxxii. Here the man is pronounced blessed **whose sin the Lord will not count to him.** That clearly means, not the man who has no sin, but the man **whose breaches of the Law are forgiven, whose sins are covered.** To turn the statement round, that man is blessed who, though he does not possess righteousness, yet has righteousness **counted to him.** The argument is verbal, and, as such, good enough for those who with Paul accepted the precise wording of Scripture as an infallible basis. But it is also more than verbal, in so far as it connects the idea of justification with the experience of forgiveness. If a man knows what it is to be a sinner, and yet to be forgiven, he knows what it is to be justified by grace.

And now a further point.   The Jewish objector might argue: 9-12
whatever may be the meaning of the words, ' **counted as right-
eousness,**' Abraham did, as a matter of fact, accept the obligations of the (as yet unwritten) Law, since he ' established the
covenant in his flesh ' (Ecclus. xliv. 20) by being circumcised.
But, says Paul, the promise to Abraham, and the faith by
which he accepted it, are recorded in Gen. xv.; his circumcision
in Gen. xvii.   At the moment, therefore, when his **faith was
counted to him as righteousness,** he was as uncircumcised
as any Gentile.   (The Old Testament critic might put the point
differently: the early-prophetic stories of Abraham know nothing of his circumcision, which is mentioned only in the late
priestly document.)   A palpable hit, if the letter of Scripture is
to be the final court of appeal.

It follows, then, that **the promise made to Abraham that
he and his offspring should inherit the world did not** 13
**reach him through the Law, but through the righteous-
ness of faith.**   Indeed, it is only on such terms that the promise 14
is worth anything at all.   A promise contingent on the fulfilment
of a law which no one fulfils in its entirety is a delusion.   The
argument is given in a fuller and clearer form in Gal. iii. 7-14
(to which I have referred on i. 17).   Here it is summarized in
the sentence: ' the Law produces Wrath ' (or, as Moffatt paraphrases, **what the Law produces is the Wrath, not the** 15
promise of God; but the paraphrase is somewhat loose); i.e.
the Law only furthers that process of sin and retribution described in chaps. i. and ii.; for **where there is no law there
is no transgression either.**   That is to say, (a) **what the
law imparts is the consciousness of sin** (iii. 20) and so it
gives the quality of guilty **transgression** to sinful acts for
which in its absence **a** man was not held responsible; and
(b) it provokes by its prohibitions the desire for sinful things, as
explained in vii. 7-25.   It is one of Paul's favourite topics, but
here it is a little aside from the main argument.

In verse 16 we come to the point which shows the real importance of the case of Abraham.   Paul wishes to show that
the Gentiles are to be reckoned among the **offspring** of Abraham to whom the promise was made.   If it was given to Abraham **on the score of what he did,** i.e. as a reward for his
keeping the Law, then only those who kept the Law could
have any share in it, and in any case the Gentiles were excluded.
But, according to Scripture, it was promised that Abraham 16-
should be **a father of many nations,** which Paul, by an   17

extension of the original meaning, takes to mean the spiritual ancestor of Gentiles as well as Jews. And so it was important to show that **all turns upon faith,** and the promise is **a matter of favour,** or grace, **to make it secure for all the offspring, not only for those who are adherents of the Law, but also for those who share the faith of Abraham.** Once again we observe how for Paul the universality of the Christian religion is bound up with justification by grace through faith.

The nature of faith is now illustrated from the story of Abraham. The fundamental proposition, **Abraham believed God and this was counted to him as righteousness,** occurs in Gen. xv. 6. The occasion is the promise made to him that he should have a son, and that his posterity should be as num-

17 erous as the stars. He was a childless man of a hundred years (Gen. xvii. 17). Reflecting on this situation, Paul concludes that to accept such a promise meant belief in **a God who**

19- **makes the dead live and calls into being that which does**

21 **not exist.** Conscious of his own **utter impotence,** Abraham relied simply and completely on the all-sufficient power of God. **His faith won strength as he gave glory to God and felt convinced that He was able to do what He had promised.** Thus, from a somewhat artificial treatment of Scripture, Paul has deduced a fine definition of what faith is. He then applies

24 it, not without a trace of the same artificiality, to the faith of a Christian. As Abraham believed in **a God who makes the dead to live,** so **we believe in Him who raised Jesus our Lord from the dead.**

25 The concluding verse of the chapter is rhetorical rather than logical in form: no antithesis is intended between ' **delivered for our trespasses,**' and ' **raised that we might be justi-fied.**' Somewhat after the manner of Hebrew parallelism, the meaning is ' He died and rose again in order that we might be delivered from the guilt of our sins.' The verse serves to bring the argument back, after the digression about Abraham, to the point reached in the previous chapter.

This discussion of the case of Abraham was, no doubt, important in Paul's apologetic against Jewish opponents within and without the Church; but for us it throws little light, except incidentally, on his main theme. It served to rebut objections which were serious to him, but have little interest and no weight for us, while the artificial method of argument from Scripture makes the whole exposition seem remote and unenlightening.

Perhaps the chief positive truth which emerges is that when Paul speaks of faith he is referring to something which did not begin with Christianity, but is an original and permanent element of all genuinely religious life, even though in some forms of religion, as in the extreme legalist form of Judaism, **faith is empty of meaning.**

III. THE RIGHTEOUSNESS OF GOD
IN SALVATION
(v. 1–viii. 39)

With chap. v. we enter upon the central section of the epistle. In iii. 21–iv. 23 we have learnt that the righteousness of God is revealed in the justification of men, by which they are given a new status before God. But justification is only the initial stage of God's dealings with men for their salvation. It is that which makes possible their entrance into the experience of salvation in the full sense. The transition from justification to salvation (or to ' sanctification,' as the Reformation theologians said) is made in v. 1–11, the kernel of which is the statement, **' much more, now that we are justified, shall we be saved by Him.'** Salvation is more than a new status; it is a new life; and that in two senses: it is a new life as being deliverance from death, with the assurance of glory to come; and it is a new life as being deliverance from the bondage of sin, with freedom to do the right. Salvation is eschatological, and it is ethical. This opening paragraph, v. 1–11, contains in brief the theme of the whole argument down to viii. 39. The following paragraph, v. 12–21, expounds the corporate nature of salvation, realized through Christ as our Representative. In vi. 1 we begin a special discussion of the ethical character of salvation, in view of certain misunderstandings to which Paul's teaching had been exposed; and this discussion is maintained, in various ways, down to viii. 13. Then what we may call the eschatological aspect is again uppermost, and the section is brought to a close with an eloquent affirmation of the certainty of salvation.

The INWARD EFFECT OF
faith that God will take
us at our worst and help
us to live at our best
through Jesus Christ - for

V. I–II: JUSTIFICATION AND SALVATION:
THE THEME STATED *through Him not below*

v As we are justified by faith, then, let us enjoy the peace
1   we have with God through our Lord Jesus Christ.
2   Through Him we have got access * to this grace
    where we have our standing, and triumph in the
    hope of God's glory. Not only so, but we triumph
    even in our troubles, knowing that trouble produces
4   endurance, endurance produces character, and char-
5   acter produces hope—a *hope* which *never disappoints* us,
    since God's love floods our hearts through the holy
6   Spirit which has been given to us. For when we
    were still in weakness, Christ died in due time for
7   the ungodly. For the ungodly! Why, a man will
    hardly die for the just—though one might bring one-
    self to die, if need be, for a good man. But God
8   proves His love for us by this, that Christ died for
    us when we were still sinners. Much more then,
9   now that we are justified by His blood, shall we
10 be saved by Him from Wrath. If we were reconciled
    to God by the death of His Son when we were enemies,
    much more, now that we are reconciled, shall we
11 be saved by His life. Not only so, but we triumph
    in God through our Lord Jesus Christ, by whom we
    now enjoy our reconciliation.

The excursus of chap. iv. is now ended, and Paul returns to
the point in the argument attained at iii. 26, yet with the added
content gained in the discussion which has immediately pre-
1 ceded. We are **justified by faith,** by faith which is a simple
trust in the power and goodness of God, like that of Abraham.
2 To put it otherwise, **we have got access to this grace where
we have our standing.** This standing, or status, which is
1 the effect of justification, is one of **peace with God,** in place of
the state of hostility between Him and us in which our sin had
placed us. By **peace,** Paul means something more than the
inward feeling of peace of mind or conscience. It is a matter
of our relation to our total environment, in a world where it is
possible to be actually at cross-purposes with the will of God

* Omitting τῇ πίστει with B D G, the Old Latin, and Origen.

which alone gives meaning to life. In such a condition no one, it is true, can possess real peace of mind, but it is the condition itself that must be dealt with. While the condition remains, it is impossible for a man, as experience (supported by psychological analysis) sufficiently attests, to get right by efforts of his own; for he finds life itself (which is a divine order) against him. In response to faith (which is an abandonment of the self to God), God Himself intervenes to give a new relation to Himself and to life. He gives peace in place of enmity as an actual condition in the spiritual world. It is this which Paul describes (verse 10 below; cf. 2 Cor. v. 18–20) as ' reconciliation ': not primarily a change in our feelings, but a change in our relations within a real spiritual world—a **standing in grace** to which we have got **access** through Christ.

But, once realized, this change in our **standing** has characteristic effects in the empirical life of moral endeavour and the feeling-tone which accompanies it. There is a new hopefulness—for that **glory of God** of which we all **come short** (iii. 23), is now known to be attainable, and the knowledge gives a sense of elation: **we triumph in the hope of God's glory.** This elation is not damped down by the troubles which 2 may still attend us; for, being at peace with God, we no longer 3 feel that things are against us in a world which He rules. On the contrary, untoward circumstance is so accepted that it furthers our moral progress: **trouble produces endurance, endurance produces character.** Here, in fact, we are first 4 introduced to the theme which is to play a large part in the further argument: the theme of the working-out of justification in moral progress (what Reformation theology described as ' sanctification '—improperly, so far as Pauline usage goes). Here it is merely sketched, in order to make the point that the hopefulness of the Christian is not an ungrounded optimism, but a **hope which never disappoints us, since God's love floods our hearts through the holy Spirit which has been given to us.**

The meaning of this very fundamental statement is not simply that we become aware that God loves us, but that in the same experience in which we receive a deep and undeniable assurance of His love for us, that love becomes the central motive of our own moral being (cf. 1 John iv. 19: **We love because He loved us first**). Since the nature of God Himself is love, in giving us love He imparts to us something of His own nature, or, in Pauline language, His Spirit. Thus love is (here, as in 1 Cor. xii. 31–xiii. 1) the primary 'spiritual gift.' It is at this point that the originally legal and forensic concept of justification decisively enters the sphere of moral experience. That which justifies is the love of God for the undeserving (see what follows), and in justifying us that love becomes the moral principle by which we live.

The whole theme of the ethical aspect of salvation receives full treatment in the course of the epistle, but the brief sketch which appears at this stage of the argument should be given its full weight. It covers the ground completely, in its summary way. Salvation, initiated by the loving act of God, is real for us so far as divine love rules us as the moral motive. When we are so ruled, the experience of life is experience of victory over **trouble,** or untoward circumstance, resulting in steady growth of **character;** and experience of increasing hopefulness in view of what the love of God has already done, not only for us, but in us. Only when the attitude of the soul is essentially a loving attitude can the injuries of fortune and of our fellow-men be borne with an **endurance** which is not embittered but joyous, and the only secure ground for hopefulness is an experience of what love can do.

6   The ruling idea of the foregoing verses has been the love of God, manifested in the act of justification, and becoming the basis of a new experience of life in the believer. The apostle now returns to the idea of the loving act by which we are justified, in order to exhibit more fully and impressively the surpassing quality of divine love. It was **when we were still in our weakness,** without virtue or merit of our own, that 7 **Christ died for the ungodly.** This is a form of love going beyond the limits of the natural sentiment of love in man. Under the influence of that sentiment a man may die for his fellow-man, but only if that fellow-man seems worthy of such a love, if he is judged to be **a good man.** For there is in real downright goodness that which naturally evokes the sentiment of love, and within that sentiment the instinct of self-preservation may be in abeyance. To enforce his point, Paul makes a curious distinction between such downright goodness and mere justice. ' The Head is a beast,' said the schoolboy, ' but he is a just beast.' Such a just man we may admire for his strict uprightness and correctness of behaviour, but he does not naturally become the centre of a sentiment of love. As he is

himself a model of stern duty, the knowledge that he 'expects every man to do his duty' may key his followers up to the point of making the last sacrifice; but it is a strain; **a man will hardly die for the just.** If a man does reach that point, his self-sacrifice depends on outstanding worthiness in the person for whom it is made: **one might bring oneself to die, if need be, for a good man.** It is characteristic of the sacrifice of Christ that it depends on no such worthiness. **Christ died 8 for us when we were still sinners,** not good men, not even just men. This is the measure of the love of God.

Observe the perfect naturalness with which Paul passes from the sacrifice of Christ to the love of God. For him it is matter of course that God Himself was at work in what Christ did. There could never have been for him any question of setting mercy in Christ against justice in God. The love which we see revealed in Christ is qualitatively divine, and if we believe in God at all, then that love is the love of God. We know divine love experimentally, he has said, when it becomes a motive in our own hearts, when we, in our measure, love with the love of God. In His perfect measure, Christ loved us with the love of God; indeed, it is because divine love became incarnate in Him that it **floods our hearts.** Thus Christ's self-sacrifice could never be thought of as something through which an angry God might be induced to treat us lovingly, since it is the love of God Himself, existing from all eternity, which was expressed in the sacrifice of Christ. Thus the principle of the Cross, so far from being set over against the righteousness of God, is inherent in His character and attitude towards us.

Two observations may here be made. First, Paul's analysis of the normal motive to self-sacrifice in men is sufficiently accurate for his purpose. A sense of the worth of the beloved object does seem to be necessary to the formation of a sentiment of love strong enough to provide the motive. But it may be that the instinctive impulse underlying the sentiment can sometimes of itself create the worth of the object, as, for instance, when a parent sacrifices himself for a child who is 'worthless' in the eyes of anyone else. It is, perhaps, this characteristic of parental love which more than anything else justifies the use of the term 'Fatherhood' to describe the relation of God to men. However this may be, Paul has made his point, that there is something inherently divine in a love which can go to the utmost lengths of self-sacrifice for the undeserving.

The second observation is that the Gospels indicate this conception of the love of God as the most characteristic thing in the teaching of Jesus. God, said Jesus, **'is kind even to the ungrateful and the evil,'** and acting out this conception of the divine character He won the reputation of **a friend of taxgatherers and sinners.** 'The summons,' says a great Jewish scholar, ' not to wait till they meet you in your sheltered and orderly path, but to go forth and seek out and redeem the sinner and the fallen, the passion to heal and bring back to God the wretched and the outcast—all this I do not find in Rabbinism; *that* form of love seems lacking.' [1] Evidently that was Paul's experience too of the Rabbinism in which he was brought up, and the revelation of ' *that* form of love ' in the self-sacrifice of Christ gave him an altogether new sense of the love of God.

9–
10   Justification, or reconciliation, is, as we have already been told, the initial act of a process; but it carries with it the assurance that the process will be completed. To enforce this point, Paul uses a double *a fortiori* argument. If while we were sinners, and so hostile to God, we were, nevertheless, the objects of His justifying and reconciling love, now that through His grace we are in good standing before Him, there can be no doubt that His love will follow us all through. This is expressed in two ways.

9   First, Christ, whose death (the supreme manifestation of divine love) was the ground of our justification, will save us from the **Wrath.** As we have seen, this term stands for the process by which sin brings its own retribution, a process conceived as reaching its consummation at the Last Judgment. From this process the divine love, which has already acquitted us of our past sins, will surely save us. We may observe that if **Wrath** stood for an act and attitude of God, there would be no need for this **' much more ';** for justification means that God is not in a wrathful attitude towards us. But, since **Wrath** is an objective principle and process in the moral order, we still need at all points the help of Christ to overcome sin and destroy its baneful effects. (A possible false inference from this verse is refuted in chap. vi.)

10   Secondly, if the death of Christ, a single event in history, has had such results, we may rely upon the continuing power of His life in communion with those whom He loves. The **' much**

---

[1] C. G. Montefiore, in *The Beginnings of Christianity.* Vol. I., p. 79.

more ' here has great significance. It shows that, in spite of the emphasis which Paul felt he must lay upon justification (partly because it was at this point that he had to meet opposition), he found the real centre of his religion in the new kind of life which followed upon justification. It was life ' in Christ,' or ' in the Spirit '; life in the love of God, as mediated to us by ' the Lord the Spirit.'

And so, after this meditation upon all that God in Christ 11 has done, is doing, and will do for us, we return to the note upon which the section began: **we triumph in God.**

LENT II 63 pm.

V. 12-21: ADAM AND CHRIST: SIN AND DEATH AND THEIR REMEDY

Thus, then, sin came into the world by one man, and 12 death came in by sin; and so death spread to all men, inasmuch as all men sinned. Sin was indeed 13 in the world before the Law, but sin is never counted 14 in the absence of law. Nevertheless, from Adam to Moses death reigned even over those whose sins 15 were not like Adam's transgression. Adam prefigured Him who was to come, but the gift is very different from the trespass. For while the rest of men died by the trespass of one man, the grace of God and the free gift which comes by the grace of the one man Jesus Christ overflowed far more 16 richly upon the rest of men. Nor is the free gift like the effect of the one man's sin; for while the sentence ensuing on a single sin resulted in doom, the free gift ensuing on many trespasses issues in acquittal. 17 For if the trespass of one man allowed death to reign through that one man, much more shall those who receive the overflowing grace and free gift of righteousness reign in life through One, through 18 Jesus Christ. Well then,

    as one man's trespass issued in doom for all,
      so one man's act of redress issues in acquittal and life for all.

    Just as one man's disobedience made all the rest 19 sinners, so one man's obedience will make all the rest righteous.

Law slipped in to aggravate the trespass; sin in- 20

21   creased, but grace surpassed it far, so that, while
sin had reigned the reign of death, grace might also
reign with a righteousness that ends in life eternal
through Jesus Christ our Lord.

Paul has now to deal with a difficulty which was felt by
those to whom he preached, and is still felt by many. You say,
' We are saved by what Christ did. But, granted that He lived
a wonderful life, and died a death of perfect self-sacrifice, we
can understand that He has thereby given an inspiring example,
yet, after all, He was an individual person in history: how can
His conquest over sin and *His* achievement of the human ideal
be effective for other individuals? ' Paul bases his answer on
a current doctrine of Jewish rabbis, that, through the Fall of
Adam, all men fell into sin (see 2 Esd. iii. 21–22, iv. 30, etc.).
Similarly, he says, through the moral achievement of Christ all
men may rise to goodness. It is a good enough argument for
those who accepted the rabbinic doctrine of the Fall. But
stated thus crudely it does not help our difficulty.

It is not, however, to be so lightly dismissed. What lies
behind it is the ancient conception of solidarity. The moral
unit was the community (clan, tribe, or city), rather than the
individual. If an Achan broke *taboo* (Josh. vii.) his whole clan
fell under the curse. Thus the whole of humanity could be
thought of as the tribe of Adam, and Adam's sin was the sin of
the race. With the growing appreciation of the ethical significance of the individual, the old idea of solidarity weakened.
But it corresponded with real facts. The isolation of the individual is an abstraction. None of us stands alone. What we
are and what we do is largely affected by the forces of heredity
and environment, i.e. by the place we occupy in the structure
of society as an historical whole. For good or ill we start with
predispositions which are the result of lives lived by other people.
There are outstanding representative men in history whose
words and deeds have perpetuated their influence through
whole periods and whole civilizations. If we think of Adam as
a man representative of all humanity, we approach Paul's
thought. But Adam is a myth (though for Paul he *may* have
been real); not so Jesus Christ, who certainly is a Figure of
history and has determined in a unique degree the course which
mankind has followed—the Representative Man in a special
sense.

But the thought of Paul does not move wholly on this level.

For him there is a real unity of mankind, a sort of mystical **unity in Adam** (1 Cor. xv. 22); and so also there is a mystical unity of redeemed humanity **in Christ.** Adam is a name which stands to him for the ' corporate personality ' of mankind, and a new ' corporate personality ' is created **in Christ** (see Rom. xii. 5; 1 Cor. xii. 12; Eph. ii. 10, iv. 4–16). All that Christ did and suffered He did and suffered as ' inclusive Representative ' of the new humanity which emerges in Him (see 2 Cor. v. 14–17). This idea is very fundamental to Paul's thought about the person and work of Christ. In Gal. iii. 16 he finds it by a characteristic piece of rabbinic exegesis, in the Scripture which promises the blessing to Abraham **and to his offspring.** The word ' offspring ' is collective (as Paul well knew), but the fact that a singular noun is used suggests to him that the true Heir of the promise is one Person, Christ, while we all share in the blessing by becoming incorporate **in Christ.**

Thus Paul's doctrine of Christ as the ' second Adam ' is not so bound up with the story of the Fall as a literal happening that it ceases to have meaning when we no longer accept the story as such. Indeed, we should not too readily assume that Paul did so accept it. The subtler minds of his age (like Philo of Alexandria, and the Egyptian Greek who wrote the Hermetic tract *Poimandres*) treated it as a symbolic allegory, and Paul's too was a subtle mind (see also notes on vii. 7–13). It is enough for him and for us to recognize that the wrongdoing of an individual is not an isolated phenomenon, but part of a corporate, racial wrongness which infects human society as we know it, and affects the individual through heredity and environment. This is the fact that Paul has in mind when he says **sin came into the world by one man.** If we take the words as expressing primarily a theory as to the way in which, as a matter of historical fact, man began to be sinful, it is doubtful whether it is consistent with the account of the origin of sin in the pagan world which he has given in i. 18–32. He is not really concerned about origins, but about the facts as they are: **in Adam** humanity is corporately sinful (see also note on vii. 14).

In attributing the prevalence of sin among men to Adam's transgression, then, Paul is following the rabbinic doctrine in which he was brought up. It was, further, part of that doctrine that **death came in by sin.** It is not at all clear that the story of the Fall as we have it in Gen. iii. means that Adam was immortal, but lost his immortality as the penalty of disobedience. But it was so understood by Jewish thinkers of Paul's time. 'God created man for incorruption,' says the Book of Wisdom (which was probably newly published when Paul was a student), ' but by the envy of the devil death entered into the world ' (ii. 23–24); and in 2 Esd. iii. 7 (written about A.D. 100) we read, ' Unto him [Adam] Thou gavest Thy one commandment; which he transgressed, and immediately Thou appointedst death for him and in his generations.'

Obviously, we cannot accept such a speculation as an account of the origin of death, which is a natural process inseparable from organic existence in the world we know, and devoid of any moral significance. For the reason why the Jewish mind felt death to be unnatural and pecularly horrible, we must probably go back to the stage in which the Jewish religion knew nothing of a life after death, so that death meant separation from God. (' The dead praise not the Lord, neither any that go down into silence '—Ps. cxv. 17.) This feeling, no doubt, Paul shared, and it is for him one of the greatest blessings of Christianity that bodily death no longer has this character, but to be ' absent from the body ' is to be ' present with the Lord ' (2 Cor. v. 8). But he is here speaking of death apart from Christ, of bodily death as the symbol of final separation from God, which we might describe (though Paul would not have used this language) as spiritual death. The death with which he is really concerned is the state of the man who is **dead in trespasses and sins** (Eph. ii. 1; cf., in this epistle, vii. 9–10, viii. 6). It is the corruption of the personality, and the corruption of the grave sets the seal upon it. Sinful man is dead while he lives, and bodily death is his fitting end. Thus ' the sting of death is sin ' (1 Cor. xv. 56—accidentally misquoted in Moffatt's note there), and only ' in Christ ' is the sting drawn.

Thus for the purposes of the present passage we may take **death** to be a comprehensive term for the disastrous consequences of sin, physical and spiritual. In this sense we may accept Paul's statement that **death came in by sin, and so death spread to all men, inasmuch as all men sinned.** Sin, we recall, is for Paul not necessarily an act for which an individual is guiltily responsible, but an objective condition in
13 which **we come short of the glory of God.** He here draws a careful distinction between sin, in this broad sense, and **trespass, or transgression,** which is a voluntary, responsible,

guilty infraction of a known command. Sin, indeed, **is never counted in the absence of law**—that is, it does not carry guilt, where there is no intention to act contrary to what is known to be right. Adam's sin was a **transgression**; he knowingly did what he was forbidden to do. In the generations which followed, men sinned—that is, they **came short of the glory of God**—but in many cases their **sins were not like Adam's transgression;** in so far as they were not clearly conscious of the distinction between right and wrong. But, though their sin was thus **never counted in the absence of law,** the baleful effects of sin in the objective order of things fell upon them. For the order of things takes no account of the perfectly valid excuses which a man can find for his wrongdoing in ignorance or lack of evil intention. Thus, **from Adam to** 14 **Moses, sin reigned even over those whose sins were not like Adam's transgression.**

Paul is thoroughly realist in his thinking here. The problem of evil is indeed something which goes beyond questions of individual responsibility, and salvation is more than a device for freeing an individual from his guilt: it must cut at the root of that corporate wrongness which underlies individual trans- 15- gression. This is, according to Paul, what has actually been 17 effected by the work of Christ. In Him men are lifted into a new order in which goodness is as powerful and dominant as was sin in the order represented by Adam; or, rather, it is far more powerful and dominant; **for if the trespass of one man allowed death to reign through that one man, much more shall those who receive the overflowing grace and free gift of righteousness reign in life through One, through Jesus Christ.** The ground of this 'much more' is probably in part the sense which the normal human mind always retains, that somehow good is more real and vital than evil; but more directly it rests on the contrast between the order of sin and retribution, which is an almost mechanical scheme of cause and effect (like what we call the laws of nature), and the order of grace, which is the perpetual outpouring of a personal love towards man. This is the true 'supernatural' in religion. We live our lives within an order of physical and psychological laws, but our **inner man is renewed day after day** (2 Cor. iv. 16) by a communion which transcends that order, because there is in it a divine spontaneity—for 'grace' is essentially spontaneity (see notes on ix. 15-16)—which does not, indeed, suspend the operation of natural law, but

GRACE

creatively brings new facts into play and so alters the total situation.

18–19
Observe that, in his summing-up, Paul includes in one statement both justification as a forensic acquittal from guilt, and actual salvation from sin. Christ's **act of redress issues in acquittal,** but also, His **obedience will make all the rest** actually **righteous.** The latter is his real point in the present argument. While justification, or **acquittal,** is to be accepted as a present fact, without which the process of salvation is not even begun, the full attainment of actual righteousness lies in the future—as will be fully manifest in what follows.

Here, then, Paul is dealing with sin and its cure in the broadest way, apart from complications introduced by law and the consequent sense of guilt. Sin, even when it is not **counted** as guilt, presents a problem. The solution of the problem is **20** found in **overflowing grace.** Law, with all its consequences, is a secondary element in the problem. It **slipped in to aggravate the trespass,** i.e. to increase (or actually to create) the guilt of sin. What Paul means, he does not stop here to explain: the subject comes up for full treatment in chap. vii. In the light of that fuller treatment we may say that law acts in two ways: (i.) it brings the consciousness that acts done hitherto without evil intent are nevertheless sinful, and so makes a man responsible for the sin he commits; and (ii.) it provokes in the mind a reaction against its prohibitions, which issues first in a greater tendency to sin.

vi. 1–viii. 13: THE NEW LIFE IN CHRIST

Paul has now made good his position that salvation comes by faith as the response of man to the grace of God mediated through Christ and His Cross, and not at all by any human achievement of righteousness in obedience to a code of precepts. But such a position is necessarily open to grave misunderstanding. Such a misunderstanding has already been alluded to in iii. 7–8: **Why should we not do evil that good may come out of it?** There the difficulty was rather dismissed with contempt than seriously tackled. Now the point has come at which it can be, and must be, adequately dealt with. Paul has just said, with reiterated emphasis, that through faith in Christ we have entered into an order in which grace is overwhelmingly stronger than sin. It **justifies the ungodly,** and confers **life eternal** upon the sinner. He now imagines someone drawing from this an inference with which he had no doubt often been confronted, whether by converted pagans with an imperfect grasp of the ethical seriousness of their new religion, or by Jewish-Christian opponents to whom it was a *reductio ad absurdum* of his whole position: the inference **that we are to remain on in sin, so that there may be all the more grace.**

It is no merely frivolous or perverse misreading of Paul's meaning, but a genuine difficulty which crops up again and again in Christian history. If God has done everything for us, and our efforts avail nothing for salvation, why make the effort to live a good life? If His grace is given to the unjust and the ungodly, why strive against injustice and ungodliness? Thus we find that when fresh emphasis has been laid upon the free grace of God, in times of religious revival, there has sometimes appeared the sinister by-product of a fanatical antinomianism, like that of the Münster Anabaptists in the first flush of the Reformation; and much more commonly a complacent acquiescence in a low or narrow moral standard combined with warm religious emotion. In our time there is a widespread feeling that the religious fervour of a past generation, to which the pious look back with regret, was often accompanied by a neglect of social ideals and duties which makes its value questionable. Many are inclined to fall back upon the maxims of the religion of all sensible men: Try to be good, and God will help you; do your best, and He will approve. That would have seemed to Paul an evasion of the deepest problem, as the whole argument of this epistle shows. His method of meeting the difficulty is to penetrate more radically into the nature of the evangelical experience itself, and to show how irrational it is to suppose that anyone who has saving faith should continue in sin. He starts from a consideration of baptism, as the sacramental initiation into the Christian life, and shows how it involves the death of the old sinful self and the emergence of a new self (vi. 1–14). He then illustrates this by two social analogies, drawn from slavery and marriage (vi. 15–vii. 6). Then, leaving analogy and illustration, he proceeds to a psychological analysis of what actually happens to a man who is saved (vii. 1–25), and passes from this at once to a meditation upon the new life as a life controlled by the Spirit of God indwelling (viii. 1–13).

vi. 1-14: *Union with Christ in Death and Resurrection*

vi.

1   **Now what are we to infer from this? That we are to ' remain on in sin, so that there may be all the more grace '? Never: How can we live in sin any longer,**

2   **when we died to sin? Surely you know that all of us**

3   **who have been baptized into Christ Jesus have been baptized into His death! Our baptism in His death**

4   **made us share His burial, so that, as Christ was raised from the dead by the glory of the Father, we too might live and move in the new sphere of Life.**

5   **For if we have grown into Him by a death like His, we shall grow into Him by a resurrection like His,**

6   **knowing as we do that our old self has been crucified with Him in order to crush the sinful body and free us from any further slavery to sin (for once dead,**

7   **a man is absolved from the claims of sin). We**

8   **believe that as we have died with Christ we shall also live with Him; for we know that Christ never**

9-10   **dies after His resurrection from the dead—death has no more hold over Him; the death He died was**

11   **for sin, once for all, but the life He lives is for God.**

12   **So you must consider yourselves dead to sin and alive to God in Christ Jesus our Lord. Sin is not to**

13   **reign, then, over your mortal bodies and make you obey their passions; you must not let sin have your members for the service of vice, you must dedicate yourselves to God as men who have been brought from death to life, dedicating your members to God**

14   **for the service of righteousn ss. Sin must have no hold over you, for you live under grace, not under law.**

In order to understand the argument here, we must bear in mind the teaching of the last chapter, that Christ is the inclusive Representative of the people of God, or redeemed humanity, which constitutes in union with Him a sort of corporate personality, as natural humanity may be regarded as a corporate personality ' in Adam,' its inclusive representative. That which Christ did and suffered on behalf of mankind is the experience of the people of God as concentrated in Him. Now, Christ

died and rose again, and **as One has died for all, then all
have died** (2 Cor. v. 14)—all, that is to say, who are incorporated
in that people of God which is 'the Body of Christ.' We
become members of the Body of Christ in virtue of faith. Upon
the ground of such faith the primitive Church admitted believers
to its membership by the sacrament of baptism.

For Paul, as for all early Christian teachers, baptism was
highly significant as the initiation into the Body of Christ. As
he is addressing people who were baptized upon conversion, in
adult years, the question of the validity of baptism apart from
the conscious assent of the baptized person does not arise. Nor
would it have been natural for Paul or any contemporary to
consider the question whether faith without baptism made a
man a member of Christ's Body, while the case of a person
seeking baptism without faith (however rudimentary) would
have seemed to him too abnormal to deserve notice. The
position was simple: the Church was a society with its own
forms of organized life, and it had always recognized faith by
administrating baptism, and thereby conferring membership of
the Body. Hence Paul could appeal directly to baptism as a
fact with a generally recognized significance, and draw from it
conclusions regarding what entrance into the people of God
involved. He is not, in the present passage, expounding the
nature of a sacrament as such, but exploiting the accepted
significance of the sacrament for a paedagogical purpose—to
bring home to the imagination a truth deeply rooted in experience, but difficult to put into purely intellectual terms. **Surely
you know,** he says, **that all of us who have been baptized** 3
into Christ Jesus have been baptized into His death! The
very symbolism of the sacrament emphasizes that fact. Immer-
sion is a sort of burial; emergence from the water is a sort of
resurrection. Paul does not indeed draw out the suggestion
of the symbolism, but it lies near the surface. The whole
sacrament is an act by which the believer enters into all that
Christ did as his Representative, in that He **was delivered
up for our trespasses and raised that we might be
justified.**

All this Paul could have said without any appeal to baptism
at all, for it follows directly from his teaching about Christ
as the second Adam; but the reference to baptism is of great
value paedagogically. For here, in this sacrament, is something actually done—a step taken which can never be retraced.
Before it a man was not a member of the Church, the people

of God: now he is a member. If he should thereafter be unfaithful, that would not simply be a return to his former condition. Something has happened, something overt, definable, with a setting in time and space, attested by witnesses. And behind that lies a similarly definite event in the inner
5 life. He has **grown into** Christ. He is now **in Christ.**

In verse 11 we have the first instance in this epistle of Paul's characteristic use of that phrase, the formula of what has been called his ' Christ-mysticism.' The context in which it here occurs offers a clue to its meaning. It is the baptized person who is **in Christ.** He has been baptized into the Church, into the Body of Christ, and so **into Christ.** He has become one of that company of people who embody the new humanity of which Christ is the inclusive Representative (cf. xii. 5: **for all our numbers, we form one Body in Christ**). So the ' Christ-mysticism ' of Paul is not exactly analogous to what is usually called mysticism. The typical mystic has an intensely individual experience of ineffable union with God (*solus cum Solo*), conceived as the One or the All. Paul's sense of union with Christ is conditioned by the experience of life in a society controlled by His Spirit, as well as constituted historically by His act. It is a sense of being included in the ' corporate personality ' of Christ which is manifest in the Church. This idea is no doubt rightly called mystical, but it is mystical with a difference. To be **in Christ** does not depend on states of abstraction or ecstasy—though Paul knew such states (see 2 Cor. xii. 2–5). It depends on active fellowship with others who are also ' members of Christ.' That is not to deny the deep inwardness of the relation for every individual ' member.' In each ' member ' as in the whole Body, Christ lives and works.

The particular aspect of this union with Christ to which Paul
6 here desires to call attention is the sharing of His death. **Our old self has been crucified with Him.** That is the meaning of our incorporation into His Body by baptism. It means a
9 passing out of the old order into **the new sphere of Life.** In solidarity with Him we have died and risen again. Hence, inasmuch as **we know that Christ never dies after His resurrection from the dead—death has no more hold over him,** we believe also that the life which is now ours will never end. The dominion of death (which **reigned from Adam**

to Moses, and still more decisively after the coming of law) is 8
broken. Thus the first conclusion we draw from our incorporation in Christ is the assurance of immortality. That,
indeed, is for Paul the one basis of belief in an after life. (He
has no doctrine of the natural ' immortality of the soul,' such
as Plato taught. As all die in Adam, so shall all be made
alive in Christ, 1 Cor. xv. 22.) So strongly did he state this
belief that at Thessalonica, and apparently at Corinth, it was
a shock to the Church when some of its members died. If he
told them bluntly that in baptism they had died and risen from
the dead, they may well have inferred that they would in consequence be exempt from bodily death. Here, however, he speaks
more guardedly. His argument indeed demands that the death
and resurrection of the Christian is sacramentally complete; but
when he comes to speak of the resurrection as an actual thing,
he uses the future tense: we shall grow into Him by a
resurrection like His; as we have died with Christ, we 5, 8
shall also live with Him. (Note that Paul constantly uses
with Christ of the future state of Christians, as distinct from
their present state in Christ—cf. 1 Thess. iv. 17; Phil. i. 23.)
In principle we are already in the new sphere of Life; we
shall be actually so in the future.

So far there is nothing which definitely answers the difficulty
from which this section started. All that is so far established is
that in becoming a Christian a man has definitely passed into
a new order of life, over which death has no sway. It has not
yet been shown that a man, having secured entrance into the
deathless order, may not go on sinning. But we remember
that for Paul death was the most unmistakable token of the
sinful condition of mankind: it was sin that reigned the
reign of death (v. 21). The escape from the power of death
must therefore mean in some way an escape from the power of
sin. And if we consider the death of Christ more closely, we
see that the death He died was for sin. The sense of these 10
words, which is not here developed, must be understood from
other passages in which Paul speaks of the life and death of
Jesus in relation to the condition of the world. Mankind, as
we have seen, was bound in the servitude of Sin, established in
the ' flesh.' Thus the natural, flesh-and-blood life of man was
the territory, so to speak, of Sin, and all dwellers on that territory
Sin claimed as his own. (This personification is implicit in the
language of our passage.) Christ, by His incarnation, became

a denizen of ' the flesh.' Sin put in his claim. In other words, Jesus was tempted to sin, as we are all tempted, in such forms as sin might take for one in His situation. But instead of yielding, and acknowledging Sin's dominion, as we all do, He rendered a perfect **obedience** to God—the makeweight to Adam's **disobedience** (v. 19)—and **stooped in His obedience even to die** (Phil. ii. 8). Jesus, in plain terms, died rather than sin; and so His death, instead of being a sign of the victory of Sin over man's true nature, was a sign of the complete rout of Sin in a decisive engagement. Whereas for other men death had been the sentence of their condemnation, Christ **condemned sin in the flesh** (viii. 3).

We have shared Christ's death, a death **to sin.** Our (sacra-
6 mental) death, therefore, is also a death to sin. Its effect is **to crush the sinful body and free us from any further slavery to sin.** It is important to bear in mind the characteristic sense in which Paul uses the term **body,** which is most clearly brought out in 1 Cor. xv. It is not the structure of flesh and blood as such. The flesh-and-blood structure may pass away, leaving not a vestige, and yet the body remain self-identical. As it now partakes of the perishable substance of ' flesh,' it may in future partake of the imperishable substance of ' glory ' or **splendour,** and yet remain the same ' body.' Such is Paul's metaphysic. The **body** is the individual self as an organism (neither flesh nor spirit being individual, and ' soul ' being merely the animating principle of the flesh, or physical structure). Thus the **sinful body** is the self as the organization of the sinful impulses inherent in the flesh.

Paul's metaphysic is hardly likely to commend itself to the thought of to-day. But his conception of the body, as the organized individual self, may be illustrated by the concept of the ' sentiment ' in modern psychology.[1] The instinctive impulses of our common human nature are conceived as organized in sentiments by reference to ends, or ideals. The individual personality is built up by means of a hierarchy of sentiments, and in proportion as they are truly harmonized with one another under a dominant sentiment, the self is unified and becomes a mature and effective personality. But each sentiment functions as a sort of sub-self, or image of the self, with its affections, ideas, and duties. If the sentiments are seriously at

---

[1] I would refer especially to Shand's *Foundations of Character* for an admirable treatment of the sentiment.

war with one another, we have a more or less acute case of
divided personality. A bad sentiment may be disintegrated,
and the instincts organized anew about more worthy ideals.
The growth of personality is a process of replacing bad sentiments by more worthy ones, i.e. by sentiments harmonious with
the immanent end of the personality, and consequently tending
to the unity of the self.

If now we think of the **sinful body** as a self organized out of
bad and disharmonious sentiments, **to crush the sinful body**
will be to disintegrate these bad sentiments, and so destroy
the self as built out of them, in preparation for the organization of a new self about the centre supplied by Christ to the
believer. That, at any rate, might be an alternative way of
describing the facts which Paul has in view. It does justice to his
insistence that a real death of the self is involved in the
sacramental death to sin by which a man enters the Christian
community.

To enforce his point, he is prepared to apply to this death 7
to sin, any proposition which would be accepted as true of
actual death. Thus, **once dead a man is absolved from
the claims of sin.** He is probably thinking of the rabbinic
maxim: ' When a man is dead, he is free from the Law and
the Commandments.' He may also have in mind the fact that
a dead man may not be prosecuted for crimes committed in his
life. His point, at any rate, is that in **the new sphere of Life**
the power of sin over a man is broken.

Now, therefore, follows the momentous conclusion. It has
been shown (1) that baptism into the Body of Christ means a
real sharing of His death and resurrection, and (2) that the
death of Christ was a death to sin, and His resurrection a
passing out of the sinful order of ' the flesh.' The inference is
that the member of Christ's Body has passed out of the sinful
order into a new order of which the centre is God, His righteousness, His love and grace. An intelligent appreciation of
these facts will produce in the Christian a new attitude to life. 11
He will now **consider** himself **dead to sin and alive to God.**
Those who raised the objection from which this argument
started ignored this necessary implicate of faith. They supposed
that a man who became a Christian under Paul's teaching,
that God justifies the ungodly on the ground of faith, would
still consider himself to be within the sinful order, and free to

sin, since **sin increased, but grace surpassed it far.** But faith, if it is the real thing, sets up such a relation to Christ that this attitude to life is altogether out of place. **There is a new creation whenever a man comes to Christ; what is old is gone, the new has come** (2 Cor. v. 17).

It is to be observed that in this account of the process of salvation the objective and the subjective aspects of the matter both appear. The ground of the whole process is the death of Christ (which, looked at from the inward side, is an act of the love of God). That is an objective fact: it is something that happened, in face of the whole world. Its benefits are appropriated by faith, a subjective attitude on the part of man. Faith is expressed in baptism, another objective fact, whereby the believer enters into the fellowship of Christ's people. The baptized person is then called upon to take up an attitude to life agreeable to the inward meaning of his baptism. He must **consider** himself **dead to sin and alive to God.** If Paul had held the view that the sacrament in itself, as a rite (a *drōmenon,* or thing done, as they said in the Greek mysteries), automatically conferred the new life, he could have said, *sans phrase,* ' You *are* dead to sin and alive to God.' He does, indeed, sometimes use this kind of language (e.g. Col. iii. 1). For on the ideal or purely religious plane, the Christian, by faith and by his solemn incorporation into Christ's people, *has* left the old life behind and entered upon the new. But Paul was realist enough to recognize that it did not by any means automatically follow that the Christian ceased to sin. His letters are full of exhortations to those who, *ex hypothesi,* have died to sin, but who are far from having realized the Christian ideal in practice. So here he insists that, while baptism has objectively placed a man within the **sphere of Life,** it rests with him to recognize this fact in a deliberate re-orientation of his own mind. Unless he ' considers himself dead to sin,' he is in effect not dead to sin, in spite of his baptism. Nevertheless, he *has* entered into a new set of relationships, which make it possible, natural, and all but inevitable to consider himself as sharing the risen life of Christ. The steady intention of mind and will is needed to make explicit in fact what is already given in principle. To use the psychological terms suggested above, the dominance of the bad sentiments has been broken, and all the materials are present for the formation of a new dominant sentiment, but it is actually formed only by deliberate attention to the object of that sentiment, which in this case is God, and His righteousness, love, and grace, as revealed in Christ.

Here follows a series of imperatives or hortatives driving ¹²⁻¹⁴ home the need for working out ethically all that is involved in being **in Christ.** The maxim all through is: ' *Werde das was Du bist* ' (' Become what you are '). The Christian is a member of Christ: he must see to it that in the empirical life of moral endeavour he becomes more and more that which a member of Christ should be. In human nature apart from Christ, **sin reigned.** By His life of perfect obedience, and His victorious death and resurrection, the reign of sin over human nature has been broken. It was broken for the individual when by baptism he entered into union with Christ in His death and resurrection. Yet it is possible that, though sin *need* no longer reign, the man will nevertheless allow it to reign. It is possible for him still to **let sin have** his **members for the service** 13 **of vice.** The seat of sin was the body of flesh and blood, which thereby became **a sinful body.** The Christian still possesses a flesh-and-blood body, so long as he is alive in this world. It *need* no longer be **a sinful body,** but it is still **a mortal body.** While the body remains fleshly, and so mortal, 12 it is still possible for sin to reign in it. **Sin** may still **reign in your mortal bodies and make you obey their passions.** The natural instincts, though released from bad sentiments, may yet assert themselves in wrong ways, unless by constant attention to the higher ideal they are organized into a new dominant sentiment. The negative warning, therefore, against falling under a renewed dominance of sin passes into a positive 13 admonition: **You must dedicate yourselves to God, as men who have been brought from death into life, dedicating your members to God for the service of righteousness** (cf. vi. 19-22, xii. 1). The **members** of the **mortal body**—that is, the various organs of our physical frame, with their faculties and instincts, through which the individual personality functions—are to be dedicated, severally and as a whole, to the service of God and His righteousness. As they are so dedicated, the mortal body itself ceases to be a sinful body, and becomes a temple of the holy Spirit (1 Cor. vi. 19—the whole of 1 Cor. vi. 9-20 provides a commentary upon this verse of Romans. Antinomian fanaticism has constantly taken the view that, the spirit being sanctified, the body does not matter. Paul guards against such a perversion of his teaching).

It might be said that the exhortation **dedicate yourselves to God** is no more than an echo of the precept of the Law: ' Ye shall be holy, for I am holy.' No doubt, where that precept occurs in the Pentateuch, the meaning of ' holiness ' is more than half ritual *taboo*; but spiritually-minded Jews, following the prophetic tradition, knew that it was a call to dedicate the whole life to righteousness. Then is Paul's appeal for righteousness in the Christian life simply a reassertion of the Law? In one sense, yes. For he recognized that the Law was in its intention holy, just, and good (vii. 12). But the Law (as he has already briefly stated, v. 20, and is to expound at 14 length in vii.) not only gave no power to break the yoke of sin, but actually provoked to sin, so that **under law** the effort to be really holy could never succeed. But to exhort Christians to dedicate themselves to God **as men who have been brought from death to life** is a different matter. They face the moral task free from the burden and the power of the sinful past, within a new order in which they are **under grace.** The grace of God gave Christ to die and rise again, and by union with Him they have entered into the **new sphere of Life,** which is a sphere of that **overflowing grace** which, as we have seen, has power to create good vastly exceeding the self-propagating power of evil (v. 16-17). And so to the conclusion of the whole matter. So far from the objection having weight, that if men live **under grace, not under law,** they will be likely to **remain on in sin, so that there may be all the more grace,** that is the very reason why they will not—or, at any rate, *should* not—sin. That is the sense given by Moffatt's translation: **Sin must have no hold over you.** But the verb in the Greek is future, and although the Greek future can have a hortative force, there seems no need to give it such a force here. Verse 14 is perhaps best taken as a statement: Granted that you **consider yourselves dead to sin and alive to God;** granted that you **dedicate yourselves to God;** then **sin** *will* **have no hold over you.**

Such then are the lines on which Paul's reply runs. We cannot fully judge of its adequacy before reading his further elaboration of it in the sections which follow, and expecially the penetrating psychological analysis of vii. 7–25. But he has said enough to make any such misinterpretation of his teaching as that suggested in vi. 1 look ludicrous. And he has said enough to convince us that he is not spinning a theory or

indulging a fantasy when he speaks of salvation through Christ.
He keeps close to experience and to facts. He confidently
assumes that his readers will know what he means when he
speaks of **living and moving in the new sphere of life.**
It was not only his own experience; it was not only that of
converts he had won; it was that of Christians in general.
The life and fellowship of the Christian community, where
every man had personally committed himself to God in Christ,
did offer a totally new environment, which at every point
helped to bring the grace of God home to a man, so that he
felt himself in a new order, and was prepared to live accordingly.
Only where this was true could Paul's argument from baptism
carry its full weight, as an appeal to recognized facts.

vi. 15-23 : *An Illustration from Slavery*

What follows, then? Are we 'to sin, because we live 15
under grace, not under law'? Never! Do you not 16
know you are the servants of the master you obey,
of the master to whom you yield yourselves obedient,
whether it is Sin, whose service ends in death, or
Obedience, whose service ends in righteousness? 17
Thank God, though you did serve sin, you have
rendered whole-hearted obedience to what you were 18
taught under the rule of faith; set free from sin, 19
you have passed into the service of righteousness.
(I use this human analogy to bring the truth home to
your weak nature.) As you once dedicated your
members to the service of vice and lawlessness, * **so**
now dedicate them to the service of righteousness
that means consecration. When you served sin, you 20
were free of righteousness. Well, what did you gain 21
then by it all? Nothing but what you are now
ashamed of ! The end of all that is death; but now 22
that you are set free from sin, now that you have
passed into the service of God, your gain is conse-
cration, and the end of that is life eternal. Sin's 23
wage is death, but God's gift is life eternal in Christ
Jesus our Lord.

The illegitimate inference from Paul's teaching about grace 15

---

* Omitting εἰς τὴν ἀνομίαν, which Hort brackets, as a gloss introduced to complete the parallel of εἰς ἁγιασμόν.

is now re-stated, in order that its falsity may be driven home by a fresh illustration. There is no advance in principle in this section. The reply to the objector is the same: that through faith in Christ a man passes from the sinful order into a new order of life in which sin has no place. In vi. 1–14 this was expressed by saying that he had through baptism died with Christ, and entered into the new sphere of life: conversion is represented as a death of the old self. In this section an illustration is drawn from the institution of slavery, and conversion is represented as a change of masters.

In order to get the full force of the argument we must bear in mind that the word translated **servant** is properly ' slave,' and **service** is ' slavery.' Slavery was an institution without parallel in our civilization. Among us the servant is an employee. His employer has a certain claim upon his time and energies, represented by the wages he pays him. Outside that contractual obligation the servant is free to dispose of his time and labour as he chooses. There is no reason why he should not serve two masters: he may sit at a desk during the day, and play a fiddle in an orchestra in the evening. The position of a slave was entirely different. He belonged to his master, who alone had a claim upon his time and energies, and could dispose of him as he thought fit. The slave could not be under obligation to anyone other than his master. He was as independent of all other persons as if he were a free man. It is this exclusive relation between master and slave that gives point to the illustration.

16   We should therefore read: **You are the** *slaves* **of the master you obey, of the master to whom you yield yourselves obedient.** The masters here in question are Sin on the one hand (verse 17) and Righteousness on the other (verse 18), and the maxim holds good: ' No one can be slave to two masters ' (Matt. vi. 24). One or the other claims exclusive obedience, whether it be Sin or Righteousness. That is straightforward enough, but in his first statement of the matter, in verse 16, Paul has confused the matter by substituting **Obedience** for Righteousness, and making **righteousness** the aim or outcome of the slavery to **Obedience,** as **death** is the outcome of the slavery to **Sin.** This is probably little more than an inadvertence in dictating, partly due perhaps to the fact that the righteousness of Christ has been described as obedience, in contrast to the disobedience of Adam; so that the state of the Christian is thought of emphatically as obedience, in contrast to the sinful state of

disobedience. But it is certainly not felicitous to suggest that
the master who is obeyed is Obedience! Paul soon feels this,
and passes over into the more natural antithesis of Sin and
Righteousness.

The idea of slavery to Sin is one of Paul's constant ideas, and
is in harmony with all that he has said before about the reign
of Sin in the flesh over all who are **in Adam.** But when he
comes to speak of the transfer of the slave to his new master, his
thought moves on a lower level than heretofore. He speaks as
though conversion were simply the acceptance of the ethical 17
teachings of **a rule of faith,** with the result that, **set free** 18
from sin, you have passed into the slavery **of righteous-**
ness (for **service** here, as we have seen, translates a word which
means ' slavery '—as it does not in verse 13 above.) It is no
wonder he feels the need to apologize for such an expression.
I use this human analogy, he says, **to bring the truth home**
to your weak nature. (For similar apologetical expressions
cf. iii. 5; Gal. iii. 15.) The apology cannot be called tactful,
but it shows that Paul is conscious that his illustration is not
going very well. Slavery to righteousness, indeed! Would not
that more aptly describe life under the Law than the condition
of Christian freedom? However, it serves to introduce the
salutary admonition which follows. **As you once dedicated** 19
your members to the slavery **of vice and lawlessness, so**
now dedicate them to the slavery **of righteousness that**
means consecration. There is a certain strength of appeal
in the thought of a life deeply and irrevocably committed one
way or the other—as irrevocably committed as a slave bought
in the market—and some readers who recalled how thoroughgoing they had been in the **service of vice and lawlessness**
might be led to feel afresh how thoroughly they were committed, by accepting the **rule of faith,** to the **service of**
righteousness. But it is all rather impersonal and sub-
Christian. It does, however, certainly effect its immediate
purpose, of proving that Paul was as far as possible from teaching
that we are free **to sin, because we live under grace, not**
under law.

Still pursuing the metaphor of the transfer of a slave, the
apostle moves to a fresh point which is not directly relevant to
his main purpose at present, but serves to enforce his exhortation—the point that the results of the transfer of allegiance are
infinitely worth while. **Set free from sin,** he has said, **you**
have passed into the slavery **of righteousness.** Formerly, 20

when you were the slaves of **sin, you were free from righteousness.** But what was that ' freedom ' worth? **What did
21 you gain then by it all? Nothing,** he replies, **but what
you are now ashamed of! The end of all that is death**
(as was amply shown in earlier chapters). What of the new
22 ' slavery,' which is also freedom from sin? **Your gain is
consecration, and the end of that is life eternal.** In the
description of this new slavery we note a subtle change of phrase.
It is no longer **the service of righeousness,** but **the service
of God.** It is true that the idea of ' slavery ' to God is one
which will later have to be corrected into the more adequate
idea of sonship to God. But, even so the thought is struggling
back from the impersonal level of obedience to a **rule of faith,**
and of slavery to **righteousness,** to Paul's habitual level of
thought on which the Christian life is essentially a personal
relation to God in Christ. The way is thus prepared for the
culminating statement of this paragraph: **Sin's wage is death,
23 but God's gift is life eternal in Christ Jesus our Lord.**
Here the contrast between God and Sin is hardly more important than the corresponding antithesis between **wage** and **gift.**
The old order, **in Adam,** was one in which man was subject to
a quasi-mechanical process of cause and consequence, sin
bringing forth more sin, and leading inevitably to spiritual
catastrophe. The new order **in Christ** is one of **overflowing
grace,** in which everything comes to man as a gift of the love
of God. Eternal life is not won by man's **service of righteousness,** in the sense in which death was deserved by his sin: both
righteousness and eternal life are God's gift, even though man
must appropriate them by moral endeavour. We are thus
back on the full evangelical level, from which Paul's thought
only temporarily and uneasily descends.

vii. 1–6: *An Illustration from the Law of Marriage*

vii.

**Surely you know, my brothers—for I am speaking to
1   men who know what law means—that the law has
hold over a person only during his lifetime ! Thus
2   a married woman is bound by law to her husband
while he is alive; but if the husband dies, she is done
3   with the law of ' the husband.' Accordingly, she will
be termed an adulteress if she becomes another
man's while her husband is alive; but if her husband
4   dies, she is freed from the law of ' the husband,' so**

**that she is no adulteress if she becomes another
man's. It is the same in your case, my brothers.
The crucified body of Christ made you dead to the
Law, so that you might belong to another, to Him
who was raised from the dead that we might be 5
fruitful to God. For when we were unspiritual, the
sinful cravings excited by the Law were active in
our members and made us fruitful to Death; but 6
now we are done with the Law, we have died to what
once held us, so that we can serve in a new way, not
under the written code as of old but in the Spirit.**

We are now to have another illustration of the general thesis
that the Christian has passed out of the power of sin. Only in
this illustration the place of sin is somewhat unexpectedly taken
by law. We have already learned that **law slipped in to
aggravate the trespass,** but it is only in the latter part of
this chapter that we shall discover just what Paul meant by
that (though a hint is given, as we shall presently see, in verse
5). In order to follow his illustration we must grant him that
to be really free from sin one must also be free from law. The
illustration is taken from the institution of marriage, as regulated
by both Jewish and Roman law. It is particularly addressed
to men who know what law means; but whether Paul
intended this as a compliment to Romans, who at the centre
of government should know what the great system of Roman
law meant, or contemplated rather Jewish-Christian readers,
who knew the Law of Moses, is a question impossible to answer.
The provisions of both laws are the same so far as this particular
matter is concerned.

The illustration, however, is confused from the outset. Paul
begins by announcing (as he had already announced in vi. 7) 1
the legal principle **that the law has hold over a person
only in his lifetime.** But the particular instance he chooses
does not, as a matter of fact, exemplify this principle. **A married woman is bound by law to her husband while he is 2
alive; but if the husband dies, she is done with the law
of the husband.** ('**The law of the husband**' means,
according to current legal phraseology, that section of the
code which regulates the rights and duties of husbands, much
as we speak of 'the law of property.') Here it is not the dead
husband, but the living wife, who is freed from the obligations
of the law. She is therefore free to marry again. What then,

is the application of the illustration, or metaphor, or allegory, or whatever it is? Broadly speaking, what seems to be in Paul's mind is the idea that a man was wedded to Law (which means wedded to Sin), but by death he is free to be wedded to Christ. Thus ' law ' plays a double part. The whole story is an example of the working of a law, and, at the same time, ' Law ' is a character in the story! To make confusion worse confounded, it is not Law, the first husband, who dies: the Christian, on the 4 other hand, is **dead to the Law.** The illustration, therefore, has gone hopelessly astray. The only *tertium comparationis* that remains is the bare fact that, in one way or another, death puts an end to obligations. We shall do best to ignore the illustration as far as may be, and ask what it is that Paul is really talking about in the realm of fact and experience.

We may start with verse 4, which bears the weight of the argument. It is essentially a re-statement of the position maintained in vi. 1–11. The Christian is dead in union with his crucified Lord. **The crucified body of Christ made you dead to the Law.** The literal translation of these words is ' You were made dead to the Law through the body of Christ.' Dr. Moffatt has taken the view that ' the body of Christ ' means the actual body which was crucified—' the body of his flesh ' (**his mortal body,** as he renders it in Col. i. 22). But, for Paul, the Body of Christ is the Church (1 Cor. xii. 27; Eph. i. 23, iv. 12, v. 30, and similarly Rom. xii. 5). The question arises here, as it does in 1 Cor. x. 16, xi. 29, whether ' the body of Christ ' means the actual body which died on the cross or the Church as forming His mystical Body. The answer probably is that Paul took so seriously the idea of the Church as embodying the ' corporate personality ' of Christ, that in the death of Christ on the cross he always saw the death of the whole people of God to sin, law, and the flesh. All Christians, as **participating in the** [mystical] **body of Christ** (1 Cor. x. 16), have been crucified with Christ (Gal. ii. 20). Thus we may render the present passage [1]: ' As belonging to the Body of Christ, you have died with Christ to the Law.' We have then an exact parallel to the thought of vi. 1–11. In any case, the result of this death, of Christ for us, and of ourselves ' in Him,' is that we **belong to Christ** (as the wife belongs to her husband) —**to Him who was raised from the dead**—for it is to a living husband that the wife belongs. It would be better, then, to

---

[1] After Schweitzer's paraphrase in *Die Mystik des Apostels Paulus,* p. 186.

put a comma after the word ' dead.' The object of this union with Christ (rather than of His resurrection as such) is **that we might be fruitful to God.** The idea of a fruitful marriage union suggests this addition, which enforces the point that the reasonable and proper result of conversion to Christianity is a morally fruitful life (and not an indifference to morality **because we live under grace, not under law**). The first ' marriage ' was indeed a fruitful one: **when we were unspiritual** (literally, ' in the flesh '), **the sinful cravings excited by the Law were active in our members and made us fruitful to Death.** Here Paul is anticipating his account, in the next section, of the actual effects of living under the Law: it excites our sinful cravings. That is what justifies him in equating subjection to law with subjection to sin.

With verse 6 the illustration of marriage is forgotten, and that of slavery comes up again. We are, as in vi. 22, slaves of God—but slaves **in a new way, not under the written code as of old, but in the Spirit.** That would serve as an explanatory footnote to what is said in vi. 15–23 about ' slavery ' to righteousness—it is not slavery in the sense of a blind and irresponsible subservience to a **written code,** but one informed by the spontaneity of the Spirit—and therefore not properly ' slavery ' at all, but allegiance to a God ' whose service is perfect freedom.' This idea will be magnificently developed in chap. viii.

The two lines of illustration, then, which Paul offers, have not proved very felicitous. He lacks the gift for sustained illustration of ideas through concrete images (though he is capable of a brief, illuminating metaphor). It is probably a defect of imagination. We cannot help contrasting his laboured and blundering allegories with the masterly parables of Jesus, unerring in their immediate translation of ideas into pictures, or rather their recognition of the idea in the picture which life itself presents. Paul flounders among the images he has tried to evoke, and then with unconscious humour pleads that he is trying to stoop to the **weak nature** of his correspondents. We are relieved when he tires of his unmanageable puppets, and talks about real things. His allegories of the slave and the widow give him an excuse for coming back again and again to the things he really wants to say, and he brings each section to a triumphant conclusion. **Sin's wage is death, but God's gift is life eternal in Christ Jesus our Lord. . . . We can** serve in a new way, not under the written code as of old, but in the Spirit. Those two sentences are no bad summary of the Pauline Gospel.

vii. 7–25: *Sin and Salvation in Experience*

What follows, then? That 'the Law is equivalent to
7 sin'? Never! Why, had it not been for the Law, I would never have known what sin meant! Thus I would never have known what it is to covet, unless the Law had said, *You must not covet.* The command
8 gave an impulse to sin, and sin resulted for me in all manner of covetous desire—for sin, apart from
9 law, is lifeless. I lived at one time without law myself, but when the command came home to me, sin sprang to life and I died; the command that
10 meant life proved death for me. The command gave
11 an impulse to sin, sin beguiled me and used the com-
12 mand to kill me. So the Law at any rate is holy, the
13 command is holy, just, and for our good. Then did what was meant for my good prove fatal to me? Never! It was sin; sin resulted in death for me by making use of this good thing. This was how sin
14 was to be revealed in its true nature; it was to use the command to become sinful in the extreme. The Law is spiritual; we know that. But then I am a
15 creature of the flesh, in the thraldom of sin. I cannot understand my own actions; I do not act as I want
16 to act; on the contrary, I do what I detest. Now,
17 when I act against my wishes, that means I agree that the Law is right. That being so, it is not I who
18 do the deed but sin that dwells within me. For in me (that is, in my flesh) no good dwells, I know; the wish is there, but not the power of doing what is
19 right. I cannot be good as I want to be, and I do
20 wrong against my wishes. Well, if I act against my
21 wishes, it is not I who do the deed but sin that dwells within me. So this is my experience of the Law: I
22 want to do what is right, but wrong is all I can
23 manage; I cordially agree with God's law, so far as my inner self is concerned, but then I find quite another law in my members which conflicts with the

law of my mind and makes me a prisoner to sin's
law that resides in my members. (Thus, left to 25
myself, I serve the law of God with my mind, but
with my flesh I serve the law of sin.)* Miserable 24
wretch that I am! Who will rescue me from this 25
body of death? God will! Thanks be to Him
through Jesus Christ our Lord!

We are now done with metaphor and illustration, and come
down to direct psychological analysis of the experience of
salvation from sin. The account is given, down to the end of
chap. vii., in the first person singular. *Prima facie*, we are
reading autobiography. It would be of great interest to know
whether we really have here a passage from the autobiography
of Paul. It is clear that, even if he is describing his own personal
experience, he means to generalize from it, for at the beginning
of chap. viii. we have both the first person plural and the third
person plural. There are other passages in the epistles where
Paul says ' I,' where apparently he might have said ' one.' For
example, in 1 Cor. viii. 13, he says, **If food is any hindrance
to my brother's welfare, sooner than injure him, I will
never eat flesh as long as I live.** In a very similar passage
in Rom. xiv. 21, he puts the same conclusion in general terms:
**The right course is to abstain from flesh or wine, or
indeed anything that your brother feels to be a stumbling-
block.** Similarly, in 1 Cor. xiii. 1-3, 11-12, the ' I ' does not
differ decisively from the ' we ' with which it alternates, and in
1 Cor. xiv. 6-19 there is a long discussion of ' speaking with
tongues ' where the repeated ' I ' might well be no more than
a convenience. Are we to say the same of Rom. vii. 7-25?

Such a conclusion might be supported by the observation
that the description of the fall into sin in verses 9-11 reads like
an allegorical interpretation of the story of the Fall of Adam in
Genesis. The importance of that passage for Paul's thought is
obvious; he has many allusions to it. Further, Philo of Alexandria, who was Paul's older contemporary, interprets it
allegorically in detail. Pleasure (the serpent) seduces the Senses
(Eve), and so Reason (Adam) is led astray: and so forth. A
slightly later writer, a pagan this time, found in the story a
parable of how Divine Humanity desired union with Material
Nature, and so fell; with the result that man as we know him,

---

* Restoring the second part of verse 25 to what seems its original and logical
position before the climax of verse 24.

though the divine spark is in him, is yet mortal (Tract *Poimandres* in the Hermetic Corpus, lately edited and translated by Walter Scott). It would thus be entirely natural for Paul to treat the biblical story as an allegory of the fall into sin which is a part of each man's individual experience; as another first-century writer said, ' Each of us has been the Adam of his own soul ' (Apocalypse of Baruch liv. 19). Paul read in Genesis how Adam at first lived in innocence. A command was given to him, intended to prevent him from forfeiting his immortality, according to the rabbinic interpretation. The serpent, subtly turning this command to his own ends, seduced Adam (through his wife —but, for Paul here, that is not significant). He transgressed the command, and death was the result. ' Which things,' as Paul might have said, ' are an allegory ' (cf. Gal. iv. 24). Translated into terms of individual experience, the story runs: **I lived at one time without law myself, but when the command came home to me, sin sprang to life and I died; the command that meant life proved death for me. The command gave an impulse to sin, sin beguiled me, and used the command to kill me.** It fits like a glove; and there are enough verbal echoes of the Greek translation of Gen. iii. to make it likely that Paul actually had the passage in mind. Such an exposition of the story of the Fall, as a parable of individual experience, is a commonplace in modern preaching. It is not always realized that Paul interpreted it so; but such is probably the case.

Are we, then, to conclude that in the passage before us the account of the fall into sin is nothing more than an allegorized version of an Old Testament story? And that the whole passage is not autobiography, but an ideal construction? Probably not. First of all, we may observe that when a man sets out to allegorize the Old Testament, he finds there what he puts in. Philo found one thing, the author of *Poimandres* another, according to their several prepossessions. The reason why Paul found there a story of how an individual fell into the power of sin and death was that he had had experience of it, and the old story fitted his experience. We may further ask whether the use of the first person singular is likely, after all, in view of Paul's general usage, to be a mere literary convention. It is probable that in 1 Cor. viii. 13 he means a good deal more than ' If food is a hindrance to one's brother, one will abstain from flesh,' for he sums up the whole discussion with the words: **Such is my own**

rule, to satisfy all men in all points, aiming not at my own private advantage but at the advantage of the greater number—at their salvation. Copy me, as I copy Christ (1 Cor. x. 33–xi. 1). The ' I ' is of substantial significance: he commends his own practice for imitation by those who know him. In writing on the same point to the Romans, who did not know him, he puts the maxim in general terms, referring them directly to the example of Christ (xv. 2–3). Similarly, in 1 Cor. xiii. and xiv., where the discussion turns upon spiritual gifts—' speaking with tongues,' and the like—it is by no means without significance that Paul should offer himself as a case in point; for he claimed such ' spiritual gifts ' himself; and where he is on the whole rather depreciating such gifts as ' speaking with tongues,' it is both tactful and effective to take his own case as an example. It will in fact be found on examination that Paul rarely, if ever, says ' I ' unless he is really speaking of himself personally, even if he means to generalize from the particular instance. Certainly, when he is describing religious experience, his ' I ' passages bear the unmistakable note of auto-biography. Who can doubt that in Gal. ii. 19–21, or Phil. iii. 7–14, to mention no others, we are reading personal confessions of the most intimate kind? If further proof were needed that our present passage is of the same type, we need only observe the emotion which breaks out at the close: **Miserable wretch that I am ! Who will rescue me from this body of death?** A man is not moved like that by an ideal construction.

We may take it, then, that this passage does describe Paul's own experience. The next question is, To what period of his life does it refer? Two views have been taken: (1) that it describes his condition at the time of writing, and therefore may describe the condition of any Christian; (2) that it describes his condition before his conversion, culminating at the moment at which he was ' apprehended by Christ Jesus.' *Prima facie* the present tense of the verbs in verses 14–25 suggests the former view. It is, no doubt, possible for a Christian to find himself in this miserable state of inward division and impotence, in need of falling back afresh on the redeeming grace of God; and Paul himself confessed that to the end there was struggle and insecurity (1 Cor. ix. 26–27; Phil. iii. 13). But the setting of this confession in the argument of the epistle seems to rule out the view that Paul is describing anything but the momentous beginning of his Christian career. He is continuing an argu-

ment to show that **under grace** a man is free from the power
of sin. He has already said that the Christian has **died to sin,**
and moves in **the new sphere of Life.** He has compared him
to a slave bought by a new master, and to a widow set free to
marry again. It would stultify his whole argument if he now
confessed that, at the moment of writing, he was **a miserable
wretch, a prisoner to sin's law** (verses 24, 23). He would
have thought it quite abnormal that any Christian should feel
so, and there is nothing in his own confessions elsewhere to lead
us to suppose that, with all his sense of struggle and insecurity,
he ever had such an experience as this after his conversion. We
conclude that Paul is clinching his argument by the undeniable
evidence of his own experience that he was once **dead in
trespasses and sins,** but has now found life and liberty.

This long argument, which may seem merely proving the
obvious to most readers who take the chapter at its face value,
has been worth while if it justifies us in accepting this immortal
description as an authentic transcript of Paul's own experience
during the period which culminated in his vision on the road
to Damascus. As such it will be treated in the detailed commentary which follows, while we shall, of course, bear in mind
that Paul is presenting an individual case as typical.

The formal transition from the last section is made in verse 7.
Paul has given two illustrations of what happens in conversion.
In the first, the part of the enslaving power is played by Sin; in
7 the second, the corresponding part is taken by Law. This
naturally raises the question, Does it follow **that the Law is
equivalent to sin?** It is easy to see how shocking such a suggestion would be to any Jew. What?—the sacred Law, the
best thing he had ever known in his religious life—the Law
which commanded, ' Thou shalt love the Lord thy God, and
thy neighbour as thyself ' (cf. xiii. 9)—the Law **equivalent to
sin? Never!** says Paul. He has already briefly defined the
relation he considered law to bear to sin, in iii. 20: **What the
Law imparts is the consciousness of sin.** This he repeats
here in slightly different words, and proceeds at once to exemplify his meaning. **Thus I should never have known what
it is to covet, unless the Law had said, You must not
covet.** A man has many instinctive desires, which in the raw
state, so to speak, are morally indifferent. But in relation to an
ethical ideal some are right and some are wrong. If there is,
as Paul firmly believed, an objective ethical ideal, immanent

in the very nature of man as a spiritual being (cf. ii. 14-15), then desires which conflict with it are (in his sense of the word) sinful, whether a man is conscious of the ideal or not, though he may not be guilty personally (cf. v. 13). When however he becomes conscious of a Law, which sets forth an ethical ideal, and in the light of it stigmatizes certain desires as wrong, then the **consciousness of sin** awakes. The man may still cherish the wrong desires. If he does, he is not only sinful (in Paul's sense), but guilty.

In the next verse, Paul takes a further step, without making 8 it clear that it is a further step. Not only does Law bring the **consciousness of sin;** in his own experience Paul found that **the command gave an impulse to sin.** Paradoxical as it may appear, this is quite a common experience. Let Augustine, a master of introspective psychology, as well as the greatest interpreter of Paul, supply us with an example. In the second book of his *Confessions* he recalls a youthful prank. ' There was a pear-tree near our vineyard, laden with fruit. At dead of night we rascally youths set out to rob it and carry our spoils away. We took off a huge load of pears—not to feast upon them ourselves, but to throw them to the pigs—though we ate just enough to have the pleasure of forbidden fruit. They were nice pears, but it was not the pears that my wretched soul coveted, for I had plenty better at home. I picked them simply in order to be a thief. The only feast I got was a feast of iniquity, and that I enjoyed to the full. What was it that I loved in that theft? Was it the pleasure of acting against the law, in order that I, a prisoner under rules, might have a maimed counterfeit of freedom, by doing with impunity what was forbidden, with a dim similitude of omnipotence? ' [1] That is to say that the desire to steal was aroused simply by the prohibition of stealing. **The command gave an impulse to sin, and sin resulted for me in all sorts of covetous desire.**

It is highly significant that Paul has chosen for his example the one prohibition of the Decalogue which deals with the inner life, and not with overt action. Let us suppose that a man, confronted by a list of prohibited acts, sets himself, either in fear of the penalty, or because he is conscientious, to avoid them. If the motive is strong enough, he may succeed in disciplining himself into strict conformity. But can he by a similar process control the desire to do these forbidden things? There

[1] Abridged from the long passage, *Conf.* II. 4-6 (my translation).

is a saying of Eleazar ben Azariah, who lived about A.D. 100: ' One should not say, " I have no desire for mixed garments, or swine's flesh, or illicit sexual relations." One should say, " I have a desire for these things, but since my heavenly Father has forbidden them to me, what can I do? " ' [1] Finely said (if one grants that these things are on the same level). But it does not touch the problem of the tenth commandment of the Decalogue. That, obviously, was where the shoe pinched for Paul. It is one of the most important teachings of modern psychology, and one most readily verifiable by analysis, that the attempt to repress an instinctive desire, directly, seldom succeeds in its object. If the desire is repressed, it is likely to form a ' complex ' below the threshold of consciousness, and to break into the conscious life in fresh and perhaps even more deleterious forms.

We are now to trace the natural history of sin from its beginnings in the conscious life. **I lived at one time without law myself,** says Paul. To bring out the full force of this we need in English some stronger word than ' **lived,**' for, when we say ' I lived,' we may mean no more than ' I spent my time.' Paul means ' I was alive '—' I lived my own life,' with powers and faculties at full stretch. He is describing a happy childhood —happier and freer in retrospect, no doubt, than it ever really was. Do we not all look back to a golden age, before school, before parental authority was felt as restrictive, before the troublesome conscience awoke? ' I lived my own life, without law ': nothing could more aptly set before us the lusty little boy, discovering every day new powers in himself, new opportunities for fun and mischief. We speak of the ' age of innocence,' but the little innocent is in actual fact greedy, interfering, quarrelsome, completely regardless of the rights or conveniences of other people. But **sin is never counted in the absence of law.** Soon, however, in a Puritan home like Paul's, ' shades of the prison-house begin to close upon the growing boy.' He became aware of the precepts and prohibitions of the Law. His desires were thwarted and repressed. The instincts asserted themselves in rebellion, and imperious desires for forbidden things forced themselves into his mind. **When the command came home to me, sin sprang to life and I died.** It is hardly necessary to say that the ' death ' here spoken of has nothing whatever to do with the sacramental

[1] Quoted by Dalman, *Worte Jesu,* 1898, p. 79.

death to sin spoken of in vi. 2. It describes the condition of impotence resulting from unsuccessful moral struggle, but with a side-glance at the story of the Fall of Man in Genesis, where transgression dooms man to death. For the old story had now come true in Paul's own experience: **The command gave an** 11 **impulse to sin**—or, to keep closer to the Greek, ' sin found a base of operations in the command ' (the metaphor being a military one, continued in verse 23, where both the word **' conflicts '** and the phrase **' makes me a prisoner '** are directly taken from the vocabulary of the army). In other words, **sin beguiled me [' as the serpent beguiled Eve '** (2 Cor. xi. 3—the same verb)], **and used the command to kill me.**

This account assumes that the Law did represent an objective moral ideal, with which wrong desires based on misdirected instinctive impulses were in conflict. Thus, in spite of the disastrous outcome, **the Law at any rate is holy, the command is holy, just and for our good** (cf. Deut. vi. 24, a passage which Paul may well have had in mind). Thus the idea that **the Law is equivalent to sin** is refuted. The conflict would not have arisen but that the Law represented a good with which the evil came in conflict (this is already implied, but is made clearer in what follows).   13

But, granting this, did not Law after all produce these disastrous results, and is it not therefore in effect an evil thing? **Never !** replies Paul. **It was sin; sin resulted in death to me by making use of this good thing.** Moreover, the Law served a useful purpose: by arousing sin to activity it showed what a heinous thing it was. **This was how sin was to be revealed in its true nature; it was to use the command to become sinful in the extreme.**

But this strange fact, that sin should use so essentially good a thing as law to destroy a man, needs some further explanation. 14 The explanation lies in a sphere beyond the conscious individual self. **I am a creature of the flesh. The flesh** is the common stuff of human nature which we inherit. In accordance with Hebrew thought in general, Paul does not think of it as necessarily evil, but as in itself powerless for moral ends. **In me** 18 **(that is, in my flesh) no good dwells.** But this powerless substrate of human nature has fallen under the power of sin— whether through Adam's transgression (as suggested in v. 12, in accordance with at any rate one type of rabbinic teaching) or because men, though **they knew God,** turned to idolatry of the creature, and so fell under the dominion of **the elemental**

14 **spirits of the world** (Rom. i. 23, Gal iv. 3). Thus by no choice of his own a man, as **a creature of the flesh, is in the thraldom of sin.**

We might put it in this way: the instincts with which a man is born are not individual, but racial. In themselves they are morally indifferent; they are certainly not evil, but equally certainly they do not by themselves lead men into those ways of living by which the true ends of personality are attained. They are part of our inheritance from a brute ancestry, and, though they are capable of becoming the raw material of personality, for that they need to be organized into sentiments by being directed to true ideals. But human society in its actual and historical forms is such that true ideals are obscured, and the formation of true sentiments is fatally hindered by the environment by which we are so largely determined. This may seem a pessimistic judgment. In a society which, like our own, has had for centuries a real though diluted Christian tradition, it is no doubt less true than it was in Paul's world. And he tends to exaggerate, and to paint things in a clearer black-and-white than nature shows (the admission of ii. 14–15 should not be forgotten). But when all discount has been allowed, is it not true that the world into which we are born is under the dominion of false gods? Is it not true at this moment that, although the experts know the kind of thing which could and should be done to deal with the present world-wide depression, yet envy, hatred, greed, and fear so rule the peoples that little can be done? All this is in the ' flesh ' that we inherit; we are given a bias from the first by a heredity and environment tainted with these things. Paul is right in seeking at a level deeper than individual choices for the roots of our moral malady.

So we come back to the point at which the restraints of law begin to make themselves felt. Because of the bias towards the lower desires, which Paul has thus accounted for, the growing boy discovers in himself a reaction against the law. But as he grows up, there is something in him which after all wants to be good. Only, wrong desires have already been provoked. False sentiments have been formed. He cannot act as he would wish. He is plunged in moral perplexity. **I cannot understand** [or, perhaps, ' recognize,' or ' acknowledge '] **my own actions; I do not act as I want to act; on the contrary I do what I detest.** That is a well-recognized condition. It is succinctly described by Ovid in the familiar lines: ' *Video*

meliora proboque; Deteriora sequor.' Aristotle distinguished four
stages in the moral history possible to a man: the first (*akolasia*,
or downright wickedness), in which he neither knows nor desires
what is good; the second (*akrasia*, or incontinence), in which he
knows what is right, but fails to do it; the third (*enkrateia*, con-
tinence or self-control), in which he succeeds in doing right by
constant effort and struggle; the fourth (*sophrosyne*, or temper-
ance), in which the personality is so harmonized that the right
is done without a struggle. The second stage corresponds with
the condition Paul is here describing. Aristotle regards it as
definitely better than the first stage, and so no doubt would
Paul, though his line of approach is different.

Paul is concerned to examine this condition more closely. 16
First, he says, it is clear that **when I act against my wishes,
I agree that the Law is right.** That is important to him, in 17
view of the question with which he started in verse 7. Further,
**that being so, it is not I who do the deed, but sin that
dwells within me.** That suggests a very intense experience of
divided personality. So complete is the separation between the
will to do and the deed, that the man feels that some alien power
in him is actually performing his actions. Paul is not meaning
to shuffle out of responsibility for his actions by ascribing them
to the alien power. What he wishes to show is how completely
he is under **the thraldom of sin**—so completely that he sins 22–
against his wish. Yet all the time there is another part of him 23
which rebels against this thraldom, the **inner self,** which is
here characterized as the **mind**—or better, ' reason,' for the
Greek word is the one current in this sense in the philosophers.
As the ' flesh ' is related to the lower creation, so the reason is
related to the higher order which is spiritual. The Law itself,
as being God's law, belongs to this spiritual order. The spiritual
part of man, therefore, is able to recognize the ideal presented
in the Law, and to assent to it, while because of the **thraldom
of sin** the flesh revolts against it. **This is my experience of
the Law: I want to do right, but the wrong is all I can
manage; I cordially agree with God's law, so far as my
inner self is concerned, but then I find quite another law
in my members which conflicts with the law of my
reason, and makes me a prisoner to sin's law that resides
in my members.**

Verse 25*b*, which follows here in Moffatt's version, re-states
the same conclusion in slightly different words: **Thus, left to
myself, I serve the law of God with my** reason, **but with**

my flesh I serve the law of sin. All our MSS. of Paul's epistles give the verse after 24–25*a*, but Dr. Moffatt is surely right in saying that its logical position is before the climax of verse 24. For it is scarcely conceivable that, after giving thanks to God for deliverance, Paul should describe himself as being in exactly the same position as before. It is easy to conjecture various ways in which the displacement may have come about. For example, it is possible that an early reader of the epistle jotted down in the margin a more succinct and epigrammatic paraphrase of the somewhat cumbrous statement in verses 22–23, and that the next copyist incorporated the note in the text at the wrong place. Or again, the mistake may have arisen in the first writing of the epistle. Paul, we know, dictated his letters to an amanuensis (cf. xvi. 22). At what a headlong speed must he have dictated this chapter, as he approached the emotional climax! It is conceivable that he himself repeated the statement of verses 22–23 in the more succinct form of verse 25, and that the amanuensis got confused, and made his fair copy in the wrong order. However this may be, we do seem to have here one of the cases (which, all New Testament scholars recognize, occur occasionally) where a primitive corruption of the text has affected all our surviving MSS., and we cannot avoid trusting our own judgment against their evidence.

We may therefore take verses 22, 23, and 25*b* as describing the state of a man who has reached desperation in the moral conflict—describing, if the argument above was right, Paul's own state when he set out for Damascus. He recognizes and affirms the moral ideal intellectually, with the ' reason '; but he has not succeeded in forming harmonious sentiments directed towards this ideal. His instinctive impulses remain attached to unworthy sentiments, and act only through low desires. But these instinctive impulses, whether rightly or wrongly directed, provide the only driving force for effective action. Thus the mere acceptance of the ideal by the reason brings no power to approximate to its realization. The will itself is impotent because of the division within the personality. ' The development of Will takes place when the self is so organized that it can act as a whole ' (Hadfield, *Psychology and Morals*, p. 102. Chaps. ix.–xi. of this book admirably illustrate Romans vii.). There is therefore no true freedom of the will so long as the self is divided, the ' reason ' paying homage to the ideal while the ' flesh ' is 24 dominated by ' the law of sin.'

That this condition of division and impotence is a miserable one, everybody knows. It is particularly miserable for a religious man, such as Paul was before his conversion. He recognized the ideal as **God's law.** He knew that only in communion with God was there any happiness or satisfaction for him. Without Him, he was **dead.** But there is no communion with God in a merely intellectual homage to His law, while all the instinctive impulses and desires are organized into a **body of death.** (The meaning of the phrase is sufficiently clear if we recall the **sinful body** of vi. 6 in the light of vii. 9, 13; it is not the same as the **mortal body** of vi. 12.) As Paul, in his vivid description, recalls his condition in the past, he is overcome with the poignant emotions of his despair: **Miserable wretch that I am ! Who will rescue me from this body of death?** With equal vividness he feels over again the emo-25 tions of his deliverance: ' I thank God through Jesus Christ our Lord! ' (I cannot think that Moffatt's paraphrase here improves upon the simplicity of the Greek. There is no formal answer to the question of verse 24, and the dramatic force of the passage is impaired by supplying one.) How the **rescue** came, we must gather from other places in the epistle, including the immediately following verses. But, apart from all explanation, this great personal confession finds its fitting climax in a simple outburst of praise to God. The one thing that is clear is that, when Paul could do nothing, God did everything for him, and all that was left for him was to give thanks.

WHITSUNDAY

viii. 1–4: *The Saving Act of God*

In the preceding section, Paul has given an account of the state of a man who is in the bondage of sin and death, ending with a personal testimony that this state is brought to an end by act of God. He now proceeds to give an account of what God has done, and of its results in a new state of life. The key-word of this whole chapter is the word **spirit.** It has already been used sporadically (some five times in all), but in this chapter it occurs over twenty times. Thus we see at once that the new state can only be described in terms of **spirit** (as the old state was characterized by **flesh**). Our word **spirit** is derived from the Latin *spiritus*, which corresponds fairly well in meaning and use with the Greek word *pneuma*. The fundamental sense of *pneuma* is ' air in motion,' whether as the wind in nature or as the breath in a living thing. In the refined

materialism of popular Stoic philosophy in Paul's time the
term was applied to an inconceivably tenuous form of matter,
superior to the elements of earth, water, air, and fire. It was
supposed to pervade the universe, as the breath pervades the
body. It is this that Virgil was thinking of when he wrote
(*Aen.* vi. 724–726):

> *Principio caelum ac terram camposque liquentes,*
> *Lucentemque globum lunae, Titaniaque astra,*
> *Spiritus intus alit.*
> (First, heaven and earth, and ocean's watery plains,
> The moon's bright orb and the Titanic stars,
> A breath within them nurtures.)

There is, however, little trace of this philosophical conception
in Paul's thought, though some of his expressions may show
something of its influence.

His real background is, first, the Old Testament; and,
secondly, the experience of primitive Christianity. The Hebrew
word which corresponds to *pneuma* has the meaning ' strong
breath,' or ' blast ': the idea of power is inseparable from it.
All actions and qualities of men which seemed to be beyond their
natural capacity (to be ' supernatural,' as we say) were attributed to a ' strong breath ' coming upon them from without—
the frenzied courage and strength of the warrior, the inspiration
of the prophet, the wisdom of the ideal king. It was the ' strong
breath ' of Jehovah, the living, mighty God. Thus ' spirit ' is
the supernatural or divine element breaking into human life,
over against the powerless, perishable ' flesh ' (cf. Isa. xxxi. 3:
' The Egyptians are men and not God; and their horses *flesh* and
not *spirit* '). Now, among the early Christians there was an
overwhelming sense of such divine power breaking in: **they
were all filled with the holy Spirit** (Acts ii. 4). They found
in it the proof that they were living in a new age, inaugurated
by the resurrection of Christ. This power found expression in
apparently supernatural phenomena like ' speaking with
tongues ' and ' mighty works.' Paul had experience of these
abnormal manifestations of ' spirit,' but he found that beneath
them there were ' gifts of the Spirit ' more real, more important,
and more enduring—namely, intellectual and moral endowments for the service of God in His Church, and, above all, the
divinely given power to live after the pattern of Christ. In a
closely knit argument in 1 Cor. xii.–xiii. he comes to the conclusion that the supreme manifestation of the Spirit in men is

DEFINITION: St Paul's

meaning of Spirit

love, or charity. Similarly, in this epistle (v. 5) he says **God's love floods our hearts through the holy Spirit which has been given to us.** So much it is well to bear in mind in reading this chapter: by ' spirit,' Paul means the supernatural or divine element in human life, and his test for it is the presence of a love like the love of God in Christ.

viii.

Thus there is no doom now for those who are in Christ 1
Jesus; the law of the Spirit brings the life which is 2
in Christ Jesus, and that law has set me free from
the law of sin and death. For God has done what 3
the Law, weakened here by the flesh, could not do;
by sending His own Son in the guise of sinful flesh,
to deal with sin, He condemned sin in the flesh, in 4
order to secure the fulfilment of the Law's require-
ments in our lives, as we live and move not by the
flesh but by the Spirit.

Paul now applies to his readers and to Christians in general 1 the truth which he had found in his own experience: **there is no doom now for those who are in Christ Jesus** (harking back in that expression to vi. 1-11). The language he uses is that of the law-court; but he is not here thinking of a simple acquittal from the guilt of past sin, but of a real liberation 2 from the present power of sin. The trouble was that a man was **a prisoner to sin's law;** but now **the law of the Spirit brings the life which is in Christ Jesus, and that law has set me free from the law of sin and death.** In vii. 6 he had contrasted the **Spirit** with the **written code** of the Mosaic Law; here, however, it is not the Mosaic Law that is in view, but that **other law in my members which conflicts with the law of my mind.** ' Law' is not used in its strict sense of a code, but in the sense of a principle or system, and so he can speak of the **law** (that is, the principle or system) A **of the Spirit.** As **sin's law** (the sinful principle or system) brought death, so **the law of the Spirit brings life;** as **sin's law** made him a prisoner, so **the law of the Spirit has set** him **free.**

This liberation is, as was implied in vii. 25a, the work of 3 God. **God has done what the Law, weakened here by the flesh, could not do.** What was it then that the Law could not do? It could not destroy the ascendancy of sin in the ' flesh,' even though it could win the homage of the reason.

God, then, **condemned sin in the flesh.** Once again the metaphor is from the law-court. To 'condemn sin' clearly does not mean, as it means in our common usage, to express moral disapproval of sin: *that* Law *could* do, and it could win the assent of the reason to such disapproval. What Paul means is something more than that. Think of the various aspects in which sin has appeared: it was the master who held a slave; it was the militant enemy who took a prisoner; but the slave found a new master and the prisoner was set free. We need here another metaphor which will express a similar idea. Sin is now a litigant at law, and the case goes against him: he is **condemned.** His claim has failed, and his adversary gets the verdict. The adversary is man (who in the other figures was the slave and the prisoner of sin); but it is man as represented by Christ, not by Adam. That is why the metaphor must run on different lines: Christ never was a slave or a prisoner, but as man He *was* exposed to the assaults of sin. He, the Son of God, was sent **in the guise of sinful flesh, to deal with sin.**

Since Paul has assumed that *all* flesh, as such, is now under the dominion of sin, he cannot here say outright (as the Fourth Evangelist could) that Christ became flesh. He is somewhat embarrassed by his twofold use of the term 'flesh,' (1) as a purely physical (or metaphysical) term, for the material element in human nature, morally indifferent, and (2) as a psychological and ethical term, for the sum of the instincts wrongly directed (which as active in the individual constitutes **the sinful body**). Elsewhere, indeed, where there is no danger of misunderstanding, he does speak of the 'flesh' of Christ, notably in Col. i. 22 (where the phrase is, literally, 'the body of His flesh'); cf. also, in this epistle, i. 3, ix. 5 (where the word translated **natural descent** is the ordinary word for 'flesh'). But he prefers to avoid such expressions, especially in such a context as the present, where he is using 'flesh' so distinctly in its moral connotation. But in saying that Christ came **in the guise of sinful flesh,** he does not mean to deny that Christ lived a truly human life. Indeed he would have said that Christ lived—and lived in the flesh as a physical condition —the only truly human life, and made it possible for those who are 'in Him.' Fallen humanity **in Adam** is not the only humanity. Man as God meant him was created in the image of God, and Christ is 'the image and glory of God' (1 Cor. xi. 7), and so He is **the heavenly Man** (1 Cor. xv. 49). When

CHAPTER VIII, VERSES 5-13

Adam sinned, he lost the image, and so we **all come short of
the glory of God.** But in so far we are less than human.
Christ then came, in all the glory of true humanity, **in the
guise of** that **flesh** which **in Adam** is **sinful, to deal with
sin** within that same sphere of physical life in which Adam
had lost the glory. That is the way in which Paul's thought
runs.

Christ therefore entered the sphere which Sin had claimed
as his own (for we must needs personify Sin if we are to carry
out the metaphor). Sin pressed his claim against Christ, but
lost his case. Christ was not condemned; Sin was. For Christ
brought into the sphere of the ' flesh ' the unimpaired power of
the ' Spirit.' And hence it follows that those also who are ' in
Christ ' are no longer condemned.

If we desire to translate metaphor into fact, we must be
guided by the Gospel story, of which Paul was certainly not
ignorant. There Jesus is first anointed with the Spirit; then
meets temptation in the wilderness, and repels it. The rest of
the story is the inevitable working-out of His great refusal to
submit to sin, ending in His death, which as a pure act of
self-sacrificing obedience to the divine will, is a victory over sin,
countersigned by His resurrection. To which Paul only adds
that He did all this as the inclusive Representative of a new
humanity, so that it belongs to all who are ' in Him ' (cf. vi.
1–11). The result, therefore, was **to secure the fulfilment** 4
of the Law's requirements (in so far as **the command is
holy, just and for our good) in our lives, as we live and
move not by the flesh, but by the Spirit.**

viii. 5–13: *Life in the Spirit*   B

> **For those who follow the flesh have their interests
>   in the flesh,**   5
> **and those who follow the Spirit have their interests
>   in the Spirit.**
> **The interests of the flesh mean death,**   6
>   **the interests of the Spirit mean life and peace.**
> **For the interests of the flesh are hostile to God; they
> do not yield to the law of God (indeed they cannot).** 7
> **Those who are in the flesh cannot satisfy God. But** 8
> **you are not in the flesh, you are in the Spirit, since** 9
> **the Spirit of God dwells within you. Anyone who**

10   does not possess the Spirit of Christ does not belong
to Him. On the other hand, if Christ is within you,
though the body is a dead thing owing to Adam's
sin, the spirit is living as the result of righteousness.

11   And if the Spirit of Him who raised Jesus from the
dead dwells within you, then He who raised Christ
from the dead will also make your mortal bodies
live by His indwelling Spirit in your lives.

Well then, my brothers, we owe a duty—but it is not to

12   the flesh! It is not to live by the flesh! If you live
by the flesh, you are on the road to death; but if by

13   the Spirit you put the actions of the body to death,
you will live.

Here follows a series of antitheses, setting the condition of
the man who is ' in Christ ' in contrast with the evil condition
described in chap. vii. The contrast has already been drawn
in various ways—slavery and freedom, death and life, and so
forth. The fresh element in the present passage is the identification of the new life with life **in the Spirit,** as contrasted
with the *flesh*. If we recall that ' Spirit ' fundamentally means
for Paul divine or supernatural power for the ends of love as
seen in Christ, it is evident that there is here a real step forward
in the exposition. The trouble of the man described in vii. 7–13

5   was that although his reason consented to the law of God his
real **interests** were **in the flesh.** (The translation is a happy
one, in view of the use of the term ' interest ' by psychologists.)
His affections and desires were engaged to lower aims. His

8   **interests,** therefore, were **hostile to God. Those who are**

6   in this sense **in the flesh cannot satisfy God,** as we have
already learnt; and so **the interests of the flesh mean**

5   **death.** All this is in vii. 7–13. But on the contrary, **those
who follow the Spirit have their interests in the Spirit.**
The full meaning of this must be read in the light of v. 5–8:
**God's love floods our hearts through the holy Spirit
which has been given to us.** On the psychological level (on
which Paul's thought is now moving) that means that the Ideal
is presented in a form which engages the **interests,** the desires
and affections, of the whole man, and liberates all his instinctive
impulses from base attachments for the service of a worthy

6   dominant sentiment, that of love to God and man. Thus from
death he has passed to **life and peace.** Here **peace** stands
for the condition of inward harmony when all elements of the

See p.
135 for
DEFN

personality are organized about a single centre, and division and conflict are at an end. (It is not the same thing as the **peace with God** of v. 1, but rather its consequence.)

All this Paul now applies explicitly to his readers. **You are** **not in the flesh but in the Spirit, since the Spirit of God dwells within you.** (The ease with which Paul passes from **in the Spirit** to **the Spirit within you** may be partly due to the familiar use of the word in Greek, to which I have referred, to denote a kind of rarefied atmosphere; you can live in an atmosphere, and at the same time breathe it in.) This is true of all Christians, for **anyone who does not possess the Spirit of Christ does not belong to Him.** Paul could with confidence write in such terms even to a church to which his specific teaching was strange, for it was the universal assumption of primitive Christianity, attested by all parts of the New Testament, that when a man came to Christ he received a supernatural gift of divine power; and this assumption must have corresponded with general experience. The effect of the gift might not go very far; Paul has cause to complain to his Corinthian converts: **I could not discuss things with you as spiritual persons** (1 Cor. iii. 1); but his appeals always rest on the assumption that the gift is there, if a man will only make use of it. Once again it is a case of *werde das was Du bist* (cf. notes on vi. 12–14).

Observe, however, how Paul has passed insensibly from **the Spirit of God** to **the Spirit of Christ.** In the next verse he takes a further step, and, with no perceptible change of meaning, speaks of **Christ within you.** This apparent equation, **Spirit of God = Spirit of Christ = Christ within you,** is characteristic of Paul among New Testament writers. We may perhaps trace the lines of his thought thus: First, for Paul as for all Christian thinkers, Christ was in the fullest way the manifestation of God, and His whole life and person the expression of the divine Spirit. Further, it was the common postulate of primitive Christianity, as we have seen, that the Church was a fellowship of the Spirit, a community of those who had received the Spirit of God through faith in Christ. The one Spirit constituted the one Body. But, for Paul, with his 'mystical' outlook, that Body was the Body of Christ, manifesting the new humanity of which He was the inclusive Representative. Hence in every member of it, possessing the Spirit of God, Christ was in some measure present and active, since the man was a member of His Body (as the whole of any organism is in some sort active in every part of it). Thus the community might be indifferently regarded as constituted by the Spirit of God, or by Christ as a 'corporate personality'; and the individual as possessed by the Spirit of God, or by Christ dwelling in His member. Christ Himself, as the 'second Adam' was a 'life-giving Spirit' (1 Cor. xv. 45), and Paul could speak, not only of **the Spirit of the Lord,** but, in the next breath, of the **Lord the Spirit** (2 Cor. iii. 17–18). Behind this rather subtle train of thought there must have been direct experience. Paul was immediately aware that when he was in close touch with Christ, that divine energy or power which he recognized as the Spirit, was released within him; and conversely, the full moral effect of that power was realized only through reference to Christ as revealing the eternal Love. **In Christ, in the Spirit, the Spirit within, Christ within** were in effect only different ways of describing the one experience, from slightly different points of view. This is not to say that Paul, in a strict theological sense, identified Christ with the Spirit. But his virtual identification of the experience of the Spirit with the experience of the indwelling Christ is of the utmost value. It saved Christian thought from falling into a non-moral, half-magical conception of the supernatural in human experience, and it brought all 'spiritual' experience to the test of the historical revelation of God in Jesus Christ.

Down to verse 9, Paul has been portraying salvation in ethical terms, as the end of bondage to sin, and the attainment of moral freedom. This is, indeed, the main theme of the whole section which begins with vi. 1, where the allegation that his doctrine implies **that we are to remain on in sin, so that there may be all the more grace,** sets the whole argument in motion. But, as we have seen (v. 12), the problem of sin was intimately bound up in Paul's mind with the problem of death; and as in vi. 1–14 the idea of resurrection from (bodily) death was interwoven with the idea of moral renewal in Christ, so here we have a similar association of ideas. Because a man has the Spirit of Christ, we have been told, he is able to **satisfy God,** by living a life of true righteousness. What then is the effect of this life in the Spirit in relation to the heritage of death which every son of Adam has?

10   To this question Paul gives two replies: (1) **If Christ is within you, though the body is a dead thing owing to**

Adam's sin, the spirit is living as the result of right-eousness. By this difficult sentence he apparently means something like this: In so far as the man's ' body ' (his organic individuality) was identified with the ' flesh ' (the natural instincts as perverted to the ends of sin), it came within the maxim: **Death spread to all men, inasmuch as all men sinned.** Well, let it die, and good riddance to it! But the real man is no longer identified with this **sinful body,** for, having **joined himself to the Lord,** he **is one with Him in spirit** (1 Cor. vi. 17), and **spirit** in its very essence **is living** (the literal translation is ' the spirit is life '). We may compare the statement in 1 Cor. xv. 45 that Christ is a **life-giving spirit,** and the confession of Gal. ii. 20: **It is no longer I who live, but Christ lives in me.**

But (2) this does not mean that the ' body,' or organic 11 individuality as such, is doomed to perish, for **if the Spirit of Him who raised Jesus from the dead dwells within you, then He who raised Christ from the dead will also make your mortal bodies live by His indwelling Spirit in your lives.** The ' body ' (or organic individuality) is not inseparably identified with **sinful flesh;** it is indeed at present **mortal,** but it is capable of being made immortal. **As there is an animate body, so there is a spiritual body.** It was in this **spiritual body** that Christ was raised; and the same power by which He was raised is at work for those who are **in Him.** So, when the end of this life comes, **what is sown is mortal, what rises is immortal . . . sown an animate body, it rises a spiritual body . . . and when this mortal body has been invested with immortality, then the saying of Scripture will be realized, Death is swallowed up in victory.** The whole passage, 1 Cor. xv. 35–55, from which I have quoted, forms a perfect commentary on the verse with which we are dealing. Only it is necessary always to bear in mind that by ' body ' Paul does not mean anything material, but the organic principle which makes a man a self-identical individual, persisting through all changes in the ' substance ' through which he realizes himself, whether material or non-material.

Here, then, is Paul's doctrine of ' immortality.' Of a natural ' immortality of the soul,' in the sense which our thought has inherited from Plato, he knows nothing. The race of Adam is doomed to death; life must be the gift of God; and life God gives, by giving His Spirit to those who are in Christ. The critical moment is not the moment of bodily death in hope of a blessed resurrection; it is the moment at which the man came to be **in Christ.** From that moment he is immortal, not, so to speak, in his own right, but because **Christ lives in** him. When bodily death comes, it is only a matter of being 'absent from the body, present with the Lord.' The life after death is not a new life: it is the life he has been living all the time **in Christ,** only lived under different conditions. This sense of a sort of interpenetration of two worlds, the deathless order being already present in moral experience, is a distinctively Christian contribution to the problem of a future life; it has singularly little to do with the kind of thing that often bulks most largely in modern discussions of the problem.

Paul has now brought to a conclusion the argument which started in vi. 1 as an attempt to rebut the allegation that his doctrine of salvation by grace through faith was non-moral. The general line of his reply is sketched in vi. 1-14. In substance he did not need to add anything further, in order to dispose of the objection. But he felt the necessity to make his position abundantly clear, and so, starting afresh with a restatement of the objection, he traversed the whole ground anew, first by way of illustration and then by an elaborate analysis of the actual experience of salvation. He has now arrived once more, laden with the treasures gathered on his devious journey, at the point where he was in vi. 11, vi. 23, and vii. 6 (his four ways of stating the conclusion should be compared). It would now be natural for him to pass to an elaboration of the theme of vi. 12-14, an exhortation to make full use of the unlimited possibilities of the new life of freedom, by moral effort. And, in fact, he seems to have been on the point of doing so. Verses 12-13 would naturally form an introduction to a section dealing with Christian ethics in practice.

We may compare the movement of thought in the Epistle to the Galatians. In chaps. ii.–iv. of that epistle he has dealt with much the same range of subjects as in Rom. iii. 21–viii. 11: justification by grace, the faith of Abraham, the place and function of law, union with Christ through baptism, bondage and freedom, flesh and spirit. His conclusion in Gal. v. 1, is a proclamation of **the freedom for which Christ set us free.** This may be set alongside Rom. viii. 1-2. In Galatians there follows a short digression dealing with the particular situation of his correspondents, and then, in his characteristic way, Paul returns to his point in v. 13: **Brothers, you were called to be free;** and then passes to the admonition, **Do not make your freedom an opening for the flesh, but serve one another in love.** And so he enters upon a short outline of Christian ethics, the principle of which is, **Lead the life of the Spirit; then you will never satisfy the passions of the flesh.**

So here, in Rom. viii. 12, he begins, **Well then, my brothers, 12 we owe a duty—but it is not a duty to the flesh ! It is not to live by the flesh !** And as in Gal. v. 17-18 he supports his precept by a short note on flesh and spirit, so here he supports it by the observation (which recapitulates what has gone before), **If you live by the flesh, you are on the road to death; but if by the Spirit you put the actions of the 13 body to death, you will live.** Here the **body** is the **sinful body** of vi. 6, the individuality as identified with the ' flesh ': according to vi. 6 it is ' crushed '; according to viii. 10 it is **a dead thing.** Nevertheless, its **actions** still need to be **put to death** in detail. As we might put it, although a new dominant sentiment has been formed, the mental and physical habits acquired under the old *régime* persist as tendencies, and must be fought by self-discipline, as Paul confesses in 1 Cor. ix. 25-27.

We are already thoroughly on the plane of moral practice, and we seem to be well launched on a course of direct ethical teaching. But Paul remembers that there is much more that should be said of life in the Spirit, on the purely religious plane. In particular, he has said nothing of the fact that the man who has the Spirit is a son (and not, as suggested by vi. 22, a slave) of God. In Galatians this topic had a large and important place in the discussion which preceded the directly ethical section, and it is equally important to his purpose in Romans. Accordingly, the true sequel to 12-13 is held up for a time. We get the section on Christian ethics at last in chaps. xii. sqq., with a different introduction; but it is well to bear in mind that vi. 1-viii. 13 is not complete without xii. 1-xv. 6.

viii. 14-17: THE SPIRIT OF SONSHIP

For **the sons of God are those who are guided by the 14 Spirit of God. You have received no slavish spirit 15 that would make you relapse into fear; you have**

16   **received the Spirit of sonship. And when we cry,
'Abba! Father!', it is this Spirit testifying along
17   with our own spirit that we are children of God;
and if children, heirs as well, heirs of God, heirs
along with Christ—for we share His sufferings in
order to share His glory.**

Verse 14 seems to be a mistranslation. The grammatical
structure of the Greek makes it clear that **'sons of God'**
(which has no article) is the predicate, and not the subject, of
the sentence. We should read therefore, 'Those who are
guided by the Spirit' (i.e. the persons described in viii. 1–11)
15 'are sons of God '—that is the new point. **You have received
no slavish spirit,** he goes on; the expression ' slavery to God,'
therefore, in vi. 22 was only an accommodation to the illustration, and needed apology just as much as the companion expression ' slavery to righteousness ' in vi. 18. Such a spirit
would make you relapse into fear—fear of the Wrath
(i. 18). But, as we learn from 1 John iv. 18, **love in its fulness
drives all dread away,** and the life of the Spirit is in the
sphere of love. No; **you have received the Spirit of sonship.** Similarly, in Gal. iv. 7, Paul says, **You are** slave **no
longer, but son.** That is the fundamental contrast in his
mind.

Here, again as in Galatians, he supports his statement by
16 an appeal to the language used by Christians. **When we cry
' Abba! Father!' it is the Spirit testifying along with
our own spirit that we are children of God.** (So in Gal.
iv. 6: **It is because you are sons that God has sent forth
the Spirit of His Son into your hearts crying ' Abba!
Father!'**) The word *Abba* is one of the Aramaic expressions
of the primitive Church which passed over into Gentile usage—
in this case possibly through the liturgical use of the Lord's
Prayer. Similarly, the Aramaic *Marana tha* (cf. 1 Cor. xvi. 22)
is retained in the Greek liturgy of the *Didache*, or *Teaching of the
Twelve Apostles*, as we still retain in liturgical usage *Amen*,
Hosanna, and *Hallelujah*, and much as the Roman Church in its
Latin liturgy has the Greek *Kyrie eleison*. But Paul is surely not
speaking here of a mere liturgical usage. The ' cry ' **Abba!**
is adduced as evidence that **we are children of God,** not as
evidence that such was the official doctrine of the Church
expressed in its liturgy.

We know that in the churches of the Pauline mission people

under the stress of strong spiritual excitement or exaltation
would break out into loud cries, often unintelligible to the
hearers (see 1 Cor. xiv.). These cries, which seemed independent of the thought or will of the speaker, were regarded as
utterances of the Spirit within him. Paul did not deny this,
though he rather deprecated the intrusion of such unintelligible
cries into the services of the Church. But where the utterances
had a clear and unmistakable meaning he would certainly have
given them full value as the authentic voice of God in the soul.
It is probable that in 1 Cor. xii. 3 he refers to such an utterance:
No one can say ' Jesus is Lord,' except in the holy Spirit.
Similarly here it is probable that he has in mind the cry **Abba !**
uttered by Christians under obvious spiritual stress. This is
no doubt strange to our way of thinking. The conditions which
Paul has in view are those associated with what is called ' religious revival,' when many of the customary restraints and
inhibitions are broken up, and the inner life is much nearer to
the surface than at ordinary times. And have we not known
cases when a man labouring under strong religious emotion has
said something which leaves us with an awed feeling that we
have heard words almost from another world? Are we to deny
all validity to such emotional experience of religious things?
True, such emotion may also accompany states of mind which
are untrue and irreligious. Paul even knew of cases where a
man, apparently ' in the Spirit,' cried **' Cursed be Jesus ! '**
(1 Cor. xii. 3). In such a case he says roundly that, whatever
spirit was at work, it was not the Spirit of God. True, also, that
the strongest religious emotion may be found without being
accompanied by the ethical fruits of religion; but that is just the
situation that Paul has before him, both here and in Galatians.
In effect he says, ' If you have so strong an emotional sense of
being a child of God, why do you not live like a child of God? '
As we live by the Spirit, let us be guided by the Spirit
(Gal. v. 25).[1] Paul does not base his faith on what is called
' religious experience ' of an emotional and non-rational kind,
but he is prepared to appeal to such experience as corroborative
evidence for the individual who has it. That one is inwardly
possessed with a sense of the nearness, the love, and shelter-
ing care of God, so that one is moved, as if involuntarily,
to cry ' Father! ' is a fact of some weight when one comes

---

[1] This is connected with the whole question of true and false ' inspiration ' which
I have discussed in chap. iii. of my book *The Authority of the Bible.*

to give an account of the spiritual universe in which one lives.

It is a striking, even to modern ears a startling, statement of Paul's that only *some* men—namely, **those who are guided by the Spirit of God**—can rightly be called **children of God.** It is commonly believed that Christianity teaches that **all** men are children of God. And yet Jesus Himself is reported as recommending a certain course of action, **that you may be sons of your Father in heaven;** which surely implies that those who do not live in this way are *not* sons of the heavenly Father (Matt. v. 45). There is a vast deal of confusion in the popular notion of the ' Fatherhood of God.' In many religions men have been regarded as the offspring of God, sometimes in a crudely literal sense, sometimes more philosophically as a sort of emanation from the Divine Being. This idea is almost wholly strange to the Bible. I can find only three possible places in the New Testament in which it is even suggested (Luke iii. 38; Acts xvii. 28; and James i. 18), and of these the only clear case is a quotation from a heathen poet! The biblical doctrine all through is that God *created* man in His image, so that the natural, universal, and permanent relation of man to God is one of creaturely dependence. The New Testament knows only one Son of God in the absolute sense (' begotten, not made,' as the Creed has it).

The fact is that in the Bible the terms ' Father ' and ' son,' as applied to God and man in their mutual relations, are of the nature of metaphor. Israel is in the Old Testament the ' son ' of Jehovah. But no Old Testament writer supposed that Israel was descended from Jehovah, as the Dorian kings were descended from Heracles, or the royal line of Wessex from Woden. No; ' *like as* a father pitieth his children, *so* the Lord pitieth them that fear Him.' The Fatherhood of God means that God loves, cares for, and disciplines His people. With the expansion of monotheism, God is thought of as (in this sense) the Father, not of Israel alone, but of mankind. In the teaching of Jesus, God is doubtless the Father of all men, in the sense that He loves, cares for, and disciplines them all, being kind even to the unthankful and the evil. Similarly, the idea of sonship connotes loyalty, obedience, imitation, and responsive love. Israel was adopted as the son of Jehovah when the people bound themselves to obey His Law. So, in the teaching of Jesus, men become the sons of God when, like Him, they love

imitation

their enemies, when they are merciful as their Father is merciful, when they receive the Kingdom of God as a little child. Hence we get the paradox that God is the ' Father ' of all men, but not all men are His ' sons.' Paul's teaching is in harmony with this. He teaches that God loves men, in the fullest possible sense, while they are yet sinners, but they are ' adopted ' as sons of God only when they enter into union with Christ and are **guided by the Spirit of God.**

Responsive Love

In verse 17 we have an extension of the idea of sonship which here comes in rather abruptly. For its setting in Paul's scheme of thought we have to turn to Galatians. According to the argument of that epistle a promise was made to Abraham by which an ' inheritance ' of blessing devolved on his **' offspring.'** Thus the **Israel of God** was the ' heir ' of the promised blessing. Like many a human heir, the people of God in its minority was **under guardians and trustees,** and no better than a slave; for the Law **held us in ward and discipline till such time as Christ came. But,** Paul goes on, **when the time had fully expired, God sent forth His Son ... that we might get our sonship. . . . So you are servant no longer but son, and as son you are also heir, all owing to God** (Gal. iv. 1–7). This gives the background for our present passage: **we are children of God; and if children, heirs as well, heirs along with Christ.** The ' inheritance ' is the future blessedness of perfected existence; but already we possess (Eph. i. 14) **the pledge and instalment of our common heritage,** in possessing the Spirit. And the present sufferings of the Christian, which are inseparable from his being **in Christ,** are all on the way to the consummation: **we share His sufferings in order to share His glory.** And so Paul's thought is turned more definitely and emphatically than before, from the present to the glorious future at which he had hinted in vi. 5, viii. 11.

i.e. to reign with Him

to enter into the glory of His reigning

viii. 18-25: THE HOPE OF GLORY

Present suffering, I hold, is a mere nothing compared to 18
the glory that we are to have revealed. Even the 19
creation waits with eager longing for the sons of
God to be revealed. For creation was not rendered 20
futile by its own choice, but by the will of Him who
thus made it subject, the hope being that creation 21

as well as man would one day be freed from its
22 **thraldom to decay and gain the glorious freedom**
23 **of the children of God. To this day, we know, the entire creation sighs and throbs with pain; and not only so, but even we ourselves, who have the Spirit as a foretaste of the future, even we sigh to ourselves as we wait for the redemption of the body that means our full sonship. We were saved with this hope in**
24 **view. Now when an object of hope is seen, there is no further need to hope. Who ever hopes for what**
25 **he sees already? But if we hope for something that we do not see, we wait for it patiently.**

At this point the argument rises to a new level. We have heard Paul declaiming against the vices of the age like a satirist, speculating on the knowledge of God and the conscience of man like a philosopher, arguing from Scripture like a rabbi, and analysing experience like a psychologist. Now he speaks with the vision of a poet. He views the universe with an ' eye that hath kept watch o'er man's mortality.' The lot of man here is suffering, and Christians are not exempt from it. **Even we**
23 **ourselves, who have the Spirit as a foretaste of the future, even we sigh to ourselves** with a deep sense of dissatisfaction and incompleteness. In this we not only share the common lot of man, but we are at one with all Nature.
22 **The entire creation sighs and throbs with pain.** This is, no doubt, a pessimistic mood, but, if it is one-sided, it rests on insight into the facts. The pain of the animals is not different from our pain; and if

> *The woods decay, the woods decay and fall,*
> *The vapours weep their burden to the ground,*
> *Man comes and tills the field and lies beneath,*
> *And after many summers dies the swan,*

the scientific mind may see in it all no more than a natural cycle of change, but the poet cannot but feel deep pathos in this **thraldom to decay** in man and Nature alike. Is there any clue to its meaning?

Yes, says Paul, the clue is to be found in the spiritual life of
23 man. **We sigh to ourselves** because we are waiting for something. **We wait for the redemption of the body that means our full sonship.** Of the redemption of the body he has already spoken (viii. 11; see also 2 Cor. v. 1–8). Only

The Experience of the Spirit

when it is complete shall we be, in full actuality, that which
we now are in principle, sons of God. As another New Testament writer puts it, **We are children of God now, beloved;
what we are to be is not apparent yet, but we do know
that when He appears we are to be like Him—for we
are to see Him as He is** (1 John iii. 2). This is our hope,
and, as Paul has already said, it is **a hope which never disappoints us, since God's love floods our hearts through
the holy Spirit which has been given to us** (v. 5). So here
he says the Spirit, which is **the Spirit of sonship**, is a foretaste
of the future, a pledge of **the redemption of the body that
means our full sonship.**

But further, this experience of the Spirit (an experience of
sonship to God, of life and freedom, of the love of God) is a
ground of hope for the whole universe, since man cannot be
isolated from the rest of Nature. The universe too is waiting 19
for something. **Even the creation waits with eager longing 20
for the sons of God to be revealed.** Its present condition is
by the will of God—we cannot give any further answer to the
question, Why? But in all its travail there is an element un-
suspected by those who do not look at it with the eyes of faith
—an element corresponding to hope in the human heart, and
that too is there by will of God. **The creation was not
rendered futile by its own choice** (as was man, who transgressed God's command), **but by the will of Him who thus 21
made it subject, the hope being that creation as well as
man would one day be freed from its thraldom to decay
and gain the glorious freedom of the children of God.**
If we are to state in prosaic terms of metaphysics what Paul
thought would happen, we must say that he shared with many
of his contemporaries the belief that, in the Good Time Coming,
the material universe would be transfigured into a substance
consisting of pure light or glory, thus returning to its original
perfection as created by God. But Paul has made of this a truly
poetical conception, as little as possible dependent on any
particular metaphysics. What it means, in the realm of logic
and fact, it is impossible to say, nor can one argue about its
truth.

Hush thou!
These things are far too sure that thou should'st dream
Thereon, lest they appear as things that seem.

We turn from the vision of the universe charged with a 24

solemn expectancy (like the world on Christmas Eve in Milton's
ode) to man again, in whom expectancy has become conscious
hope. Such hope, Paul adds, is a positive good. Like faith and
love, it is one of the things that ' abide ' (1 Cor. xiii. 13). Like
faith, it links us with the unseen (which is the eternal—2 Cor.
iv. 18, v. 7): **When an object of hope is seen, there is no
further need for hope. Whoever hopes for what he sees
25 already? But if we hope for something that we do not
see, we wait for it patiently.** ' It is good that a man should
both hope and quietly wait for the salvation of the Lord ' (Lam.
iii. 26).

viii. 26–27: THE SPIRIT WITHIN—OUR HELPER

26 **So too the Spirit assists us in our weakness; for we do
not know how to pray aright, but the Spirit pleads
for us with sighs that are beyond words, and He
27   who searches the human heart knows what is in the
mind of the Spirit, since the Spirit pleads before
God for the saints.**

The present condition, then, of the Christian in this world
is one of much suffering and weakness, with a painful sense of
incompleteness, tempered by a sure and certain hope. That
hope is based upon the Spirit which makes him a son of God.
In this he has not only a **foretaste of the future,** but a present
26 help: **the Spirit assists us in our weakness.** Paul has said
that **we sigh to ourselves as we wait for the redemption
of the body.** This inarticulate aspiration is the deepest form
of prayer, and it is itself the work of the Spirit within. **The
Spirit pleads for us with sighs that are beyond words.**
When we would pray, we know too little of our own needs or of
God's purposes to **pray aright.** But not even in prayer is the
human intelligence or will the determining factor (any more
than we can be ' justified ' by our own deeds). An inarticulate
aspiration is itself the work of the divine in us, and though we
ourselves may not be conscious of its meaning, God knows what
27 it means, and answers the prayer, **since the Spirit pleads
before God for the saints.**
This profound conception of prayer as the divine in us
appealing to the God above us is of a piece with Paul's whole
conception of the Christian life as one in which the divine

initiative is displayed at every point. If we are conscious of God as our Father, it is the Spirit of God **testifying along with our own spirit.** Our knowledge of God and His ways is, so to speak, God within us recognizing Himself. **What human being can understand the thoughts of a man, except the man's own inner spirit? So too no one understands the thoughts of God except the Spirit of God. Now we have received the Spirit . . . that comes from God, that we may understand what God bestows upon us** (1 Cor. ii. 9–16). It is in the same sense that the Spirit is thought of as the real author of all virtues and graces in the life of the Christian. They are **the harvest of the Spirit** (Gal. vi. 22). Love, which is the supreme and all-inclusive virtue, is **the love that the Spirit inspires** (xv. 30) or **love in the Spirit** (Col. i. 8; cf. 1 Cor. xiii.). When we recall how Paul equates **the Spirit of God within you** (viii. 9) with **Christ within you** (viii. 10), we approach, by a new line, what he means when he says, ' **It is no longer I who live, Christ lives in me.**'

This ' mysticism ' of Paul, if we are to call it so, is anything but a vague philosophy of immanence such as has been popular in recent times, or such as was taught by the Stoics in Paul's day. The Spirit stands for the immanent Divine, but its correlative is the transcendent Divine for whom Paul in the main reserves the name ' God.' Prayer is, indeed, the activity of the Divine Spirit within us, but it would lose its significance for Paul if it did not ascend to God above us. In the verses which now follow he emphasizes the transcendence of God, His absolute sovereignty and unconditioned will, as the ultimate basis of all our hopes of salvation. The practical importance of this emphasis may be illustrated from one of the great Stoics of a time not far removed from Paul's. The noblest of them all, perhaps, was the Emperor Marcus Aurelius. His *Meditations*, the revelation of a very rare spirit, are touched all through with a profound melancholy. ' The real explanation of the chronic depression of the Emperor Marcus Aurelius,' wrote A. E. Taylor, ' is surely plain enough. What weighs most on that melancholy personage is the sense of the untold possibilities of moral degradation attendant on the possession of irresponsible power. He can never forget the " bad emperors " who began their reigns well to all appearance, and is always in a shiver lest, to use his own words, he should " end as a Caesar." If

Stoicism as a system is really answerable for his inability to rise above these fears, it is, I think, because the doctrine offers only a " god within " and no " God without " to whom one can look for grace against temptation.' [1] What Paul might have said to him or to any Stoic is contained in what follows.

viii. 28-30: GOD ABOVE—OUR ASSURANCE

28
29
30

We know also that those who love God, those who have been called in terms of His purpose, have His aid and interest in everything. For He decreed of old that those whom He predestined should share the likeness of His Son—that He might be the firstborn of a great brotherhood. Then He calls those whom He has thus decreed; then He justifies those whom He has called; then He glorifies those whom He has justified.

In verse 28 the A.V. has ' All things work together for good to them that love God.' The Moffatt version represents another way of construing the Greek: literally, ' With those who love God he co-operates in all things for good.' Some MSS. insert ' God ' as the subject of the verb; but it is also possible that the subject is ' the Spirit '—the dominant subject of verbs in the preceding verses. Either construction could claim some support from parallels in Greek writers, but it seems more consonant both with Paul's argument here and with the general tendency of his thought to affirm the co-operation of God, or of the Spirit, than of ' things.'

Some readers may regret the loss of a text which expresses the truth in a form so congenial to the ' modern mind,' which thinks of the universe as an orderly system, and likes to believe that ' it will all come right in the end.' But this is not the attitude of Paul or of any other New Testament writer. He has just told us that the creation is expectant of deliverance from **the thraldom of decay;** but that is not because he finds in it any inherent tendency to get better and better, until it arrives at the

one far-off divine event
To which the whole creation moves.

Just as the redemption of man is an act of God, a sheer act of free grace on His part, so he expects the redemption of the creation to be an act of God, free and unconditioned—or, rather, he expects it as the result of the same act of God, in a fuller stage of realization. The hope that is embedded in its structure is not a natural tendency towards progress, but is conditional upon a hope in man which is due solely to an act of God in history. It would not occur to Paul to look to 'things' to 'work together' for the salvation of man. What he does look for, and find, is God's co-operation with us *in* things, even things which are hostile to us. His meaning is clear from the final section of the chapter. He brings before us various things such as calamity and death, which threaten the well-being of men. He does not say calamity is 'somehow good,' because it belongs to a general scheme which will all come right in the end. He says it cannot separate us from the love of God. In calamity, as in all things, God will co-operate with us for good. There is no situation, however desperate, in which a man can find himself, where he cannot find God, and **have His aid and interest.**

Whether this comes to the same thing, I should not like to say. It is clear that the point of view is different. And I suspect that some such changed point of view is called for in our day through the decay of the evolutionary optimism of the nineteenth century. After all, the Second Law of Thermodynamics, with its applications as expounded by some recent authorities, seems to suggest a universe which is 'running down' through the constant degradation of its energy. No doubt its elements 'work together,' but, whether 'for good,' science does not seem so sure. It is more than ever a venture of faith to say that they work together for good in particular cases, 'for those who love God.' It is a venture of faith also to say that He co-operates with us in all things; but it is a faith more clearly within the limits of human experience, and more securely verifiable. At any rate, it was Paul's faith, which is our present point.

We observe that Paul promises God's co-operation to **those who love God,** for which he then immediately substitutes **those who have been called in terms of His purpose.** The reason of the substitution is not far to seek. To say, simply, that with those who love God He co-operates, might leave us free to suppose that by our love to Him we have merited His help. To suppose any such thing would be for Paul the last heresy. He is always turning our attention from our own feeling, will, and act to the will of God. That those who are called according to God's purpose love Him, is for Paul a matter of course, but their love for Him is not the determinative fact. He would have agreed with another New Testament writer who says: **Love lies in this, not in our love for Him, but in His love for us—in the sending of His Son. . . . We love, because He loved us first** (1 John iv. 10, 19). This love for us is shown, according to Paul's teaching, by the fact that we <u>have been called in terms of His purpose</u>. That is not a matter of subjective feeling, but of fact. <u>Jesus lived and died</u>; His resurrection brought the Church into being; <u>the preaching about Him reached a particular individual at Rome; he responded by faith,</u> and was by baptism incorporated in the Church. That was a series of verifiable events. <u>They happened by the will of God, and expressed</u> His purpose. The Roman Christian, therefore, might know himself **called in terms of His purpose,** and so might be sure of **His aid and interest in everything.** That is Paul's meaning. The only point in this chain at which the subjective comes in is the point at which faith is demanded. But faith, as Paul understood it, amounts to the negation of all that is merely subjective: it is the opposite of any assertion of the human personality, whether in thought or feeling or will; it is to ' stand still and see the salvation of God.' <u>Thus Paul sets the ground of a man's hope</u> of salvation entirely <u>outside himself, in the purpose of God</u> as manifested in the world of facts. This is different from any kind of religion which seeks assurance from exalted states of feeling, or the apprehension of occult revelations, or the performance of meritorious actions. Feelings may pass, revelations may be illusion, and who can reckon the merit of an action? But <u>the purpose of God is known to us in the realm of fact.</u> There is <u>the fact of Christ and of His Church</u>; <u>there is the fact</u> that <u>we have heard His Gospel and not withstood it. That is</u> our calling; and, as Paul says, **it is all the doing of God** (2 Cor. v. 18).

The rest of the chapter is a meditation, in the spirit of prophecy, upon the significance of this free and unconditioned act of God ' for us men and for our salvation.' It is not theology; it is part of the *data* for theology; it is the direct witness of the Spirit **testifying along with our own spirit.** The basic fact is that we **have been called in terms of His purpose.** That, as we have seen, is a fact verifiable in history and experience. Behind it lies a fact beyond human history and experience, beyond time and space, in the world of the unseen and eternal. It has its being in **the depths of God,** which only **the Spirit fathoms** (1 Cor. ii. 10). **He decreed of old that those whom He predestined should share the likeness of His Son.** [29]

The idea of the predestinating decree of God is one which, when treated as a theological dogma, raises grave intellectual difficulties. We remember that the devils in Pandemonium

> *reasoned high*
> *Of providence, foreknowledge, will and fate ;*
> *Fixed fate, freewill, foreknowledge absolute ;*
> *And found no end, in wandering mazes lost.*

It is doubtful whether the human intellect has been more successful in solving the problems. Yet discuss them we must. In chaps. ix.-xi., Paul does make some attempt at a philosophical discussion of the place of freewill within the divine purpose. Here, however, he is not on the level of philosophical discussion. ' The idea of " election," ' says Professor Otto— ' namely, the idea of being elected and predestined by God to *salvation*—crops up as a pure expression of the religious experience of grace. A man who is the object of grace, when he looks back upon himself, feels more and more that he has become what he is by no act or activity of his own, that grace came to him without his own will or power, that it took hold of him, drove him, led him on. Even his most intimate, his freest, acts of decision and assent become to him, without losing their quality of freedom, something that he *experienced* rather than *did*. Before any act of his own, he sees redeeming love seeking and choosing him, and recognizes an eternal decree of grace on his behalf.' [1] Augustine, and Calvin after him, had this profound intuition of the electing grace of God, but they both, and especially the latter, made the mistake of erecting upon it a rigid dogmatic system, and thereby laid snares for the feet of believers. The best commentators upon this passage of Paul are not the theologians, but the greater hymn-writers of the Church. We shall read it best, not with an eye to logical implications and philosophical problems, but with a mind receptive of the

---

[1] Otto, *Das Heilige*, p. 109—my translation ; Otto's italics.

29 tremendous affirmation that our salvation is rooted in **the depths of God.**

We are called upon, then, to contemplate the eternal decree of God that men **should share the likeness of His Son— that He might be the firstborn of a great brotherhood.** We note here, first, that the issue of the decree is something which Paul has already declared to be a matter of experience, **that we are children of God, heirs along with Christ,** possessing an indefeasible hope that we shall **share His glory** as we now **share His sufferings;** secondly, that the reference to Christ anchors the conception of salvation to an historical revelation. There is no end to the ideas (or fantasies) of salvation that the human mind can form—unending sensual bliss, absorption into the All, crowns and harps, Nirvana, or what not. Paul holds us to the essential thing: that, whatever else it may be, salvation means **sharing the likeness of Christ,** and Christ we know. Let us recall that mankind is in trouble because **all come short of the glory of God** (iii. 23), and that, on the other hand, we **have the knowledge of God's glory in the face of Christ** (2 Cor. iv. 6). Thus, although the final realization of our salvation is something at present inconceivable—for **what no eye has ever seen, what no ear has ever heard, what never entered the mind of man, God has prepared all that for those who love Him** (1 Cor. ii. 9)—yet it is enough to know that Christ is to be **the firstborn of a great brotherhood**—a brotherhood which, as we are to be told later, will ultimately include all mankind (Rom. xi. 32). Such is the divine decree. From this decree proceeds the whole process of salvation which Paul has described, and which he now briefly recapitulates in three stages: **He calls those whom He has thus predestined; then He justifies those whom He has called; then He glorifies those whom He has justified.** It is all founded on the impregnable rock of the eternal will of God.

Ideas of Salvation

30

viii. 31-39: THE CERTAINTY OF SALVATION

31   **Now what follows from all this? If God is for us, who**
32   **can be against us? The God who did not spare His**
         own Son but gave Him up for us all, surely He will
33   **give us everything besides! Who is to accuse the**

elect of God ? When God *acquits, who shall condemn?*
Will Christ?—the Christ who died, yes and rose
from the dead ! the Christ who is at God's right 35
hand, who actually pleads for us ! What can ever 34
part us from Christ's love? Can anguish or calamity
or persecution or famine or nakedness or danger 36
or the sword? (*Because, as it is written,*
  For Thy sake we are being killed all the day long,
  we are counted as sheep to be slaughtered.)
No, in all this we are more than conquerors through
Him who loved us. For I am certain neither death 37
nor life, neither angels nor principalities, neither 38
the present nor the future, no powers of the Height
or of the Depth, nor anything else in all creation 39
will be able to part us from God's love in Christ
Jesus our Lord.

There is in the thought of the decree and calling of God an 31
immense assurance for the Christian in a world where so much
seems to be against him. **If God is for us, who can be
against us?** Of God's goodwill towards us there can be no
possible doubt, for **God proves His love for us by this,
that Christ died for us while we were still sinners** (v. 8).
That carries with it everything else. **The God who did not** 32
**spare His own Son, but gave Him up for us all, surely
He will give us everything besides !** Among other things,
we can be sure of victory over anything that threatens our
ultimate well-being. Paul now suggests some things that conceivably might do so.

First, there is the fact of our sin. For that we are sinners 33
we cannot without self-deception deny. The thought conjures
up Paul's favourite picture of the law-court: the ' accuser of
the brethren ' may bring up our sins against us, and claim a
verdict of condemnation. But he has no *locus standi* in the
court, for the issue has been prejudged. **When God acquits,
who shall condemn?** We are sinners, it is true, but we are
justified ' sinners. After all the disquisitions of chaps. vi.–viii.,
no one can suppose that that means any paltering with the
absolute claims of the moral law. As justified sinners we are
bound to the ' slavery of righteousness.' But even while we are
still striving to **put the actions of the** [sinful] **body to death**
(viii. 13), God sees in us that which in Christ we are becoming,
and acquits us.

I
SIN

34   But, after all, may not Christ Himself condemn us, His unprofitable servants? **For we have all to appear without disguise before the tribunal of Christ** (2 Cor. v. 10). What if His sentence is one of condemnation? Unthinkable, Paul replies. Christ died and rose for us (cf. iv. 25)—**when we were still sinners** (v. 8). Far from condemning us, He **actually pleads for us.** The Judge is Advocate for the defence !

It is worth while pausing here to observe that in all this Paul is appealing, not to any teaching peculiar to himself, but to the common Christian faith, as it appears in the whole New Testament. **I passed on to you,** he writes in 1 Cor. xv. 3-4, **what I had myself received** (what, therefore, was already the common Christian faith when he was converted), **namely, that Christ died for our sins as the scriptures had said, that He was buried, that He rose on the third day as the scriptures had said.** To this the primitive Church added that He is on the right hand of God (Acts vii. 55; Mark xiv. 62 —this also belonged to the tradition which Paul received; cf. Col. iii. 1, Eph. i. 20), and that He would be Judge of the quick and the dead (Acts x. 42—and, as we have seen, Paul accepted this too). Thus Paul might here very well be quoting from a primitive form of the Creed (as he probably is): ' He was crucified, dead, and buried; the third day He rose again from the dead, and sitteth on the right hand of God; from thence He shall come to judge the quick and the dead.' But lest the thought of Christ as Judge should lead Christians to fear for their salvation, he reminds them of another idea which also was deeply fixed in early Christian belief, though it did not get into the Creed. ' He ever liveth to make intercession for them,' says the Epistle to the Hebrews (vii. 25) (and elaborates the idea into a doctrine of Christ's eternal Priesthood); ' If any man sin,' says 1 John (ii. 1), ' we have an advocate with the Father, Jesus Christ the righteous.' Behind it lies a word of Jesus Himself: ' Whosoever will confess Me before men, him will I confess before the face of My Father which is in Heaven ' (Matt. x. 33). And, indeed, even without any explicit statement the followers of Jesus knew that, whether on earth or in heaven, He must be the Friend of sinners. Thus we stand entirely on the ground of the original preaching of the Gospel. Paul is only making a peculiarly effective application of the common belief of all Christians, and one whose truth to fact he has already established by careful argument.

What, then, is the application to ourselves (to translate Paul's poetry into prose)? No sober and self-respecting man can be other than concerned about his own failure to live up to high ideals. The more morally sensitive he becomes, the more concerned he will be. Least of all can a Christian, who takes seriously his calling in Christ, make light of his sinfulness. He cannot have a good conscience. 'The good conscience is an invention of the devil,' says Dr. Schweitzer.[1] **Although I am not conscious of having anything against me,** said Paul (1 Cor. iv. 4), **that does not clear me. It is the Lord who cross-questions me.** Before that cross-examination the best of men must confess to a 'sense of sin.' But a sense of sin, although it is often recommended and cultivated by the religious, is in itself not a help, but a hindrance, to the growth of personality. Psychology can prove that to the hilt. It daunts our courage, saps our confidence, and frustrates our effort. What is the cure for it? Not to repress it, or to sophisticate ourselves out of it. The only cure is 'justification by faith'—the faith that the infinite love of God in Christ takes charge of our whole life, sins and all. We are wholly in His hand; 'there is no refuge from God but unto God'; and God is love. The Judge becomes our Advocate. Christ, who is Himself the Ideal we fail to reach (the **glory** of which **we come short**), pleads our cause. We are thus freed from the sheer negativity of the sense of failure, and set towards positive achievement. At every moment we can leave our whole past in the hands of God, with complete confidence, and make a fresh start upon the line that His will sets for us, knowing that we **have His aid and interest in everything.** ~~Some other things which conceivably might threaten our well-being~~

So much, then, for the worst of the ills that menace our security. Paul now passes to another group of ills: **anguish, 35 calamity, persecution, famine, nakedness, danger, the sword.** There is a particular pathos about some of the items in this list. Paul was writing on the eve of his last voyage to Jerusalem. He was putting his head into the lion's mouth, as he well knew (cf. Acts xx. 22–25). **Persecution** certainly, likely enough **the sword,** awaited him. He reminds himself and his 36 readers, by a citation of Scripture, after his manner, that all

[1] *Civilization and Ethics*, p. 263.

this was in the will of God. But the list is comprehensive enough: suffering, calamity, poverty, danger are very common experiences. May they not **part us from Christ's love**—which is **God's love in Christ Jesus** (cf. v. 8)? That they can part us from the present sense of God's love many would have to confess. Sometimes under calamity the whole universe seems to be against us, and it is hard to feel the love of God, or to love Him in return. But we are not dependent upon such feelings. We **have been called in terms of His purpose,** and that

37   purpose, because it is the purpose of love, determines that none of these things can overthrow us. **In all this we are more**

38   **than conquerors through Him who loved us.**

Finally, Paul sweeps together all powers, existences, or conditions in which any possibility of overthrowing our salvation might conceivably reside—**death, life, the present, the future,** and those mysterious forces which to him were real and at least half-personal beings, and to us are 'laws of Nature,' or powers of destiny, or, in any case, the terrifying mysteries of a world half known—**angels, principalities, powers of the Height or of the Depth** [1]—and declares his unshakable certainty that neither these **nor anything else in all creation will be able to part us from God's love in Christ Jesus our Lord.** There is no arguing with such a certainty. Either you simply don't believe it or you recognize it as the word of God.

We have now reached the climax of the high argument upon which Paul entered at i. 17, and the conclusion of that part of it which began at v. 1, which in a sense is all an elaboration of the theme introduced in v. 1–5. It is worth observing how closely it is all knit together, in spite of all digressions, and how at the end, Paul brings up again in organic connection the various ideas with which he has been working all through: the sovereign love of God revealed in the death of Christ; grace; justification by faith; sonship to God; liberty and life through the Spirit; the hope of glory. It all holds together. Each several idea depends upon and implies the others, and none of them can be understood, as Paul meant it, without the others. We have been told quite often enough in recent years that Paul is no theologian, that he is not even a clear or orderly thinker, but at best a wild genius who threw out suggestive ideas here and there, without ever trying to think them together. That can be understood as a reaction against the older dogmatic use of the epistles, but it is not true. Doubtless he was not a syste-

[1] See note on xi., 30–32

matic theologian, at least so far as we know. Doubtless he had
in him more of the prophet than of the doctor of divinity. But
no one can go honestly through the labour of following the
strong and coherent, though complicated, thread of argument,
from Rom. i. 17 to viii. 39, without knowing that he is in the
presence of a first-rate thinker, as well as a man of the deepest
religious insight. We have here, not a jumble of *obiter dicta*, but
a co-ordinated presentation of Christianity in a rich variety of
aspects. The chain of argument is continuous, even though it
may drag at times, and have a weak link or two. The difficulty
that we find in following it is largely due to the extensive background in Paul's own mind, which we have to divine, often
from mere hints. But we know that the background is there,
and that, even if sometimes the relation of ideas is obscure to
us, it would become clear if we knew the background. How
far the Romans followed the argument is a question to which
one would like to know the answer. They shared the general
background of Paul's thought, more or less, but they no more
than we had that personal knowledge of him which would be
necessary for a full understanding. No doubt to them, as to us,
the epistle became really thrilling when argument passed into
prophecy, and with its ' **I am certain** ' challenged, not logical
discussion but spiritual assent.

IV. THE DIVINE PURPOSE
IN HISTORY
(ix.–xi.)

At this point the way seems to be clear for the full and explicit
treatment of Christian ethics for which the theological discussion
has been preparing, and to which we have several times been
directly pointed (vi. 12–14, 19–22, viii. 4–8, and especially
viii. 12–13). The immediate sequel to viii. 31–39 is: **Well
then, my brothers, I appeal to you by all the mercy of
God to dedicate your bodies as a living sacrifice,** and so
forth (xii. 1 sqq.). But once again the sequel is postponed,
while certain theological difficulties left over from the foregoing
discussion are dealt with.

Chaps. ix.–xi. form a compact and continuous whole, which
can be read quite satisfactorily without reference to the rest
of the epistle, though it naturally gains by such reference, just

as other parts of the epistle gain by being read alongside Galatians or 1 Corinthians. It has been suggested that the three
chapters were originally a separate treatise which Paul had by
him, and which he used for his present purpose. There is a
good deal to be said for this view. The angle from which the
questions are dealt with is not quite the same as that from
which he glances at them earlier in the epistle. The method
is in some respects different. Thus, in chaps. ix.–xi. a much
larger place is given to detailed exposition of particular passages
of Scripture. Only in chap. iv. have we any close parallel to
this. Elsewhere in the epistle references to Scripture are more
allusive. The closest parallels are to be found in the Epistle
to the Galatians.

Again, the style has a character of its own. Almost everywhere in Paul's writings we overhear the tones of the living
voice, as is natural in one who was much more a preacher than
a writer; but in this section the conversational note is very
clear. The style is, in fact, that of the so-called *diatribé*, or
philosophical conversation—a technique evolved by the Cynic
and Stoic schools for popularizing philosophical and ethical
ideas. The best familiar example of its use is the *Diatribai*,
or Dissertations, of Epictetus, which were actually taken down
from oral delivery by his pupil Arrian. (His better-known
Enchiridion, or Handbook, is a compilation of selected sayings.)
They are distinguished by a familiar and lively interchange
of question and answer, ironical apostrophe and personal appeal.
If now in chaps. ix.–xi. we disregard the characteristically
Jewish and rabbinic method of argument from Scripture, the
rest reminds one very strongly of Epictetus. **'I am telling the
truth . . .' 'Then are we to infer? . . .' 'But who are
you, my man? . . .' 'What are we to conclude? . . .'
'And why? . . .' 'But, I ask . . .' 'Then, I ask . . .'
'Surely you know . . .'** and so forth all through. There are
indeed traces of this *diatribé* style in most of Paul's epistles (and
another good example is the Epistle of James), but nowhere else
is there such a long sustained passage dominated by it.

If now, bearing all this in mind, we forget for a moment that
chaps. ix.–xi. are part of a long epistle, and read them by themselves, we get the impression that we are listening to Paul
preaching. It has already been suggested that in ii. 1–iii. 20 we
have a distinct echo of Paul's preaching style, but that is in no
sense a complete sermon. Chaps. ix.—xi., on the other hand,
have a beginning and a close appropriate to a sermon, and the

preaching tone is maintained all through. It is the kind of sermon that Paul must often have had occasion to deliver, in defining his attitude to what we may call the Jewish question. It is quite possible that he kept by him a MS. of such a sermon, for use as occasion demanded, and inserted it here. As we have seen, the epistle could be read without any sense of a gap if these chapters were omitted. They are unlike the other excursuses in the epistle, in that the results gained in this discussion are not directly used in what follows. On the other hand, the discussion is certainly of value in clearing up questions inadequately noticed at the point where they come up in the main argument; and it is likely that Paul already knew that he was going to use his sermon on the Rejection of Israel when he briefly dismissed the difficulties raised in iii. 1–9. Moreover, there is a slight indication that Paul had already incorporated chaps. ix.–xi. in the epistle before he went on to xii., in the fact that xii. starts with the idea of the *mercy* of God, and '*mercy*' has been the key-word of the discussion in ix.–xi., and particularly of its conclusion, xi. 30–32; whereas the key-word of viii. is ' *love*.' And xv. 9 is only to be clearly understood in the light of ix.–xi. (see note, p. 223). In other words, chaps. ix.–xi. do not constitute a mere interpolation; though, on the other hand, they were very likely not written *currente calamo* with the rest of the epistle, but represent a somewhat earlier piece of work, incorporated here wholesale to save a busy man's time and trouble in writing on the subject afresh.

The question before us is the one which was raised in iii. 1, and almost immediately dropped. We may put it in this way: Granted that historically the Israelite nation has played a special part in the divine plan, as the bearer of a special revelation, how can it be consistent with that plan that a new way of salvation should now be revealed, which not only rules out in principle any special privileges for Israel, but, as a matter of fact and experience, is excluding the major part of the nation? To Paul's Jewish-Christian opponents, this question pointed to a *reductio ad absurdum* of his whole position. To all who accepted the historic revelation in the Hebrew Scriptures as the starting-point of Christianity (as Paul did, and all Christians at the time, so far as we know), it could not but present a serious difficulty. Paul deals with it, after a short exordium, ix. 1–5, in three stages: (i.) in ix. 6–29 he establishes the absolute sovereignty of God, and His complete freedom to choose the recipients of His favour and the instruments of His purpose, at any moment; (ii.) in ix. 30–x. 21 he reviews the history of the process of selection by which the divine plan has advanced, showing how human freewill enters into it; (iii.) in xi. 1 32 he deduces from the freedom of God, from His action in history, and from His known character, a hopeful view of future developments. He then concludes, in xi. 33–36, with a hymn of God's wisdom which may be compared with the hymn of God's love which concluded the preceding section (viii. 31–39).

ix. 1–5: THE TRAGEDY OF THE REJECTION OF ISRAEL

ix.

1 **I am telling the truth in Christ—it is no lie, my conscience bears me out in the holy Spirit when I say that I am**
2 **in sore pain. I suffer endless anguish of heart. I**
3 **could have wished myself accursed and banished from Christ for the sake of my brothers, my natural**
4 **kinsmen; for they are Israelites, theirs is the Sonship, the Glory, the covenants, the divine legislation,**
5 **the Worship, and the promises: the patriarchs are theirs, and theirs too (so far as natural descent goes) is the Christ. (Blessed for evermore be the God who is over all ! Amen.)**

The sermon (if we may call it so) starts abruptly, with no connection with what has preceded. Paul gives expression to the emotional interest in national hopes which his estrangement from his nation had not destroyed. He has spoken of the abrogation of the privilege of Israel, in a dispensation in which

1–
2 **no distinctions are drawn.** But it hurts him to speak like that; for, in actual fact, he sees that Israel as a people has no part at all in the blessings of the New Age that has dawned. Though the Gospel was offered **to the Jew first and to the Greek as well,** the Jews as a body have decisively rejected it, though individual Jews have been incorporated along with Gentiles in the Christian Church. The existing character of the Church as a predominantly Gentile community was largely the result of his own work, but that thought only embitters his

3 disappointment, and makes him feel that his own position among the saved is something which he would willingly forgo, if at that price he could secure the salvation of his people.

With a tragic pride in the vastness of the heritage thrown 4 away, he recites the privileges of the Chosen Race: **they are Israelites**—bearers of the sacred name; **theirs is the Sonship** —for God said, ' Israel is My son, My firstborn ' (Exod. iv. 22); **the Glory,** of God's manifest presence; **the covenants** with Abraham, Isaac, and Jacob, and with Moses at Sinai; **the divine legislation,** which, though it is now superseded as a way of salvation, is yet holy, spiritual, just, and good (vii. 12, 14, 16), the highest revelation in the sphere of law that ever has been or even can be; **the Worship** of the Temple, with its divinely ordered and significant ritual; **the promises,** which are the everlasting foundation of all man's faith and hope (see chap. iv.); **the patriarchs,** whose faith and obedience 5 claimed the promises; and, as the climax of all, **theirs too (so far as natural descent goes) is the Christ.** The pathos of this climax lies in the fact that all the religious privileges enumerated pointed forward to the fulfilment of the whole history of Israel in the coming of the Messiah: the Messiah came—and instead of fulfilment came frustration and disaster!

Moved by the thought of the immeasurable favour of God to His people, Paul breaks out into an ascription of praise: **Blessed for evermore be the God who is over all ! Amen !** There is another possible way of construing the words, according to which they form the conclusion of the previous sentence: ' Theirs is the Christ, who is God over all, blessed for ever.' But such a direct application of the term ' God ' to Christ would be unique in Paul's writings. Even though he ascribes to Christ functions and dignities which are consistent with nothing less than deity, yet he pointedly avoids calling Him ' God ' (e.g. 1 Cor. viii. 6; Phil. ii. 6–11; see also note on Rom. x. 9).[1] Thus Dr. Moffatt's rendering seems to be the most natural and probable. But it has been pointed out that the transposition of two Greek words (three letters in all) [2] would give a different meaning to the sentence. It might then read: ' theirs is the God who is over all, blessed [be He] for ever,' which would give a very close parallel to the constant rabbinic formula, ' The Holy One, blessed be He.' There is no manuscript evidence whatever for such an alteration of the

---

[1] The reason why Paul could not do so, while the theologians who followed him could, was not that they differed from him in their belief about the Person of Christ, but that they were Greeks and he a Hebrew; though he spoke Greek, his religious terms always bore their Hebrew colouring: and the Greek *theos* is not the precise equivalent of the Hebrew *elohim*.

[2] ὢν ὁ for ὁ ὢν.

text, but it is, I think, not impossible that this is what Paul
dictated. In that case, the climax of the privileges of Israel
is the fact that God said, 'I will be their God and they shall be
My people.' (Jer. xxxi. 33, &c.).

ix. 6–29: DIVINE SOVEREIGNTY

It is not, of course, as if God's word had failed! Far
6   from it! 'Israel' does not mean everyone who
7   belongs to Israel; they are not all children of Abra-
     ham because they are descended from Abraham.
     No, *it is through Isaac that your offspring shall be reckoned—*
8   meaning that instead of God's children being the
     children born to Him by natural descent, it is the
     children of the Promise who are reckoned as His
9   true offspring. For when God said, *I will come about*
     this time and Sara shall have a son, that was a word of
     promise. And further, when Rebecca became preg-
10 nant by our father Isaac, though one man was the
     father of both children, and though the children
11 were still unborn and had done nothing either good
     or bad (to confirm the divine purpose in election
     which depends upon the call of God, not on anything
12 man does), she was told that *the elder will serve the*
13 *younger.* As it is written, *Jacob I loved but Esau I hated.*
14 Then are we to infer that there is injustice in God?
15 Never! God says to Moses,
        I will have mercy on whom I choose to have mercy.
        I will have compassion on whom I choose to have compassion.
     You see, it is not a question of human will or effort
16 but of the divine mercy. Why, scripture says to
17 Pharaoh,
        It was for this that I raised you up,
        to display My power in you,
        and to spread news of My name over all the earth.
18 Thus God has mercy on anyone just as He pleases,
     and *He makes* anyone *stubborn* just as He pleases.
19 'Then,' you will retort, 'why does He go on finding
20 fault? Who can oppose His will?' But who are you,
     my man, to speak back to God? *Is something a man ha.*
     moulded to ask him who has moulded it, 'Why did you make
21 me like this?' What! has *the potter* no right *over the*

clay? **Has he no right to make out of the same lump
one vessel for a noble purpose and another for a** 22
**menial? What if God, though desirous to display
His anger and show His might, has tolerated most
patiently the objects of His anger, ripe and ready** 23
**to be destroyed? What if He means to show the
wealth that lies in His glory for the objects of His
mercy, whom He has made ready beforehand to
receive glory—that is, for us whom He has called** 24
from among the Gentiles as well as the Jews? As 25
indeed he says in Hosea,

> *Those who were no people of Mine, I will call ' My People,'*
>   *and her ' beloved ' who was not beloved;*
> *on the very spot where they were told, ' You are no people*   26
>   *of Mine,'*
> *there shall they be called ' sons of the living God.'*

And Isaiah exclaims, with regard to Israel, *Though* 27
*the number of the sons of Israel be like the sand of the sea, only a
remnant of them shall be saved; for the Lord will carry out His* 28
sentence on earth with rigour and despatch. **Indeed, as Isaiah** 29
foretold,

> *Had not the Lord of hosts left us with some descendants,*
>   *we would have fared like Sodom,*
>   *we would have been like Gomorra.*

The position which is being attacked in the first part of the
sermon is that God was bound, by His promise to Abraham,
to save Israel as a corporate whole, whatever the attitude or
behaviour of individual Israelites might be. As we have seen
(notes on ii.), this position was actually held, and in fact appears
to have been orthodox doctrine, though it was not unquestioned.
Paul replies by insisting that full weight must be given to the
doctrine of divine sovereignty which he shared with his Pharisaic
opponents. On the ground of this doctrine, it must be admitted
that no one has any claim upon God as of right. His mercy is
a free self-determination of His sovereign will. His promise to
bless ' Israel,' His chosen people, certainly holds good; but it
is for Him to decide with absolute freedom who shall constitute
that chosen people. If He chooses to reject the Jews and to
elect Gentiles, then the true ' Israel ' is composed of those whom
He elects. That such might indeed be His plan was actually
declared by the prophets. Therefore, even if the entire Israelite
nation is rejected, the promise has not been broken. It has been

fulfilled by God in His own way; and the rightness of that way
is something which no man dare challenge.

The argument starts from the assumption that the Jewish
nation, representing historic Israel, has forfeited its ' inheritance '
of the blessings promised to Abraham.   The Jewish objector
6 argues that this is as much as to say that **God's word had
failed,** which, he implies, is absurd; therefore the premiss
from which it is deduced is false; *quod erat demonstrandum.* Paul
denies the inference.   The term **' Israel,'** as used in the terms
7 of covenant, **does not mean everyone who belongs to** the
historic nation of **Israel;** and the term **' children of Abraham '** does not mean all who are physically **descended from
Abraham** (see iv. 11-17). Every Jew admitted this: Ishmael
was a child of Abraham, but no Jew believed that the Arabs,
his descendants, were within the covenant.   The Scripture
8– said, **It is through Isaac that your offspring shall be
9 reckoned.** And why? Because, says Paul, the birth of Isaac
was not a matter of ordinary physical generation: it was supernatural, the result of a promise of God, accepted by the faith
of Abraham (see iv. 18–22). Very well then, from the beginning
there were ' children of Abraham ' who were outside the
promise, yet that does not mean that **God's word had failed.**
The present situation is only the same thing on a larger scale.

' But,' the Jew will argue, ' this is beside the point.   The
choice of Isaac was involved in the original promise; any
further selection, such as you postulate at the present time,
is not on the same footing. Moreover, we are descendants of
10– Isaac, not of Ishmael, and therefore we are **children of the
18 promise.'**   Paul rejoins: ' So are the hated Edomites, the
descendants of Esau. Esau and Jacob were both sons of Isaac.
They were actually twins, born under exactly the same condi-
11 tions.   Yet the one was rejected, the other chosen; and this
choice took place before their birth, **to confirm the divine
purpose in election, which depends on the call of God,
not on anything a man does.'** (This contrast between the
divine call and human action is not really necessary to the
argument; but Paul cannot get away from his favourite antithesis of faith and works; his point is simply that the divine
freedom of choice is limited by nothing in the world or out of
it.)   Thus, if descent from Abraham gives a title to the ' inheritance,' Jew and Edomite are on the same footing. No Jew
could admit this.   It follows that the status of the Jew rests

upon nothing but a free determination of the divine will, and he cannot complain if, by a similar determination, God rejects the descendants of Jacob as He rejected the descendants of Esau. In neither case has **God's word failed.**

The first objection, therefore, is disposed of. Paul's position does not imply that the divine purpose has failed. But now a further difficulty arises. If this is how the divine purpose 14 works, must we not say that it was unjust, either in itself or in its method? The question was raised in iii. 5. The only answer there given was that the Judge of all the earth *must* do right, which is logically no answer at all. Nor is there a direct answer here. In effect Paul says: ' It is not a question 15– of justice, for justice would imply an inherent right of the 16 creature over against his Creator. It is a question of the mercy of God upon those who in justice have merited, and can merit, nothing at all. The mercy of God, as Scripture declares, is determined by nothing beyond itself; **I will have mercy on whom I choose to have mercy.**' This is, indeed, the quality of mercy. If it counts desert, it is not mercy. But there can, in the nature of things, be no desert on man's part before God. The ' prevenient grace ' of God is a necessary condition of any salutary activity of man. The mercy of God is an original act of His creative will.

We may illustrate this as follows. In the course of evolution in Nature, certain parts of Nature become the points at which a new stage is initiated, and as such are distinguished from other parts which remain unevolved. The life-force, or what-ever we call it, selects the objects which are to be the vehicles of its further operations, selects in the act of producing fresh forms. ' The mammal I loved; the saurian I hated ' might be written over the transition from the Secondary to the Tertiary Period. Similarly, the divine mercy, designing to bring into being a new order of mankind—**God's children**—creates selectively its own objects, by initiating in humanity at certain points—i.e. in certain individuals—the disposition which is receptive of mercy. (And, as we shall see, this selection of individuals is made with a view to the ultimate elevation of all mankind into the new order; not only so, but **the creation waits with eager longing for the sons of God to be re-vealed** and hopes **to gain the glorious freedom of the children of God.**) It is hard to see how we can get away from this position, that the initiative in salvation **is not a question of human will or effort but of the divine mercy.**

17–
18   The next step, however, that Paul takes seems to be a false step. It was not necessary for his argument, to show that God also creates *bad* dispositions in those who are not to be saved, that He not only **has mercy on anyone just as He pleases,** but also **makes anyone stubborn just as He pleases.** It was enough for Paul's purpose here that the positive working of God's redeeming purpose should be self-determined in regard to its objects. This position is guaranteed by *data* of the religious consciousness, for the truly religious man knows that any good that is in him is there solely by grace of God, whatever he may make of this in his philosophy. But to attribute one's evil dispositions to God is a sophistication. One may feel driven to it by logic, but the conscience does not corroborate it. The doctrine of sin which we have met in the earlier chapters of the epistle (particularly chaps. i. and vii.) does not admit of this solution of the problem. It was however a good *argumentum ad hominem*, for the Jewish objector would be bound to recognize the authority of the Scripture which said that God Himself made Pharaoh stubborn (Exod. ix. 12, 16), and could not complain if Paul gave it an application of which he had not thought.

The Hebrew mind tended to determinism, attributing to the omnipotent will of God, as first cause, all consequences of second causes, and this tendency was strengthened in the rabbinic period by a definite fight against dualism, which might introduce into the universe a ' second power ' over against the One God. Such dualism was familiar to the Jews through the Zoroastrian religion of Persia. But a fully ethical conception of God makes it self-contradictory to attribute evil to His will. Paul shared the tendency to determinism, but when he had fully in view the revelation of God in Christ as pure love, he could not hold that sin was the result of His action. Here his thought declines from its highest level. And, while the argument is primarily *ad hominem*, it does lead up to a doctrine for which he later makes himself responsible—namely, that by divine decree Israel was blinded to the significance of the Gospel (xi. 8). That doctrine is set forth with qualifications which partly draw the venom from it. Here he pushes what we must describe as an unethical determinism to its logical extreme, in order to force his opponent to confess the absolute and arbitrary sovereignty of God.

19   Very naturally the objector replies, ' **Then why does He**

go on finding fault? Who can oppose His will? ' (cf. iii. 7). If it is His will that men should act like Pharaoh, He cannot condemn them for doing so. In other words, a mechanical determinism annihilates morality. And, of course, the objector is right. Paul has driven himself into a position in which he has to deny that God's freedom of action is limited (not now by physical or historical necessity, but) by moral considerations. **Has the potter no right over the clay?** It is a well-worn 20-illustration. But the trouble is that a man is not a pot; he *will* 21 ask, ' **Why did you make me like this?** ' and he will not be bludgeoned into silence. It is the weakest point in the whole epistle.

But this is not Paul's last word. He must convince himself 22–and his readers that it is worth while to discuss at all the purpose 23 and action of a God whom he has just represented as a non-moral despot. The verses which follow are extremely difficult in the Greek. Dr. Moffatt has made the best of them. As I have already observed, when Paul, normally a clear thinker, becomes obscure, it usually means that he is embarrassed by the position he has taken up. It is surely so here. The general sense of the verses, however, can be made out. Although God is not responsible to human judgment, and we are not necessarily called upon to show that His action is guided by any principle but His own arbitrary will, yet actually a moral quality *can* be detected in His dealings; and that in two ways: (i.) although some men are **objects of His anger** (or, rather, in accordance with what was said on i. 18, are ' objects of retribution '), **ripe and ready for destruction,** yet these very men **God has tolerated most patiently.** The reference is to the **forbearance** of iii. 25 (see note), the **kindness, patience, and forbearance** of ii. 4. It is not indeed said here, as in ii. 4, that this kindness is intended to lead its objects to repentance. The suggestion is rather that the forbearance is no more than a stay of execution. But in the light of iii. 25, and of the conclusion in chap. xi., we may say that something more positive is really in Paul's mind. In any case, however, it is clear that there is something inherent in the character of God which leads Him to show such forbearance even to those who are not within the terms of His promise and covenant; (ii.) His plan must be judged, not by its negative effect in excluding some men, but by its positive effect in securing untold blessings for the chosen: **He means to show the wealth that lies in His glory for the objects of His mercy.**

24   And with this, Paul comes back to the point of vital interest
in the whole discussion: **that is, for us whom He has called
from among the Gentiles as well as the Jews.** Until now
the argument has moved on abstract and academic lines, using
such lay figures of the schools as Jacob, Esau, and Pharaoh;
now it suddenly touches concrete reality. <u>The objects of His
mercy</u> are to be found in the Christian Church; Paul and his
readers are among them. The freedom of choice which he has
25– vindicated as God's inalienable right has been exercised in
29 constituting a new 'Israel' of Jews and Gentiles. And this,
25 he adds, is in accordance with what the prophets said regarding
God's designs. First, that Gentiles should be included is established by Hosea's prophecy: **Those who were no people of
Mine, I will call 'My People'** (Hos. ii. 23). It is rather
strange that Paul has not observed that this prophecy referred
to Israel, rejected for its sins, but destined to be restored:
strange because it would have fitted so admirably the doctrine
of the restoration of Israel which he is to expound in chap. xi.
But, if the particular prophecy is ill-chosen, it is certainly true
27 that the prophets did declare the calling of the Gentiles.
Secondly, that only a minority of historic Israel is to form part
of the chosen people of God is distinctly taught in Isaiah's well-
known doctrine of the Remnant (Isa. x. 22–23). Here Paul is
unquestionably at one with prophetic teaching in its main
trend. His Christian experience has given him a key to the
prophets which the rabbis had largely lost.

The first stage of the argument, then, has brought us so far:
God purposed blessing for His chosen people; He has absolute
right, which no man dare impugn, to constitute that people
as He will; He has willed that it shall be composed of a remnant
of Israel, together with selected Gentiles; the assurance of all
the promised blessings to this new 'Israel' amounts to a complete fulfilment of the original promise: **it is not,** therefore,
as if God's word had failed. The four succeeding verses
make a transition to the next stage of the argument, which is
designed to show that, although no reason *need* be sought for
the course that God has chosen, since it is enough that He
willed it so, yet a reason for it *can* be found.

ix. 30–x. 21: HUMAN RESPONSIBILITY

What are we to conclude, then? That Gentiles who
never aimed at righteousness have attained right- 30
eousness, that is, righteousness by faith; whereas
Israel who did aim at the law of righteousness have 31
failed to reach that law. And why? Simply because
Israel has relied not on faith but on what they 32
could do. They have stumbled over *the stone that makes
men stumble*—as it is written,   33

> *Here I lay a stone in Sion that will make men stumble, even a
> rock to trip them up;*
> *but he who believes in Him will never be disappointed.*

x.

Oh for their salvation, brothers! That is my heart's
desire and prayer to God! I can vouch for their 1
zeal for God; only, it is not zeal with knowledge. 2
They would not surrender to the righteousness of 3
God, because they were ignorant of His righteousness and therefore essayed to set up a righteousness
of their own. Now Christ is an end to law, so as to 4
let every believer have righteousness. Moses writes
of law-righteousness, *Anyone who can perform it, shall live* 5
by it. But here is what faith-righteousness says: *Say* 6
not in your heart, 'Who will go up to heaven?' (that is, to
bring Christ down). Or, *'who will go down to the abyss?'* 7
(that is, to bring Christ from the dead). No, what
it does say is this: *The word is close to you, in your very* 8
mouth and in your heart (that is, the word of faith which
we preach). Confess *with your mouth* that 'Jesus is
Lord,' believe *in your heart* that God raised Him from 9
the dead, and you will be saved; for   10

> with his heart man believes and is justified,
> with his mouth he confesses and is saved.

No one who believes in Him, the scripture says, *will ever be* 11
disappointed. No one—for there is no distinction of 12
Jew and Greek, the same Lord is Lord of them all,
with ample for all who invoke Him. *Everyone who
invokes the name of the Lord shall be saved.* But how are they 13
to invoke One in whom they do not believe? And 14
how are they to believe in One of whom they have

15   **never heard? And how are they ever to hear, without a preacher? And how can men preach unless
they are sent?—as it is written,** *How pleasant is the
coming of men with glad, good news!*

16 **But they have not all given in to the Gospel of glad news?
No, Isaiah says,** *Lord, who has believed what they heard from*

17   *us?* **(You see, faith must come from what is heard,**

18   **and what is heard comes from word of Christ.) But,
I ask, ' Have they never heard? ' Indeed they have.**
*Their voice carried over all the earth,
and their words to the end of the world.*

19   **Then, I ask, ' Did Israel not understand? ' Why,
first of all Moses declares,**
I will make **you** *jealous of a nation that is no nation,
I will provoke* **you** *to anger over a nation devoid of understanding.*

20   **And then Isaiah dares to say,**
*I have been found by those who never sought Me,
I have shown Myself to those who never inquired of Me.*

21   **He also says of Israel,** *All the day long I have held out My
hands to a disobedient and contrary people.*

The last section left us with the fact of the Christian Church,
a predominantly Gentile community, as a concrete embodiment of the results of God's ' selective purpose.' Paul now
examines this fact, with the question in mind, Can we discern
any reason why the divine purpose should have worked in
30 just this way? In the Church we see that **the Gentiles who
never aimed at righteousness have attained righteousness . . . whereas Israel who did aim at the law of
righteousness have failed to reach that law.** The statement is more absolute than the facts warrant: not all Gentiles
have attained righteousness, nor have all Jews failed to attain;
and, again, some Gentiles did pursue righteousness (see ii.
14–15). But, broadly speaking, it is true that Greek religion
had not the predominantly ethical note which was characteristic
of Judaism; and yet Judaism, as such, is outside the Church,
while most Christians are Gentile in origin. This is a paradoxical state of affairs, and it needs explanation. It is explained
at once on the Pauline principle that **righteousness** is **by faith.**
In speaking of Christians as possessing righteousness, he is not
thinking in the first place of right conduct; in this respect
there was often much left to be desired. He is thinking primarily

of righteousness in the Hebrew, rather than the Greek, sense of
the word (see note on i. 17), as a status (being in the right,
rather than doing right). Christians possess righteousness
because they have been **called** by God (ix. 24), and, as **He
calls those whom He has decreed, so He justifies those
whom He has called** (viii. 30). That the acceptance of this
status will lead to actual righteousness of life, that indeed it is
the necessary and sole pre-condition of any real moral advance,
he has sufficiently shown in the section v. 1–viii. 13.

The Jews, then, are outside the sphere of righteousness
**simply because Israel has relied not on faith but on what
they could do.** The point is that the paradoxical state of 32
affairs exhibited in the Christian Church is absolutely inexpli-
cable except by the inscrutable fiat of God, *unless* the principle
of justification by grace through faith is accepted. The accep-
ance of that principle at once makes it possible to give an ethical
account of the matter. Already, therefore, we have advanced
from the position defended in ix. 6–23, provided we accept the
teaching of iii. 21–viii. 39.

Once again Paul appeals to Scripture for corroboration. He 32-
puts together two passages of Isaiah, viii. 14, xxviii. 16. The 33
same two passages are combined in 1 Pet. ii. 6–8. It has been
shown [1] that the combination was probably made before Paul
wrote, perhaps in a collection of proof-texts from the Old
Testament, designed to be used in controversy with the Jews.
The prophets spoke of a mysterious Stone—the Stone which the
builders rejected, and which was made the head of the corner
(Ps. cxviii. 22; Mark xii. 10; cf. 1 Pet. ii. 4); the Stone cut
without hands, which became a great mountain (Dan. ii.
34–35, 44–45), and so forth. This Stone, the earliest Christian
students of the Old Testament thought, symbolized the Messiah
and His Kingdom. The prophecies regarding it were fulfilled
in Jesus Christ, rejected and exalted, and by His Church, humble
in its beginnings but destined to become a world-power. It
must have been the same Stone, they thought, that Isaiah
spoke of—both when he spoke of the divinely laid foundation-
stone of Sion and when he spoke of the stumbling-stone—and
his twofold prophecy was fulfilled when Jesus Christ came: the
Jews refused to believe in Him, and yet He became the Foundation of the true Israel of God, the Church (cf. 1 Cor. iii. 11).
See the exegesis of the combined prophecies in 1 Pet. ii. 4–10,
and observe that it leads up to the citation of the same passage

[1] See Rendel Harris, *Testimonies*, I., pp. 18–19, 26–32.

from Hosea which Paul has just quoted, and in the same (improper) sense. The interest of all this is the evidence it gives that Paul is appealing, not to the authority of Scripture in a general way, but to a particular application of Scripture which was already traditional in the Church, and would be recognized by Jewish Christians whom he wished to persuade.

These verses, then, introduce the theme which is to be worked out at length in chap. x., which forms a compact section of the sermon. It has a short exordium of its own (x. 1-2), similar in tone to ix. 1-5, and this leads up to a re-statement of the theme: Israel is rejected, not simply on account of an arbitrary decree of God, but because they themselves chose a wrong course. He has now to show that they *could* have chosen otherwise, and therefore are responsible. In order to do this he sets out to prove (i.) that the way of faith (which they rejected) is simple and accessible to all (x. 5-10); (ii.) that this way has been so proclaimed that all Jews have had a chance to learn it (x. 11-15); and (iii.) that, in spite of this, many (most) Jews have not followed it, not because they were ignorant of it, but because they are what the prophet called them, **disobedient and contrary** (x. 16-21).

1   Paul reiterates his intense desire that his own people should be saved (cf. ix. 1-3). He has spoken severely of them, but
2 he must give them their due: **I can vouch for their zeal for God** (for **they did aim at the law of righteousness**—ix. 31);
3 but it was a mistaken zeal. **They would not surrender to the righteousness of God, because they were ignorant of** (or, rather, they failed to recognize; for it was there always to be known) **the righteousness of God, and therefore essayed to set up a righteousness of their own.** This reiterates the charge of ix. 32. The way they have chosen is a false one,
4 because **Christ is an end to law, so as to let every believer have righteousness.** He *must* have put an end to law, for otherwise 'righteousness' would not be available for **every believer;** but it is so available, as the experience of the Christian Church shows. Therefore the Jewish way of righteousness through works of the Law must be wrong.

But, granting for the sake of argument that this is so, the Jewish objector would urge: ' How on earth were the Jews to know this, and how can they be held responsible for their error?' Well, Paul replies, the **righteousness of God is**

attested by the Law and the prophets (iii. 21). For ex- 5–
ample, in Deut. xxx. 12–14 we read that the righteousness of 10
God is **close to you, in your very mouth and in your** 8
heart. That is surely something different from the righteousness described in Lev. xviii. 5: **Anyone who can perform it** 5
shall live by it. Leviticus speaks of <u>law-righteousness</u>, but
the ' **word in your heart** ' of Deuteronomy is <u>faith-righteous-
ness.</u> Such is Paul's main point. Now of course Deuteronomy,
no less than Leviticus, is speaking of the Law. But Paul is nevertheless so far justified, that the <u>ideal of Deuteronomy is far more
inward and spiritual than that of the Law of Holiness and the
Priestly Code of which Leviticus is composed.</u> The righteousness of Leviticus is, in the main, <u>hard and mechanical,</u> and its
emphasis is on <u>ceremonial with no moral value.</u> The Deuter-
onomic code, which was sponsored on its promulgation by the
prophetic school, has much more of the prophetic spirit in it:
it bases righteousness on <u>the love of God which should be
provoked by His grace towards His people.</u> Thus it shows real
spiritual insight on Paul's part that he should have recognized
(without the aid of modern criticism) that there is a *stratum* in
the Pentateuch which goes deeper than the bald legalism of
other parts, and <u>comes very near in spirit to Christianity.</u>

But unfortunately (from the standpoint of the modern reader)
Paul is not content with this. He must show that the passage
in Deuteronomy has a cryptic meaning which makes it a direct
prophecy of Christ and of the Christian faith. His view of the
Old Testament was that it contained Christian doctrine in a
veiled form. The Jews did not penetrate the veil: **Down to**
this day, whenever Moses is read aloud, the veil rests
on their heart; though whenever they turn to the Lord
the veil is removed (2 Cor. iii. 15–16). Thus Deut. xxx. 12–13, 6–
rightly interpreted, means that Christ is not an inaccessible 9
heavenly Figure (like the apocalyptic Messiah of Judaism), nor
yet a dead prophet (as the Jews thought), but the living Lord
of His people, always near. And Deut. xxx. 14, rightly interpreted, means: **Confess with your mouth that ' Jesus is**
Lord,' believe in your heart that God raised Him from
the dead, and you will be saved.

As an interpretation of Scripture this is purely fanciful. Its
interest for us is confined to the light it throws on Paul's conception of Christian faith. This is the only passage where he seems
to equate saving faith with belief in a certain proposition, and
he probably does so here only because he is approaching it

through the exegesis of an Old Testament passage. It is quite clear that for Paul faith is fundamentally a trustful attitude towards God (see note on i. 17), and not intellectual belief. But he would always have said that effectual faith is exercised only through a living Christ. **If Christ did not rise, then our preaching has gone for nothing, and your faith has gone for nothing too** (1 Cor. xv. 14). Thus faith in God through Christ implies that **God raised Him from the dead.** And this belief was included in the Christian confession of faith: **Jesus is Lord** (cf. 1 Cor. xii. 3; Phil. ii. 11). This formula was in all probability used in earliest times as the baptismal confession—baptism being at first ' in the name of the Lord Jesus ' (Acts ii. 38, xix. 5; cf. 1 Cor. i. 13), a form of the sacrament which was long recognized as valid, even after the Trinitarian form had prevailed.

The use of the title **Lord** as applied to Christ has been in recent years the subject of elaborate investigations, notably by Wilhelm Bousset.[1] It certainly began (in spite of Bousset) in the primitive, Aramaic-speaking Church, which has left us the liturgical expression *Marana tha*[2] (1 Cor. xvi. 22='Our Lord, come! '). The corresponding Greek word *Kyrios* was commonly used of the deity who was the object of a special cult (not usually of the regular State-deities). The god (Hermes, Serapis, or whoever it might be) was the ' Lord ' of his worshippers; they his ' slaves.' It thus implied both divine status and a sort of ' covenant ' relation between the god and his worshippers, who had chosen him as their special patron (or, as they would have said, had been chosen by him). But though the word is Greek, the usage is probably not Greek in origin, but rather Semitic. The Phoenicians called Tammuz ' Adonis,' i.e. Lord; and similarly the Hebrews read the name Jehovah in their Scriptures as the corresponding Hebrew word 'Adonai,' which our old version renders ' the LORD ' in capitals. For them too it denoted a God who stood in a special covenant relation with His worshippers.

This double usage forms the background of the confession ' **Jesus is Lord.**' Paul brings it into connection with ordinary pagan usage in 1 Cor. viii. 5–6, where he says that paganism

---

[1] See Bousset, *Kyrios Christos.* Among English writers who have dealt with Bousset's views may be mentioned A.E.J. Rawlinson, in his Bampton Lectures, *The New Testament Doctrine of the Christ*; and F.C. Burkitt in his little book *Christian Beginnings*.

[2] Not, as Moffatt following earlier authorities prints it, *Maran atha,* supposed to mean ' Our Lord comes,' an impossible translation of the words.

has many so-called gods, and many ' lords ' too; but Christians
have **one God, the Father from whom all comes,** and
one Lord, Jesus Christ, by whom all exists. Paul also, as
we shall presently see, freely applies passages in the Old Testament which speak of the LORD (i.e. Jehovah) to Christ.
Precise theological definition is difficult; but, with an eye on the pagan
background, we may say that for Paul's converts the confession
Jesus is Lord would suggest that He had chosen them to
belong to the community of His worshippers, and that, while
others might belong to Hermes, Serapis, and the rest, they
belonged exclusively to Him.   With the Hebrew background
in view, it would suggest that God had conferred upon Christ
His own Name as the covenant-God of Israel—the **Name
above all names** (cf. Phil. ii. 9–11)—to indicate that all
divine activity for the salvation of men is henceforward concentrated in Him.   In any case, the title ' Lord ' belongs to Christ
specifically as **head over everything for the Church, the
Church which is His body** (Eph. i. 22; cf. Col. i. 18), and
as destined Head of the whole universe (Phil. ii. 11; Eph. i. 10;
1 Cor. xv. 25).

We now take a fresh step. Not only was the Gospel implicit
in Deuteronomy, if the Jews could but see it, but it has been
explicitly declared to them (verses 11–15) and refused (verses
16–21).   The proof of this is given by way of the exegesis of a
catena of Scripture passages. All through we are left in some
doubt whether Paul means that in the time of the prophets the
Gospel was declared to the Jews and rejected by all but the
' Remnant,' or whether the prophets foretold the preaching of
the Gospel, which was actually carried out by the apostles of
Christ. Paul, we may suppose would have said that both these
things were true. The teaching of the prophets implied justification by faith and the universality of salvation, and the result
of their work exactly foreshadowed what happened when Christ
was proclaimed to the Jews: as the prophets found only a ' remnant ' to respond to their appeal, so the apostles of Christ won
only a minority of the Jewish people. The history of Israel is
all of a piece. But if we press the question, Is Paul referring to
events in (say) the sixth and fifth centuries B.C. or in the first
century A.D., we must answer that he is describing the latter in
terms of the former. Instead of arguing inductively from the
facts before him and his readers, he prefers to argue deductively
from the principles laid down by the prophets. This is because,

for his present purpose, it seemed to him less important to show what happened than to show that it was in God's purpose that it so happened. But the method adopted is inevitably strange to our way of thinking.

The starting-point is found in two complementary statements in Isaiah (xxviii. 16) and Joel (ii. 32) respectively: **No one 11, who believes in Him will ever be disappointed; Every- 13 one who invokes the name of the Lord shall be saved.** These statements, in Paul's view, affirm both justification by faith and the universality of salvation. The terms in which they are expressed imply that **there is no distinction of Jew and Greek.** The phrase used is the same as in iii. 23. There it meant: ' Jew as well as Greek has sinned '; here, ' To Jew as well as Greek salvation has been offered.' And, as in iii. 29–31, so here he shows this universality of the offer of salvation 12 to be the logical implication of monotheism: **the same Lord is Lord of them all.** But the one Lord here Paul takes to be Christ. Wherever the term *Kyrios*, **Lord,** is applied to Jehovah in the Old Testament, Paul seems to hold that it points forward to the coming revelation of God in the **Lord** Jesus Christ.

Here then is a divine promise: **everyone** (Jews included) **who invokes the name of the Lord shall be saved.** Such a promise would be an empty mockery unless all (Jews included) were given an opportunity of securing its benefits. If God gave the promise, He must have provided the necessary conditions under which men might avail themselves of it. What, then, 14 are the conditions? They are these. (*a*) You cannot invoke the name of Christ unless you believe in Him; (*b*) you cannot believe unless you have heard of Him; (*c*) you cannot hear about Him unless someone preaches the Gospel; (*d*) no one can preach the Gospel unless he is sent by God (for the Gospel is not somebody's happy idea, but the word of God). Very well then, it must be that God sent preachers of the Gospel to the 15 Jews, among others. And so He did, for the prophet says, **How pleasant is the coming of men with glad good news;** (Isa. lii. 7). Strictly this proves (*c*), but it is taken as implying (*d*). Thus at the divine end the chain (*a*)-(*b*)-(*c*)-(*d*) holds fast. If there is a breach in it, it must be at some other link.

A breach there has been, for certainly the Jews have not invoked the name of Christ and been saved. Links (*c*) and (*d*) are firm enough; this has already been proved, and now it is 18 shown that link (*b*) holds. **Have they never heard? Indeed** they have. 'Their voice carried over all the earth, and their words to the end of the world' (Ps. xix. 4—Paul ignores the fact that the words of the psalm refer to the heavenly bodies which 'declare the glory of God,' and applies it to preachers of the Gospel). It remains, therefore, that the missing 16 link must be (a); and so, indeed, it is: **They have not all given in to the Gospel of glad news? No. Isaiah says** [liii. 1] '**Lord, who has believed what they heard from us?**' (implying the answer, 'Few or none'). The proof is complete: Israel has been rejected, not because God did not give them the opportunity of salvation, but because they refused it when it was given.

Paul now adds a further point. **Did Israel not understand?** 19 (that the Gentiles were to be called, evidently). He answers that they did understand, or at least ought to have done so, for the calling of the Gentiles is distinctly declared in Deut. xxxii. 21 and Isa. lxv. 1; and incidently the latter passage is 20 followed by one (lxv. 2) which shows both that God did His best for Israel and that the responsibility for their downfall lies 21 with their own bad will: **All the day long I have held out My hands to a disobedient and contrary people.**

It is a curious line of argument, but there is much of the same kind of thing in rabbinic discussions in the Talmud. One may hope that it impressed Paul's opponents brought up in that tradition. To us it is apt to appear little better than solemn trifling. But there is more in it than appears on the surface. It is noteworthy that nearly the whole of this *catena* of quotations comes from the latter part of the Book of Isaiah. We have already had occasion to remark how important this part of the Old Testament is in the background of Paul's thought (see especially notes on i. 17). He was certainly right in holding that in essentials his closely associated doctrines of justification by grace through faith, and the universality of God's purpose of salvation, are to be found in the teaching of the Second Isaiah and his school. With this clue, we can find in this chapter a suggestion towards the interpretation of the post-exilic history of Israel. The restoration of the community after the Babylonian *débâcle* was heralded by the magnificent promises of the Second Isaiah. These were associated with a call to Israel, as the Servant of Jehovah, to accept a mission to the Gentiles. The Jews preferred to follow Ezekiel, Ezra, and the exclusivist party, and to foster a fantastic national pride upon a narrowing religion which canonized envy, hatred, malice, and all uncharitableness against the Gentile. Protests such as those uttered in the Book of Jonah and Ruth, and some of the later additions to the Book of Isaiah, were unheeded. The Book of Esther, the chauvinist Psalms, and the fiercer apocalypses represent the growingly dominant temper of Judaism. In due time this narrow religious nationalism led to the crucifixion of Jesus Christ. Paul saw rightly that in his struggle with Jewish nationalism within the Church he was fighting the battle of prophetic idealism afresh. The realization of the most spiritual of the religious hopes of the Second Isaiah, he felt, was bound up with the mission to the Gentiles to which the prophet had called his countrymen in vain.

The first two parts, then, of the sermon must be taken as complementary: first, God's plan of salvation is a free determination of His sovereign will, conditioned by nothing else than the everlasting mercy which is His nature and property; but secondly, it works through the free response of men in faith, and those whom it rejects have themselves rejected the opportunity offered to them. The Jewish nation as a whole, though they knew (or might have known) the way of God, chose their own way, and cannot complain if the divine purpose has passed them by and selected the Gentiles (as He always said He would) as the recipients of His promises. The third part examines the history of the past, the facts of the present, and the prospects of the future in the light of this twofold conclusion.

xi. 1–32: THE ISSUE OF THE DIVINE PURPOSE

xi.

Then, I ask, *has God repudiated His People?* Never! Why,
1   I am an Israelite myself, a descendant of Abraham,
2   a member of the tribe of Benjamin! *God has not
     repudiated His People*, His predestined People! Surely
     you know what scripture says in the passage called
3   'Elijah'? You know how he pleads with God against
     Israel; *Lord, they have killed Thy prophets, they have demolished
4   Thine altars; I alone am left, and they seek my life.* Yet what
     is the divine answer? *I have left* Myself *seven thousand
5   men who have not knelt to Baal.* Well, at the present
6   day there is also a remnant, selected by grace.
     Selected by grace, and therefore not for anything

they have done; otherwise grace would cease to be grace.*

Now what are we to infer from this? That Israel has 7 failed to secure the object of its quest; the elect have secured it, and the rest have been rendered insensible 8 to it—as it is written,

> God has given them a spirit of torpor,
>   eyes that see not, ears that hear not—
> down to this very day. And David says,   9
>   Let their table prove a snare and a trap,
>   a pitfall and a retribution for them;
>   let their eyes be darkened, that they cannot see,   10
>   bow down their backs for ever.

Now I ask, have they stumbled to their ruin? Never! 11 The truth is, that by their lapse salvation has passed to the Gentiles, so as to make them jealous. Well, 12 if their lapse has enriched the world, if their defection is the gain of the Gentiles, what will it mean when they all come in? I tell you this, you Gentiles, that as an apostle to the Gentiles I lay great stress 13 on my office, in the hope of being able to make my 14 fellow-Jews jealous and of managing thus to save some of them. For if their exclusion means that 15 the world is reconciled to God, what will their admission mean? Why, it will be life from the dead! If the first handful of dough is consecrated, so is the rest of the lump;   16 if the root is consecrated, so are the branches.

Supposing some of the branches have been broken off, while you have been grafted in like a shoot of wild 17 olive to share the rich growth of the olive-stem, do not pride yourself at the expense of these branches. 18 Remember, in your pride, the stem supports you, not you the stem. You will say, 'But branches were 19 broken off to let me be grafted in!' Granted. They were broken off—for their lack of faith. And you 20 owe your position to your faith. You should feel awed instead of being uplifted. For if God did not 21 spare the natural branches, He will not spare you either. Consider both the kindness and the severity

* Omitting [εἰ δὲ ἐξ ἔργων, οὐκέτι ἐστὶν χάρις, ἐπεὶ τὸ ἔργον οὐκέτι ἐστὶν ἔργον] with the Latin version and most MSS.

22   of God; those who fall come under His severity, but you come under the divine kindness, provided you adhere to that kindness. Otherwise, you will be
23   cut away too. And even the others will be grafted in, if they do not adhere to their unbelief; God can
24   graft them in again. For if you have been cut from an olive which is naturally wild, and grafted, contrary to nature, upon a garden olive, how much more will the natural branches be grafted into their proper olive?

To prevent you from being self-conceited, brothers, I
25   would like you to understand this secret; it is only a partial insensibility that has come over Israel, until the full number of the Gentiles come in. This
26   done, all Israel will be saved—as it is written,

The deliverer will come from Sion,
he will banish all godlessness from Jacob :
27   *this is My covenant with them,*
when I take their sins away.

28   So far as the Gospel goes, they are enemies of God —which is to your advantage; but so far as election
29   goes, they are beloved for their fathers' sake. For God never goes back upon His gifts and call.

30   Once you disobeyed God,
and now you enjoy His mercy thanks to their disobedience;
in the same way they at present are disobedient,
31   so that they in turn may enjoy the same mercy as yourselves.
32   For God has consigned all men to disobedience, that He may have mercy upon all.

The general tendency of the foregoing argument has been
1 to suggest that God has **repudiated His People,** the Jews, as a corporate whole. But Paul cannot accept this suggestion without further consideration. As he began the first two sections of the sermon with protestations of his loyalty to his own people, so here again he prefaces his argument with a similar protest. **Why, I am an Israelite myself, a descendant of Abraham, a member of the tribe of Benjamin,** and therefore cannot be expected to acquiesce in the final abandonment of the hope of Israel. ' The Lord will not cast off His people, neither will He forsake His inheritance,' said the

Psalmist (Ps. xciv. 14), and echoing this declaration (in the very words of the Greek version), Paul affirms, **God has not repu- 2 diated His People—His predestined People.**

In support of his conviction he first returns to the prophetic 2– doctrine of the Remnant, which he has already expounded in 4 chap. ix. But here he chooses an example earlier than the time of Isaiah, who first formulated that doctrine. As early as the time of Elijah, things looked very much as they do to-day, he suggests. Elijah, faced by widespread apostasy, thought that God had repudiated His people, for he seemed to be the only faithful Israelite left, and his death was imminent. But God showed him that he was wrong: **I have left Myself seven thousand men who have not knelt to Baal.** There was a faithful Remnant; and in that Remnant the future hopes of Israel resided. **Well, at the present day there is also a 5 remnant, selected by grace.** The apparent repudiation of Israel is not necessarily more absolute or final than it was in Elijah's time. It is true that **Israel,** as a whole, **has failed to 7 secure the object of its quest** (cf. ix. 30–31), but **the elect** (of Israel) **have secured it** (by incorporation in the Christian Church).

But the problem of the ' rejects ' in this process of selection still remains. **The rest** (not **of men,** as Moffatt, but) **of Israel have been rendered insensible to it.** Once again, Isaiah 8 (xxix. 10) and Deuteronomy (xxix. 4) are appealed to for 9– corroboration, together with Psalm lxix. 22–23. Formally, this 10 is an application of the doctrine of ix. 17–18, that God **makes anyone stubborn just as He pleases,** as He did in the case of Pharaoh. But the point of view is somewhat different. In Isaiah and Paul alike, the judgment, **God has given them a spirit of torpor,** is more like an instinctive reaction than a deliberate theological statement. When they saw how per- sistently and inexplicably blind their contemporaries were to what seemed to them the most obvious realities of the situation, they felt that here was something more than ordinary human stupidity: it was preternatural and mysterious.

We can understand their feeling. When one contemplates the behaviour of the European Governments since the war, the comment that rises in the mind is, *Quem Deus vult perdere, dementat prius.* One has the sense that some fate, bent on the destruction of Western civilization, is compelling the nations to continue in their suicidal policies, and blinding them to all the warnings of experience, all the counsels of reason. That was how Isaiah felt, in a situation not altogether unlike our own: **The Eternal has drenched you with stupor, closing your eyes and covering up your heads, till the sight of all this is no more to you than words in a sealed scroll.** History confirmed his judgment: the **stupor** continued, and the catastrophe came. *Absit omen!* Paul also felt like that about the Jewish people in his time. If we read the comments of a sober rabbi like Jochanan ben Zakkai (see his speech referred to in the notes on ii. 17–23), or of a political realist like Josephus, not to speak of the parables of Jesus, we are led to the conclusion that Paul did not exaggerate when he judged that the history of the eighth and seventh centuries B.C. was repeating itself in the half-century preceding the Fall of Jerusalem. **The Wrath is on them to the bitter end !** (1 Thess. ii. 16). A fate bent on their destruction was blinding them to all true values. But, being a theist, Paul no more than Isaiah could say ' fate '; and, shrinking from dualism, he would not say ' the devil.' Somehow it must all lie in the overruling purpose of God.

But if a place is to be found for such a conception within an ethical theism, it is necessary to be able to believe that the purpose is a recognizably good one—good for God's creatures at large, and good in the long run for the rejected nation. Paul realizes this, and proceeds to show (*a*) that the rejection is not final, (*b*) that it has immediately beneficent results in the conversion of the Gentiles, and (*c*) that in the long run the rejected Jews will share in the universal salvation of mankind towards which the divine purpose is moving. This solution of the problem is briefly indicated in verses 11–12. Israel has indeed **stumbled,** but not **to their** (final) **ruin.** Again, **by their lapse salvation has passed to the Gentiles.** This points to the historical fact that when the Jews had rejected Jesus Christ, and His apostles had failed to move them to repentance, the Church, largely under Paul's leadership, appealed to the Gentiles, and immediately found a considerable measure of success. Humanly speaking, it was because the appeal to the Jews miscarried that the Gospel was preached to the wider world. Paul, with his strong sense of a divine providence overruling all things, does not think of asking, ' What would have happened if the Jews had responded ? ' That things happened as they did must have been according to the purpose of God (and really the pastime of constructing hypothetical history is not particularly profitable, though undeniably entertaining:

what happened, not what might have happened, determines the future). And so, since he knew from the prophets (see ix. 24-26, x. 19-20) that it was God's purpose to include the Gentiles in His people, he concludes that the disobedience of the Jews was the destined way to that end. Thus **their lapse has enriched the world,** since **their defection is the gain 12 of the Gentiles.** But further, God declared in Deuteronomy: **I will make you jealous of a nation that is no nation** (x. 19 above). That means, Paul thinks, that the Jews, seeing the Gentiles entering into what they regarded as their own inheritance, will be so jealous of them that they will change their minds and enter too. By this roundabout route the rejected nation will find its way into the chosen people of God, the Church. And, as **their lapse has enriched the world,** something inconceivably glorious will result (*a fortiori*) **when they all come in.**

This theme will presently be fully worked out, but at this 13 point the preacher turns to Gentiles in his audience, with some- 14 thing of an apology. They will be surprised, he thinks, and perhaps a little affronted, that he, the apostle of the Gentiles, should be so much concerned about the salvation of the Jews. Rather tortuously he suggests that he works so hard for the conversion of the Gentiles, in order that he may prepare the way for the conversion of the Jews, because their conversion would bring such benefit to the whole world. Thus he was the instrument of the divine purpose (as declared in Deut. xxxii. 21) **to make my fellow-Jews jealous.** He certainly did make them jealous, but if he really thought that it would have any such desirable result, he was a great optimist! It is not likely that he felt this to be his motive to missionary work except for the moment, under the stress of his present train of thought.

What exactly he supposed would be the great benefit which 15 the conversion of the Jews would bring to the world he does not make too clear. **It will be life from the dead,** he says. This may be simply a very strong expression for the greatest conceivable blessing. But it may be that Paul means that the general resurrection of all mankind (as distinct from the resurrection of Christians) [1] will take place after the people of God

---

[1] See 1 Cor. xv. 23-26, where the first stage is the resurrection of Christ; the next, the resurrection of 'all who belong to Christ,' which is to take place at His Coming; and the last stage of all, the abolition of death.

has been completed by the inclusion of the Jews.[1] But Paul's use of all this eschatological mythology is fluctuating and somewhat uncertain. The general sense probably is that he cannot conceive of the process of history reaching its consummation until, as it were, the loose ends of the divine purpose have been gathered together, so that the universe must wait for its final destiny of blessedness until Israel has been brought to God.

16   But why should it be expected that Israel, at present so clearly astray from the divine purpose, should nevertheless ultimately be brought in? The ground for such an expectation is expressed in two metaphors. The first is drawn from the ritual practice of ancient religion, and the theory underlying it. In Num. xv. 20-21 it is enacted: ' Of the first of your dough ye shall give unto the Lord an heave-offering.' The idea of this rite was that, by the consecration of a portion of the people's food to their national God, the whole of that class of food was made safe for His people to eat: it was ' holy,' or free from power to ' defile ' them. The point which Paul makes is that, although the mass of dough received no such consecration, it was all ' holy ' because of the consecration of one part of it. The second illustration belongs to a similar circle of ideas. If a tree is dedicated to the Deity (sacred trees being common in most ancient religions), then all branches which it may subsequently put forth belong to Him. The application of both illustrations depends on the ancient idea of the solidarity of the tribe or nation (see notes on v. 12-21). Israel is thought of, not as a series of individuals each with his own personal responsibility to God, but as a solid whole. They are only branches springing from the root of the patriarchs: they form the mass of dough of which the faithful Remnant is the consecrated portion. All Israel therefore, whatever the behaviour of individuals in it, retains something of the ' holiness' of the patriarchs and of the faithful Remnant. **They are beloved for their fathers' sake** (xi. 28).[2]

It is difficult to reconcile this principle, as it is here applied, with Paul's strenuous denial in earlier parts of the epistle that descent from Abraham gives any right to the inheritance of

---

[1] Much as in the simpler scheme of Mark xiii. 10 it is suggested that ' the End ' will not come until the Gospel has been preached to all the Gentiles.

[2] It is to be observed that Paul applied this conception of tribal solidarity to the Christian Church: the children of Christian parents—or even of one Christian and one pagan parent—are ' holy ' (1 Cor. vii. 14) If we baptize the children of Christian parents we do so presumably because we believe that the very fact of being born into a Christian tradition is significant.

his blessing. But there is clearly a truth in the idea of solidarity to which justice must be done. Heredity, whether physical or social, does count for much in establishing certain predispositions. National character is a real thing, even though individual character must be the personal achievement of the individual; the Englishman may develop highly individual traits, but he remains ' a chip of the old block.' We might perhaps put Paul's point in this way: the innate religious capacity shown by the faithful Remnant is not an individual achievement, but is somehow dependent on their belonging to this particular stock, and having been born and bred within this particular tradition. And if so, the potentiality of such religious capacity must be latent in the stock and the tradition, and must some day come into actuality in the people as a whole. But if we say so, then we should probably have to say that the presence of such religious capacity in members of the human race indicates a corresponding potentiality in the race as a whole, since the principle of solidarity cannot be confined to one people. And although Paul does not say this, it may be the unexpressed premiss underlying his final optimism regarding mankind as a whole (see xi. 32).

The illustration of the tree and the branches is now expanded into an elaborate allegory. The tree is an olive, the most widely cultivated fruit-tree in Mediterranean lands. Suppose, says Paul, that the branches of an olive have been broken off, and that shoots of wild-olive have been grafted into the stock in their place. Apparently he supposed that in that case the grafts would bear true olives; at any rate, they would **share the rich growth of the olive-stem.** But the gardener has kept the broken branches by him, and, when the new grafts have ' taken,' he grafts the old olive-branches upon the stock once more. A truly remarkable horticultural experiment! Paul had the limitations of the town-bred man. He thought it absurd to suppose that God should care for cattle (1 Cor. ix. 9); and he had not the curiosity to inquire what went on in the olive-yards which fringed every road he walked. But, as we have remarked in his earlier illustrations (vi. 15-vii. 6), he is not really interested in the objects which he uses as figures; they are only a transparent disguise for realities. Jeremiah had said to the Jews of his time: ' The Lord called thy name, A green olive-tree, fair with goodly fruit: with the noise of a great tumult He hath kindled fire upon it, and the branches of it are broken ' (Jer. xi. 16). With this clue, the meaning of the allegory is clear: the olive-tree with the broken branches is the ' Israel of God '; the native branches are the Jews, the natural descendants of Israel; the wild grafts are the Gentiles incorporated in the people of God. The illustration shows clearly how complete, in Paul's thought, was the continuity between the Christian Church and the Israel of the Old Testament. The Church is not a new society; it is ' the Israel of God ' (Gal. vi. 16); it is the old stock of Abraham—since Christ is the destined **offspring** of Abraham (Gal. iii. 16) and Christians are **in Christ**—with new branches grafted upon it.

18   The application of the allegory is in two stages. First Paul warns his Gentile hearers against self-conceit and contempt for the Jews. The contempt that the average Roman felt for the Jews comes out in Latin literature of the period, in the speeches of Cicero, the *Histories* of Tacitus, and the *Satires* of Juvenal; and we can well believe that many Gentile Christians, at Rome and elsewhere, though they were glad enough to share the legal tolerance enjoyed by the Jewish religion, disliked any idea of connections with the Ghetto. Such anti-semitism in the Church might well lead to an indifference to the great Old Testament tradition out of which Christianity grew. So long as the leaders of Gentile Christianity were men like Paul, there was no danger of the revolt against Jewish legalism leading to a departure from the religion of the prophets. But it may well be thought that the anti-semitism of the Church in later times was accompanied by a real impoverishment of ethical ideals. Some would say that at the present time the Church would gain from closer and more respectful relations with the Jews, who have preserved, in living tradition, elements of the prophetic ideal which belonged to Christianity at the first, but were overlaid by Greek metaphysics and Roman law. It is certain that the contributions of devout Jewish scholars to our understanding of the Gospels in recent years have earned our gratitude.

Thus Paul is forestalling a real danger when he warns Gentile Christians, **Remember in your pride, the stem supports you, not you the stem;** your religious life is nourished by the
19 Old Testament tradition. It is you now, not the Jews, who are **boasting** and being **proud before God** (iii. 27, iv. 2). Those unbelieving Jews—those **branches**, as you will say, which **were broken off to let me in**—let them be an example and a warn-
20 ing rather than an occasion for self-conceit: **they were broken**

off—for lack of faith. You should feel awed instead of being uplifted; for here is a signal proof that there is in God **severity** as well as kindness. They have felt His **severity**: you 22 are the objects of His **kindness,** for it is by His free grace that 23 you have been admitted to His People. But **you owe your** 20 **position to your faith,** and **you come under the divine kindness, provided you adhere to that kindness: other-** 22 **wise you will be cut away too.** If the element of free-will needed to be emphasized to balance the emphasis on pre-destination in chap. ix., the emphasis is ample here.

The second stage of the application follows directly on the 23 conclusion of the first. If the Gentile Christian may lose his **standing in grace** (v. 2) by declension from faith in God, so also the Jew may be restored to such a standing by repent-ance: **the others will be grafted in, if they do not adhere to their unbelief.** It is, after all, far easier to graft a shoot native to the stock than to graft an alien shoot.

And so to the conclusion: **it is only a partial insensibility** 25 **that has come over Israel,** and only a temporary one, **until the full number of the Gentiles has come in. This done,** 26 **all Israel will be saved.** This, Paul says, is **a secret**—a mystery (the Greek word). By this he means a truth given by special revelation, rather than deduced by argument, and in particular he means (cf. 1 Cor. ii. 7, xv. 51; and especially Col. i. 25-27, Eph. iii. 4-12) a truth divined by religious intuition in the facts of the Gospel—the life, death, and resur-rection of Christ and the emergence of the Church. It is indeed a religious intuition that lies behind all this exposition, even though in form it is largely an argument from Scripture quite in the rabbinic manner. But Paul would have said that only the revelation which Christ had brought could give the true understanding of Scripture (cf. 2 Cor. iii. 15-16). And so he clinches his conclusion with prophecies from the Books of Isaiah (lix. 20) and Jeremiah (xxxi. 33-34—the prophecy of the 27 New Covenant, which elsewhere in the New Testament is always applied to the Church as the New Israel, and not, as here, to the salvation of the Jews). But the major premiss of 29 any argument on the subject is the fundamental conviction that God is self-consistent and unchangeable in His purpose: **God never goes back on His gifts and call.** This conviction was one of the great achievements of the Hebrew prophets. ' The Strength of Israel is not a man, that He should repent ' (1 Sam. xv. 29); ' He also is wise and will not call back His words' (Isa. xxxi. 2). Paul sums it up in the maxim: 'God is faithful' (1 Cor. i. 9, x. 13, 1 Thess. v. 24).

From our standpoint, with a far longer historical retrospect than Paul could have dreamt of, the special importance here assigned to the Jews and their conversion in the forecast of the destiny of mankind appears artificial. It is doubtful whether it is really justified on Paul's own premisses. The fact is that he has argued from the promise to Abraham on two divergent and perhaps inconsistent lines. If the promise means ultimate blessedness for ' Israel,' then *either* the historical nation of Israel may be regarded as the heir of the promise, and Paul is justified in saying that **all Israel will be saved,** *or* its place may be taken by the New Israel, the Body of Christ in which there is neither Jew nor Greek; but in that case there is no ground for assigning any special place in the future to the Jewish nation as such. Paul tries to have it both ways. We can well understand that his emotional interest in his own people, rather than strict logic, has determined his forecast. We should be disposed to say rather that in all the great religions there is a ' promise ' of man's high destiny, and that the faithfulness of God guarantees its ultimate fulfilment.

30–   The theme of xi. 11–29 is now summed up in a passage of
32   rhythmical prose recalling the parallelism of Hebrew verse, which leads up to the conclusion: **God has consigned all men to disobedience, that He may have mercy upon all.** The universal state of **disobedience** has been set forth in i. 18– iii. 20. It has been shown in the present chapter that this state of mankind is within the purpose of God, but in a sense which does not exclude the free choice of the human will. But the final aim of that purpose is a state in which God's **mercy** is as universally effective as sin has been. In other words, it is the will of God that all mankind shall ultimately be saved.

It has been thought incredible that Paul should have committed himself to such an absolute ' universalism.' Accordingly, it has been pointed out that the Greek expression for **all** has a form which need not imply a ' numerical universal '; that is, it means primarily ' mankind as a whole,' rather than ' all individual men,' and, it is urged, would not be inconsistent with individual exceptions. Further, it is alleged that Paul's argument does not justify a completely universal conclusion. He has been arguing in terms of great corporations—Jews, Gentiles, the Christian Church—and not in terms of individuals; and all that his argument warrants is that at ' the End ' the Church will consist of **all Israel** (xi. 26) + **the full number of the Gentiles** (xi. 25). The latter may mean only the full number of those elected to salvation (as in the Burial Service we pray ' that it may please Thee shortly to accomplish the number of Thine Elect '); and Paul has contemplated that some of those now within the Church may lapse from faith (xi. 22). In any case (it is said), Jews and Gentiles who died before ' the End ' are not accounted for. The last point would be met if **life from the dead** (xi. 15) refers to a general resurrection of all men at the final stage. At any rate, after the inclusion of **all Israel** there is yet a further stage, at which some inconceivably great benefit is to be received by the world (xi. 12), so that there is at least the possibility of a further act of grace for any who may not yet be saved.

But if, instead of pressing such points pedantically, we look at the trend of the discussion, we observe (as I have already pointed out) that the arguments by which Paul asserts the final salvation of Israel are equally valid (in fact are valid only) if they are applied to mankind at large. Every religious intuition and aspiration that has entered the mind of man must surely be as much a promise of God as the word that came to Abraham. He gave all men knowledge of Himself in **His everlasting power and divine being** (i. 20), and He gave them His **Law written on their hearts,** and attested by their **conscience** (ii. 14–15). They may have sinned against the light; but Israel, who sinned against the light, is to be saved, because **God never goes back upon His gifts and call** (xi. 29); and if this principle is to be invoked for the salvation of Israel, then it must hold good for all men, since **there is one God, God of the Jews, God of the Gentiles as well** (iii. 30, 29), and **no distinctions are drawn** (iii. 22). Whether or not, therefore, Paul himself drew the ' universalist ' conclusion, it seems that we must draw it from his premises.

But, further, there is evidence in the epistles that Paul expected the spiritual powers now hostile to God and to man's salvation ultimately to be reconciled to Him through Christ. Thus he says in Col. i. 16–20: **It was by Him that all things were created both in heaven and in earth, both the seen and the unseen, including Thrones, angelic Lords, celestial Powers and Rulers ... for it was in Him that**

the divine Fullness willed to settle without limit, and by Him it willed to reconcile in His own person all in earth and heaven alike. And similarly in Eph. i. 10: **It was the purpose of His design so to order it in the fullness of the ages that all things in heaven and earth alike should be gathered up in Christ.** The ' things in heaven ' clearly include the ' Thrones, Dominations, Princedoms, Powers,' those mythological beings who are always in the background of Paul's thought; ' Discarnate Intelligences,' as we might call them in the language of Hardy's *Dynasts*. They not only had a place in Jewish thought of the time, as ' angelic ' orders, but they were recognized in contemporary philosophy, both Platonic and Stoic, and so this mythology might pass in the first century for a statement of religious ideas in terms of ' science.' The Discarnate Intelligences were connected with the heavenly bodies, and thought to be agents of fate controlling human destiny. That is probably why Paul tells the Galatians that if they **observe days and months and festal seasons and years** they are **under the thraldom of the Elemental spirits of the world,** as in their pagan days (Gal. iv. 8–10; cf. Col. ii. 20–23). These **angels and principalities, powers of the Height and of the Depth,** have even now no power to hinder the salvation of Christian men (viii. 38–39); but in the future they will cease to be hostile, being **reconciled** to God in Christ (Col. i. 20). We should probably connect this with the liberation of the material universe from **thraldom** into **glorious liberty** (viii. 21). It all sounds very mythological to us: but what it really expresses is a religious conviction or intuition that, if God is what we believe Him to be, then all the evil in the world must in the end be worked out.

But if Paul believed that such a thoroughgoing redintegration of the universe was the end of the divine purpose, then he cannot but have thought that a complete redintegration of the human race was included in it; and he may be allowed to have meant what he said in its full sense: that God would **have mercy upon all.** If we really believe in One God, and believe that Jesus Christ, in what He was and what He did, truly shows us what God's character and His attitude to men are like, then it is very difficult to think ourselves out of the belief that somehow His love will find a way of bringing all men into unity with Him.

Whatever we may make of Paul's teaching here, with all its

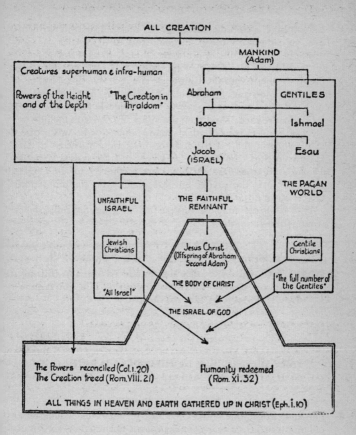

ALL CREATION

MANKIND (Adam)

Creatures superhuman & infra-human

Powers of the Height and of the Depth

"The Creation in Thraldom"

Abraham

GENTILES

Isaac

Ishmael

Jacob (ISRAEL)

Esau

THE PAGAN WORLD

UNFAITHFUL ISRAEL

THE FAITHFUL REMNANT

Jewish Christians

Jesus Christ (Offspring of Abraham Second Adam)

Gentile Christians

"All Israel"

THE BODY OF CHRIST

"The full number of the Gentiles"

THE ISRAEL OF GOD

The Powers reconciled (Col. i. 20)
The Creation freed (Rom. VIII. 21)

Humanity redeemed (Rom. XI. 32)

ALL THINGS IN HEAVEN AND EARTH GATHERED UP IN CHRIST (Eph. i. 10)

mythological and speculative elements, we must confess that it presents a broad and elevated philosophy of history. As in the world of Nature a process of ' natural selection ' is the means by which life advances to higher forms, so in the history of man a divine process of purposive selection has been at work. The process remains selective and exclusive down to the coming of Christ. On the natural, historical side (**as David's offspring by natural descent**) He represents the climax of the divine ' election '—the true **offspring of Abraham,** embodying in His single Person the ultimate Remnant of Israel. On the other side He represents a fresh incursion of the divine creative energy.

And so by His coming, the process is reversed, becoming inclusive instead of exclusive. Those who turn in faith to God through Him are incorporate **in Christ,** in His **Body:** first the handful of Jewish believers, then the Gentile converts who began to stream into the Church. The inclusive process cannot stop before the rest of mankind is gathered in: first the Gentiles, then the Jews, until at the last there will be **life from the dead** for the entire race. And then the vision broadens, to include the physical universe out of which man sprang (for he was created of the dust of the earth), and the mysterious **powers of the Height and of the Depth**—*die unbekannten höhern Wesen, die wir ahnen.* And so at last all things are **gathered up in Christ** (Eph. i. 10): the divine purpose reaches its consummation: God is all in all (1 Cor. xv. 28).

Paul's scheme may be represented diagrammatically somewhat as shown on page 195.

xi. 33–35: THE PRAISE OF DIVINE WISDOM

33 **What a fathomless wealth lies in the wisdom and knowledge of God! How inscrutable His judgment! How mysterious His methods!**

34   *Who ever understood the thoughts of the Lord?*
          Who has ever been His counsellor?

35   *Who has first given to Him and has to be repaid?* **All comes from Him, all lives by Him, all ends in Him. Glory to Him for ever, Amen!**

The vision of the future which has been presented to us is not knowledge, but faith, and faith set against a background of ignorance. *Omnia abeunt in mysterium.* The religious consciousness, after its highest flights of speculation, returns to the simple 'numinous' feeling of awe before the Mystery. 'Verily Thou art a God that hidest Thyself, O God of Israel, the Saviour!' (Isa. xlv. 15). This *Deus absconditus* remains the Object of our worship. But when we can start from the religious experience of redemption by the love of God, which Paul has eloquently expressed in viii. 18–30, the feeling of awe has a joyful and not a gloomy colour. We are assured that the **fathomless wealth** of the **wisdom and knowledge of God** is at the service of everlasting mercy, and we are content that **all comes from Him, all lives by Him, all ends in Him.**

TRINITY XIII *a.m. Chap XII*

EPIPHANY I, II or III
also 2nd Sn Sunday Evg. Purification of BVM 2.1964
verses 1-5

V. THE RIGHTEOUSNESS OF GOD
IN CHRISTIAN LIVING

(xii. 1–xv. 13)

Outstanding theological problems have now been disposed of, and Paul can proceed to the subject to which he was leading up in chaps. v.–viii. The point which he made there was that the righteousness of God is revealed, not only in 'justifying' men, or giving them a status of rightness before God, but in bringing them into a new order of life in the Spirit, from which they derive the power to lead an actually righteous life. It remains to show how a man should behave who is living in this new order. Thus Christian ethics emerges from Christian theology. It defines the way in which **the divine righteousness that rests on faith** re-shapes the conduct of men in society.

Paul is not a systematic moralist any more than he is a systematic theologian. He does not attempt to define the ethical end, or *summum bonum*, and to deduce from this a scheme of virtues. Indeed, any such scheme or genetic classification of virtues, such as Aristotle and the Stoics attempted, would be just as foreign to his conception of morality as the Pharisaic *Halakha*, or Rule of Conduct, derived from a fixed code of commandments accepted as divine and unalterable. He does not think of right conduct either as conformity with a code or as the adding of virtue to virtue in a discipline of self-culture. It is **the harvest of the Spirit**—a spontaneous reaction of the inward spirit of a man, controlled by the Spirit of God, to the successive situations in which he finds himself as he lives with other men in society. All that the Christian moralist can do, therefore, is to indicate in a general way the moral quality which conduct will exhibit in a society guided by the Spirit of Christ, and to give some examples of it. Within these limitations, Paul comes nearer to giving a systematic treatment here than in any other epistle. We may roughly divide the section up as follows: (*i.*) fundamental attitudes—self-devotion, moral insight, self-knowledge, the sense of the Body (xii. 1–9); (*ii.*) love (charity) as the dominant sentiment, creating right relations both within the Christian community and towards outsiders

I beseech you therefore by the mercies of God, because of all God's goodness & mercy that ye present your bodies - a living sacrifice,

and the pagan State (xii. 9–xiii. 10); (*iii.*) the seriousness of
the times (xiii. 11–14); (*iv.*) an example of Christian charity at
work (xiv. i–xv. 6), leading up to (*v.*) a final statement and
prayer (xv. 7–13).[1]

holy acceptable unto God, which is your reasonable service — (To put God first)

XII. 1–2: SELF-DEDICATION AND MORAL INSIGHT

xii.

1 Well then, my brothers, I appeal to you by all the mercy
     of God to dedicate your bodies as a living sacrifice,
     consecrated and acceptable to God; that is your
     cult, a spiritual rite. Instead of being moulded to
2   this world, have your mind renewed, and so be
     transformed in nature, able to make out what the
     will of God is, namely, what is good and acceptable
     to Him and perfect.

1

Christian morality is the response to **all the mercy of God,**
which has been movingly set forth in the preceding chapters.
It does not begin with a man's ambition to make himself a
fine specimen of virtuous humanity, and so, it may be, to win
the approval of God. It begins with the thankful recognition
that God, the source of all goodness, has done for him what
he could never do for himself.

The contemplation of God's mercy has moved Paul, and his
readers, to a sense of awe before the **fathomless wealth** of
the Divine Being. This sense of awe, as we have learnt from
Otto's now famous book, is the root of the religious idea of the
Holy. That idea is not one which reason forms for itself. It
is based on an instinctive awe before a Mystery beyond our
knowing and yet potent to kindle our deepest emotions. In all
theistic religions this awe is felt for God; and persons and
things are 'holy' which belong to Him and share His nature.
For Paul, as for other early Christian teachers, the Christian
man is a 'holy' person—**called to be a saint** (i. 7)—because
he is **called to belong to Jesus Christ** (i. 6) his 'Lord' (**you
belong to Christ, and Christ to God,** 1 Cor. iii. 23); and
because he possesses the 'Holy Spirit,' which is the Spirit of
Christ and of God. The ethical value of this idea of holiness

[1] In the notes on this section I have occasionally made use of paragraphs from
my essay, 'The Ethics of the Pauline Epistles,' in the volume, *The Evolution of Ethics,*
edited by Dr. E. Hershey Sneath. I am grateful to the publishers, Yale University
Press, New Haven, Conn., U.S.A., for kindly granting permission to quote from
this essay.

depends on the moral quality attributed to the Divine Being.
Already by his Jewish training Paul was compelled to think of
God's holiness in ethical terms, and when he contemplated His
mercy as revealed in Christ his sense of God's ethical holiness
was immeasurably deepened. Where this is so, the enormous
weight of instinctive emotion which attaches to the idea of the
Holy is placed at the disposal of the moral ideal. Thus the
Christian is enjoined to lay his **body** (i.e. his individual personality as an acting concrete whole; see note on vi. 6) as a **living
sacrifice** on the altar of God (as elsewhere he is bidden regard
this **body** as **the temple of the Holy Spirit**, 1 Cor. vi. 9;
cf. iii. 16). Observe that the way has been prepared for this
injunction in vi. 13, 19, 22. It means that morality is lifted out
of the sphere of convention or calculated expediency, and associated with all that is loftiest and deepest in the universe of our
experience.

To place the idea of the Holy at the centre of ethics has
certain dangers. It may easily throw the conception of right
and wrong over to the side of the irrational, and set up a system
of superstitious fears and *taboos*. The Pharisaism in which Paul
had been bred did not wholly avoid a taint of the irrational in
its ethical code. It proscribed certain foods, for example,
because of an obscure sense that they were ' unholy,' or ' unclean,' just as it proscribed murder and adultery. Paul was
saved from this chiefly because he identified the ' Spirit of
Holiness ' with the ' Spirit of Christ,' and so had a ready point
of reference in a Figure standing in the clear light of history,
with the concrete solidity of a powerful human personality;
and One whose morality in word and deed was reasonable and
humane, with no taint of *taboo* in His ideal of holiness. We may
fairly say that it is never safe to emphasize the call to holiness
as a part of Christian teaching, unless the idea of the Holy is
understood by constant reference to the Jesus of the Gospels,
His example and teaching.

The offering of the **living sacrifice**, Paul goes on, is **your
cult, a spiritual rite.** The ritual of sacrifice was in Judaism, See
as in all ancient religions, the central act of worship, by which
the holiness of God was acknowledged, and in some sense p. 79
conveyed to the worshippers. For Christians, Paul says, the
real worship of God is their self-dedication to Him for ethical
ends. As the actual liturgy of worship gradually shaped itself
in the Christian Church, with its centre in the commemoration
of the sacrificial death of Christ as described in 1 Cor. xi. 23–26,

it was powerfully influenced by the thought that the Church, as the Body of Christ, is associated, or identified, with Christ Himself in His sacrifice of obedience to God in life and death. This thought finds expression in the post-communion prayer of the Anglican rite: ' Here we offer and present unto Thee, O Lord, ourselves, our souls and bodies, to be a reasonable holy, and lively sacrifice unto Thee.' Without that thought, taken with full ethical seriousness, any ritual of sacrifice in Christianity would be a relapse into superstition.

2   With this pre-supposition, that the whole moral life of a Christian man is a self-dedication to God, we proceed to the consequences of such teaching as that of vi. 1–14, that the Christian has entered into a new order of life. Because that is so, he must, **instead of being moulded to this world, have** his **mind** (or ' reason,' as in i. 28, vii. 23–25) **renewed, and so be transformed in nature, able to make out what the will of God is.** This is one way in which the liberty of the Christian man is realized. He is not the slave of the conventional judgments of society (being **ransomed from the futile traditions of the past,** 1 Pet. i. 19), but has a fresh and independent insight into moral realities. Where morality is conceived as obedience to a code, the first of virtues is docility and a sub-missive spirit. What Paul expects of the ' slave of Christ,' whose service is perfect freedom, is independent moral insight. He expects to find such insight in simple and ordinary lay folk. He knew the risks of this demand, but he was sure that to make the demand was the way to that fullness of character which is the Christian ideal (cf. 1 Thess. iv. 9, v. 21; 1 Cor. x. 15; Rom. xiv. 5). The **children** and **heirs of God** (viii. 17) should recognize for themselves **the will of God.**

By **the will of God** he means **what is good and acceptable and perfect.** The first of these terms is the most general expression for what is of absolute worth in and for itself, and as such is common to all philosophies. The second term, not previously used, it would appear, as a technical term of ethics, is a word which has in ordinary usage the sense ' satisfactory.' The limiting words ' **to him,**' which appear in Moffatt's trans-lation, are not present in the original, and they probably do not represent Paul's intention; for he is giving a definition of what he means by **the will of God,** and to say that it is that which is **acceptable to Him** would be mere tautology. He means that God wills the kind of action which in itself gives satisfaction to all concerned. Thus the word comes near in meaning to the untranslatable Greek ethical term *to kalon* (translated, in vii. 21, **what is right**). It is properly a term of aesthetics, meaning ' the beautiful,' but as used by Aristotle and other Greek moralists it connotes that quality of fineness or nobility in moral action which moves us to an aesthetic admiration as well as to rational approval. The third term, **perfect,** belongs to the ethical vocabulary of the Old Testament, and also to that of the Stoics. The ' perfect ' man is defined by them as the man whose character is complete on all sides, possessing all the separate virtues as elements of a fully developed personality. We may recall that our psychologists regard the impulse towards completeness as ' the most compelling motive of life,' [1] and often find in it the basis of ' natural ' ethics. Thus the will of God for man is not some mysterious and irrational form of holiness (such as leads to superstitious distinctions of days and food and the like; see chap. xiv.). It consists of that kind of life which the **renewed mind** of the Christian man can see to be good in itself, satisfying, and complete.

xii. 3-8: THE SOCIAL ORGANISM

In virtue of my office, I tell every one of your number 3 who is self-important,* that he is not to think more of himself than he ought to think; he must take a sane view of himself, corresponding to the degree of faith which God has assigned to each. In our one body we have a number of members, and the 4 members have not all the same function; so too, for all our numbers, we form one Body in Christ 5 and we are severally members one of another. Our talents differ with the grace that is given us; if the 6 talent is that of prophecy, let us employ it in proportion to our faith; if it is practical service, let us 7 mind our service; the teacher must mind his teaching, the speaker his words of counsel; the contri- 8 butor must be liberal, the superintendent must be in earnest, the sick visitor must be cheerful.

If a man is to see straight in ethical matters, he must not be 3

---

[1] Hadfield, *Psychology and Morals*, chap. viii.
* I accept the ingenious conjecture that τι has fallen out after ὄντι.

hindered by any 'self-fantasy' (to use the psychological term).
A fantastical estimate of one's own worth, powers, or importance
is one of the most radical, and certainly one of the commonest,
causes of obliquity of moral vision. It is those who take themselves most seriously, and fix their ideal highest, who are most
exposed to this danger. We can therefore understand why Paul
gives so prominent a place to self-knowledge. To **take a sane
view of oneself** is the beginning of wisdom. In this, Paul is
in the line of the wisest Greeks. Only, with him, the religious
background gives a deeper meaning to the precept 'Know
thyself,' while it also points the way to put it into practice.

4-
5   For a just estimate of oneself it is necessary that one should
escape from the individualist outlook, and think of oneself as
part of a social whole. Thus the demand for self-knowledge
leads directly to an exposition of Paul's doctrine of the Christian
society as a Body or concrete organic whole. For a full account
of this doctrine we must look to 1 Cor. xii. It is there clearly
based upon the idea of the mystical unity of Christians with
Christ, which makes them, as a society, **Christ's Body, and
severally members of it** (1 Cor. xii. 27). It seems probable
that Paul was the first Greek writer to use the term 'body' in
the sense of a 'body corporate,' as we say. As we have seen
(note on vi. 6) he uses the term 'body' in a highly philosophical
way, meaning by it, not anything material, but the organization
of personality as an acting concrete individual. It was the
easier for him to give to it the extended meaning of a social
organism. But it is probable that he was led to do so under the
influence of the sacramental idea. In the Lord's Supper the
bread was designated, in the words of Christ Himself, His
'Body.' For Paul, this meant, not the 'substance' of His
natural body—which was **flesh** (Col. i. 22)—but the organic
instrument of His Personality. But in a similar sense the Church
itself could be thought of as His 'Body.' Thus in a double sense
the sacrament is **participating in the Body of Christ** (1 Cor.
x. 16; see notes on pp. 79-80, 87-88). It seems that it was
along this line that Paul developed his doctrine of the Church
as a Body.[1]

The idea is here presented without its mystical or sacramental background, simply as a doctrine of the 'social organism.' As such, it would be not unfamiliar to any Roman
readers who had a smattering of popular Stoic teaching. 'What

---

[1] See A.E.J. Rawlinson's essay, 'Corpus Christi,' in *Mysterium Christi*, edited by
Bell and Deissmann.

is the profession of a citzen?' said Epictetus (*Diss.* II. x. 4–5).
'To have no private interest of his own, and to view nothing
as a detached individual; just as the hand or the foot, if it had
reason and followed its natural bent, would have no impulse or
desire except as tending to the whole. . . . The whole is more
important than the part; the city than the citizen.' And few
Romans would not have heard the famous fable of the Belly
and the Members, by which Menenius Agrippa was said to
have put an end to a 'general strike' of the lower orders in the
early days of Rome (Livy II. 32).

The particular application which Paul makes of the idea of 6
the social organism is to suggest that all individual abilities and
faculties are endowments for functions within the body, and
must be used as such with a true sense of responsibility. In the
corresponding passage of 1 Corinthians he makes a list of
ministries in the Church to which this principle specially applies:
**apostles, prophets, teachers, workers of miracles,
healers, helpers, administrators, and speakers in 'tongues' of various kinds.** Here the list is even wider, and shows
clearly that Paul made no such hard and fast distinction between clerical and lay ministries as later emerged in the Church.
His point is that whatever special **talent** a member of the
Church may possess is a gift of the **grace** of God (or, as he says
in 1 Corinthians, 'of the Holy Spirit'), and gives no claim to
dignity or pre-eminence in the community, but marks out that
individual for a particular line of service, to which he must
devote himself.

xii. 9–21: LOVE AS THE PRINCIPLE
OF SOCIAL ETHICS

**Let your love be a real thing, with a loathing for evil and 9
a bent for what is good. Put affection into your 10
love for the brotherhood; be forward to honour one 11
another; never let your zeal flag; maintain the 12
spiritual glow; serve the Lord; let your hope be a 13
joy to you; be stedfast in trouble, attend to prayer,
contribute to needy saints, make a practice of hos- 14
pitality. Bless those who make a practice of persecuting you; bless them instead of cursing them.
Rejoice with those who rejoice, and weep with those 15
who weep. Keep in harmony with one another; 16**

17 **instead of being ambitious, associate with humble folk;** *never be self-conceited.* **Never pay back evil for evil**
18 **to anyone;** *aim to be above reproach in the eyes of all;* **be at peace with all men, if possible, so far as that depends**
19 **on you. Never revenge yourselves, beloved, but let the Wrath of God have its way: for it is written,** *Vengeance is Mine, I will exact a requital*—**the Lord has said it. No,**

20 *if your enemy is hungry, feed him,*
if he is thirsty, give him drink;
for in this way you will make him
feel a burning sense of shame.

21 **Do not let evil get the better of you; get the better of evil by doing good.**

In the passage of 1 Corinthians to which we must keep referring, the recital of typical gifts of the Spirit leads up to the conclusion that the greatest of them all is love, or charity, which is the constructive principle in society (**love builds up,** 1 Cor. viii. 1), and the bond which makes it complete (Col. iii. 14—for the social reference is evident, though it is not brought out by Moffatt's translation). Here the underlying train of thought must be the same, though the link is not expressed. We thus come to the central principle of Paul's social ethics. The word which we must, however inadequately, translate **love** is in Greek, *agapé*. It scarcely exists in pre-biblical Greek, and its specific meaning must be gathered from the Christian literature which first gave it real currency.

For Paul, *agapé* is primarily the distinctive activity of the divine Nature—the redemptive goodness of God exhibited towards the undeserving (Rom. v. 8). It is not strictly definable, nor indeed can it be fully comprehended in intellectual concepts; yet it can be known in religious experience (Eph. iii. 19). Moreover, that religious experience in which we know the love of God also implants love in our nature as an indwelling energy (Rom. v. 5). Thus love is the supreme and all-inclusive gift of the Spirit (1 Cor. xii. 31–xiii. 1). Conformably with the teaching of the Gospels, the objects of such love are God (Rom. viii. 28) and our neighbour (xiii. 8–9); but it is upon the latter that the emphasis falls, other terms being used by preference for our attitude to God (again, as in the Gospels). In 1 Cor. xiii., *agapé* is described in a series of aphorisms. It is the source of the patience and gentleness which are characteristic Christian

virtues (cf. 2 Cor. x. 1). It excludes jealousy, being thereby
sharply distinguished from some other forms of ' love.' Where
it is present, any form of egotism is excluded, whether a fantastic
estimate of oneself such as would lead to lack of respect for one's
fellows, or any kind of self-seeking such as might lead to the
anti-social vices enumerated in Rom. i. 29–31. It saves a man
from those irrational outbreaks of resentment which are (as
modern psychology can assure us) chiefly the result of an
affronted ' self-fantasy.' It breeds a generous oblivion of the
wrongs one suffers. Not only so, but it fixes the attention upon
the highest values of personality—truth and right—and produces a sense of joy in their presence which excludes any mean
satisfaction in the moral defects of others. In the presence of
the imperfections of humanity it preserves a tolerance of injury,
a belief in human nature, and an indefeasible hope of its perfection even in the fallible folk one knows. The passage which
I have thus paraphrased evidently does not attempt to give a
logically exact or exhaustive description of *agapé*. It is poetical
rather than scientific. This fact enables us to add that *agapé*
is suffused with emotion. Yet it is not simple emotion. It is,
in the language of recent psychology, a ' sentiment,' within
which various instinctive impulses and emotions are organized
and sublimated.

From this point of view it may be defined as the sentiment
for humanity as identified with its ideal values, right and
truth. We use the term ' love ' in that sense, but it is also used
in such a variety of shades of meaning that it is hardly in itself
a sufficient translation. The Latin translators felt the difficulty,
and, instead of using *amor*, adopted the less common word
caritas, which signified esteem rather than affection. The
earliest English translators attempted to naturalize this word
in the form ' charity,' but that word has become so narrowed
and even debased in usage that it no longer serves. We can
hardly do better than render *agapé* by love. In doing so, however, we must beware of a certain ' sloppy ' sentimentalism which
often haunts the word in modern religious speech. Anything
of the kind is remote from Paul's robust and even austere conception of the Christian ideal, as it is remote from the Example
upon which he modelled that conception.

The treatment of *agapé* here is more concrete and more 9
prosaic than in 1 Cor. xiii. First we have the general maxim
that love must be absolutely sincere, and that it must be marked

by **a loathing for evil and a bent for what is good.** Then the implications of such love are drawn out, first within the Christian society and then in relations between Christians and outsiders.   The division is not made quite clear, but verses 9–13, 15–16 belong to the former section, and verses 14, 17–21 to the latter.

LOVE – AGAPE

I   10   Within the Christian community, *agapé* takes the special form of *philadelphia*, or **love for the brotherhood.**   This is to be accompanied by warm feelings of **affection.**   The ' tender emotion ' of the psychologists, primarily associated with the parental instinct, is thus taken up into the exalted sentiment

15 for humanity.   There is naturally a ready sympathy with
16 joy and grief in others, and a strong impulse towards unanimity of thought and feeling.   The instinctive craving for superiority is, within the dominant sentiment, so redirected that, instead
10 of desiring superiority for himself, a man desires his associates to excel (as a parent finds fullest satisfaction in the success of
16 a child).   Personal vanity is excluded by a high estimate of the worth of others, and a readiness to undertake the humblest service (or perhaps to **associate with humble folk,** as Moffatt
13 has it).   Within a family of brothers there will be a full sharing of needs and resources, by way of hospitality and otherwise.
11–   With all this will go a particular emotional tone—one of joy,
12 fervour, hopefulness, and zeal.   Such are the marks of conduct which is not dictated by mere obedience to precept, but produced by the re-direction of instinctive energy within a dominant sentiment.

II   17   In relations with the outside world, the Christian will show respect for the moral standards of his non-Christian neighbours. The danger of a revolutionary movement in ethics, such as early Christianity was, is that in claiming independence of convention in the interests of a higher morality, unstable characters are liable to lose the support which comes from public opinion, and to abuse their independence in the direction of a morality lower than the conventional.   That this sometimes happened in the Pauline communities is clear from 1 Cor. v. 1–2.   Such a danger would be obviated if Paul's precept (borrowed from the Greek translation of Prov. iii. 4, with a significant alteration) were followed: **aim to be above reproach in the eyes of all.** The assumption is that there is a certain moral standard common to Christians and pagans—doubtless the **law written on**

[handwritten at top]: Eph. 2 13/15 But now in Christ Jesus, ye that once were far off are made nigh in the blood of Christ. For he is our peace

CHAPTER XII, VERSES 9–21 *[handwritten]:* Why made both and brake down the middle wall of partition

their hearts, which good pagans **obey instinctively**—and love requires the Christian to make the most of this as a basis for harmonious relations.

One of the primary social manifestations of *agapé* is peace. 18 Peace among men was for Paul one of the most desirable of all things: Christ had died to make it possible (Eph. ii. 14–18). Accordingly, the Christian must always strive for peaceful relations with his pagan neighbours. If collisions occur, as they almost inevitably will, the provocation must not come from the Christian side: **be at peace with all men if possible, so far as that depends on you.** The limits of possibility contemplated are, of course, the higher demands of the Christian conscience. The difficulty of keeping such a precept under the conditions of the first century is evident. Similar injunctions are given with even greater emphasis in the First Epistle of Peter, written after severe persecution had broken out. The leaders of the Church all through the period of persecution loyally stood by Paul's principle, though there are indications that their advice was not invariably followed.

Further, *agapé* demands that one shall not only refrain from offending or shocking one's pagan neighbours, but also endeavour positively to do them service. This is implied rather than stated here. It is made quite explicit in Gal. vi. 10 and I Thess. v. 15. The special difficulty in the application of this rule arises when the neighbour in question is an enemy. If 17 one suffers injury, what is to be done? First, there are to be no reprisals. The specious plea that, if injuries are overlooked, the moral order will suffer (in recent years a standard apology for war) is met by the counsel, **Let the Wrath have its way.** 19 What the Wrath is, we have sufficiently learned from chap. i. It is the principle of retribution inherent in a moral universe. God, who 'brings the Wrath upon men' (iii. 5) **will exact a requital,** without our interference. In other words, the moral order will look after itself, without the crude attempt of the individual to uphold it by 'getting even with' people who have done him wrong.

But mere abstention from revenge is not yet fully Christian. Quoting his Master, Paul says: **'Bless those who make a** 14 **practice of persecuting you.'** To bless is to wish well, and to turn the wish into a prayer. If the wish and the prayer be sincere, they will lead to beneficent action as opportunity offers; and so, **if your enemy is hungry, feed him; if he is** 20 **thirsty, give him drink; for in this way you will make**

[handwritten at bottom]: ...having abolished in his flesh the enmity, even the ... of commandments contained in ordinances ... he might create in himself of the twain one new man, so making peace—

him feel a burning sense of shame. Paul is quoting Prov. xxv. 21–22. Whether this translation represents what the original writer of Proverbs meant, is not certain; but it no doubt gives the meaning which Paul attached to the curious phrase ' will heap coals of fire on his head.' The principle involved is the law that evil can never be overcome by evil, but only by a greater good; in our common saying, ' two wrongs do not make a right.'

This is the most important thing that Paul has to say about love, or charity, in its wider application. *Agapé* is, as we have seen, in its essence that property of the divine Nature by which God is good to the undeserving, supremely expressed in that **Christ died for the ungodly.** Where the divine love **floods the heart,** there evil will be met with an unwearying beneficence which, in the end, will wear out the evil. That such will be the ultimate result is an optimistic belief which goes with the faith (set forth in chap. xi.) that the mercy of God will finally include all men; and it can be effectively held, probably, only if human nature be believed to be fundamentally good, and evil an abnormality. This Paul held, in spite of ' original sin.' The injunction, ' **Do not let evil get the better of you; get the better of evil by doing good,'** is an admirable summary of the teaching of the Sermon on the Mount about what is called ' non-resistance,' and it expresses the most creative element in Christian ethics.

xiii. 1–7: CHRISTIANITY AND THE STATE

Paul now approaches a question which was of the greatest practical importance for the early Church: what was to be the attitude of Christians to the Roman Empire, under whose rule they lived? Many Jewish Christians brought over with them a traditional resentment of the Roman rule. Jewish national feeling was running high at this time, when things were brewing up to the crisis of A.D. 66. Within the Church there was pretty certainly an anti-Roman strain of feeling. The lengths to which it could go may be judged from the virulent hatred of Rome that runs through the Revelation of John. That book was composed during a period when persecution of Christianity was a part of imperial policy, as it was not yet in Paul's time; but it is unlikely that its general attitude to the imperial power was an altogether new thing in the Church. In contemporary

Jewish apocalypses Rome already played the part of Villain in
the cosmic drama, which used to be assigned to Babylon, and
the Christian apocalypse carries on this tradition within Christianity. We can hardly doubt that the possibility existed that
the Church might be committed by Jewish-Christian extremists
to a disastrous policy of opposition to the Government. To
Christians in the capital the question was obviously one of
especial urgency. After the fire of A.D. 64 (some five years after
the time of this letter), the Roman Government fixed upon the
Christians of the city as suitable scapegoats. It is likely enough
that they acted upon an impression that these sectaries held
anarchical opinions; and we cannot deny the possibility that
some Christians had given excuse for such an impression.
However this may be, we can see how important Paul felt it to
be that he should give a perfectly clear lead to the Roman church
on this momentous question. For himself he had long ago
made up his mind. While Christians in the Jewish apocalyptic
tradition, of which ' John ' afterwards became the exponent,
identified Rome with Anti-Christ, Paul saw in the Empire the
providential instrument by which the coming of Anti-Christ
was delayed—**that which restrains him from being revealed before his appointed time** (2 Thess. ii. 6). That was
some seven or eight years ago. By this time he had developed,
as we shall see, a clear and definite doctrine of the positive value
of the Empire in the world. His position was accepted by the
Church at large. Even when Christianity had been outlawed,
the duty of loyalty to the Empire was put just as strongly in the
First Epistle of Peter (ii. 13–17). It remained the steady principle of the Church all through, although the measure of ' non-
co-operation ' which was made inevitable by the intimate
association of Caesar-worship with all acts of State gave the
appearance of an imperfect loyalty.

xiii.

Every subject must obey the government-authorities, 1
**for no authority exists apart from God; the existing
authorities have been constituted by God. Hence
anyone who resists authority is opposing the divine** 2
**order, and the opposition will bring judgment on
themselves. Magistrates are no terror to an honest** 3
**man,* though they are to a bad man. If you want
to avoid being alarmed at the government-authorities, lead an honest life and you will be commended
for it; the magistrate is God's servant for your**

4   **benefit. But if you do wrong, you may well be alarmed; a magistrate does not wield the power of the sword for nothing, he is God's servant for the infliction of divine vengeance upon evil-doers. You**
5   **must be obedient, therefore, not only to avoid the divine vengeance but as a matter of conscience, for**
6   **the same reason as you pay taxes—since magistrates are God's officers, bent upon the maintenance of order and authority. Pay them all their respective**
7   **dues, tribute to one, taxes to another, respect to this man, honour to that.**

1   For the view that secular governments are of divine institution, Paul could cite Old Testament authority (see Dan. iv. 28), and it was orthodox doctrine in Judaism. But it is noteworthy that, whenever the principle is invoked in Jewish literature, it is nearly always by way of menace to those who use their authority badly; as for example in the Wisdom of Solomon (vi. 1–11). Rarely if ever is it used as it is here, as the basis for a positive valuation of secular government as such. The inference which Paul draws from it is equally remarkable:

2   **Hence anyone who resists authority is opposing the divine order, and the opposition will bring judgment on themselves.** That is to be read, in the first instance, as a definite repudiation, on behalf of the Church, of the Zealot tendency in Judaism which was already gathering strength for the final outbreak, and might well have repercussions among Christians. Paul makes his statement quite absolute. Yet he was clearly prepared to disobey in the case of a conflict of loyalties. But he is thinking of contumacious defiance of the Empire such as was advocated by Jewish fanatics. Upon those who rebel, the legal penalty for rebellion will fall; and this, he seems to imply, is in fact the divine judgment on their action. (Paul does not consider the case of a *successful* rebel; a Roman citizen knew no successful rebels.) It is tempting to see here a reference to the saying attributed to Jesus in Matt. xxvi. 52, especially in a context where there are several reminiscences of the teaching of Jesus. Although this saying is not known to the earlier Gospel sources, it is not impossible that Paul was acquainted with it.

* Reading ἀγαθοεργῷ, Patrick Young's attractive conjecture (confirmed by the Ethiopic version). As Hort points out ' the apparent antithesis to τῷ κακῷ could hardly fail to introduce τῷ ἀγαθῷ.'

There follows a definite statement of the purpose and value 4 of civil government. It is there to support the cause of right, and to enforce just retribution on wrongdoing. Moffatt's paraphrase disguises the fact that the key-word of the passage is the now familiar term ' the Wrath,' which means the principle of retribution inherent in a moral universe. We might render it: ' You wish to be free from fear of the Government?—then continue in good behaviour and you will get credit from the Government; for it is then for you a divine agent to good ends. But, if you are behaving ill, then you have cause to fear the Government; for then it is a divine punitive agent, working for retribution upon the evil-doer.' We then get Paul's theory of civil government in its true setting. It is a part of the natural moral order, of divine appointment, but lying outside the order of grace revealed in Christ. It exhibits the principle of retribution just as it is exhibited in the natural laws of cause and effect to which the body and mind of man are subject; in accordance with which, for example, **to hinder the truth by wickedness** results in a ' reprobate reason ' (i. 18–32). The social degradation which results from sin is the most radical manifestation of ' the Wrath,' but the retributive system of justice in a non-Christian society is also a manifestation of the same principle. The Christian order of society rests on a different and higher principle, which was expounded in chap. xii., and is succinctly stated in xiii. 8–10.

The Christian takes no part in the administration of a retri- 5 butive system; but, in so far as it serves moral ends, he must submit to it. He himself lives by a higher principle, and he obeys the Government, not because he fears the retribution which follows on disobedience, but because his conscience bids him do so. The same motive justifies him in paying taxes to a 6 pagan Government (a sore point with Jews, and doubtless with some Jewish Christians). He pays them, not because he will be punished for non-payment, but because they help to maintain the moral order in a world which as yet does not know the order of grace. And here we cannot but suspect a reference to the saying of Jesus, **Give Caesar what belongs to Caesar** (Mark xii. 17). Paul paraphrases it, and enlarges upon it: **Pay them all their respective dues, tribute to one, taxes to another, 7 respect to this man, honour to that.** From the way in which he introduces the matter of tax-paying we should judge that, in virtue of the saying of Jesus, Christians in general assumed that it was their duty to pay up. He wishes to show how this duty is related to the question of civil obedience in general, and to put it upon a theoretical basis.

xiii. 8–10: LOVE AND DUTY

8
Be in debt to no man—apart from the debt of love one to another. He who loves his fellow-man has fulfilled the law. *You must not commit adultery, you must not*
9
kill, you must not steal, you must not covet—**these and any other command are summed up in a single word,** *You must love your neighbour as yourself.* **Love never wrongs**
10
a neighbour; that is why love is the fulfilment of the law.

In the discussion of civil obedience we have come upon the concept of ' duty ' (**due,** or **debt;** the words are etymologically identical). The comparative unimportance of this concept in Paul's ethics is rather striking. In many systems it is the regulative idea. Recent psychology takes the view that the sense of duty arises within a ' sentiment,' as the result of the particular direction given to instinctive impulses when they are organized about some particular ideal. This view is confirmed by the observation that the perverted counterpart of the ' sentiment,' the ' complex,' gives rise to a sense of obligation or compulsion to act in certain ways, which is psychologically indistinguishable from what moralists call the sense of duty. Now Paul finds the principle of all moral action in the ' sentiment '

8 of *agapé*, the sentiment for humanity as identified with its ideal values. It follows that *agapé* creates a comprehensive duty, or **debt,** towards all men (cf. i. 14). This debt is always outstanding. ' The debt of charity,' says Origen,[1] ' is permanent, and we are never quit of it; for we must pay it daily and yet always owe it.'

Paul has expressed himself a little obscurely in the compressed and epigrammatic sentence, **Be in debt to no man—apart from the debt of love one to another.** It might seem that he subsumes love under the more inclusive category of duty: it is a duty to pay taxes and so forth; it is a still higher duty to love your neighbour. But this cannot be his real meaning, which we might rather express as follows: Love for one's

---
[1] Quoted by Sanday and Headlam on this passage (my translation).

kind creates a sense of duty towards other men over a wide
range of relations. Many of these relations are defined by the
laws and customs of society, and the duty imposed by love can
in such cases be fulfilled by simple good citizenship—by the
payment of rates and taxes, by respect for persons in authority,
by strict observance of the law. In all these relations the
Christian should stand in debt to no man; i.e. he should dis-
charge all his obligations. But, when he has done so, he is not
discharged from the wider obligations, not imposed by law and
custom, which love for his fellows imposes on him. These can
never be defined or limited by any code of behaviour; they arise
out of the varying situations in which one is involved with other
people, and are felt as duties in so far as love for men is a dominant sentiment.

Paul illustrates his point by referring to the current summary 9
of the Mosaic Law in the maxim, **You must love your neighbour as yourself.** It is probable that the idea of thus sum-
marizing the Law was already familiar in the rabbinic schools [1]
before Jesus accepted from a rabbi the suggestion that the
whole Law could be stated in terms of love to God and to
neighbour (Luke x. 26–28; in Mark the suggestion comes from
Jesus and is welcomed by the rabbi). It is at this point that
Christianity is most organically related to the best rabbinic
Judaism. We might say that the advance made by Christianity
lay in deepening the meaning of all three terms, ' God,' ' neighbour,' and ' love,' and in this respect Paul's teaching is true to
that of his Master. In his demonstration, however, of the
validity of the summary, his thought moves pretty much on
rabbinic lines. To love your neighbour means to do him no 10
wrong (as Hillel formulated it, ' What to thyself is hateful, to
thy fellow thou shalt not do '); and hence all the ' Thou-shalt
nots ' of the Law are covered by the precept ' Love thy neighbour
as thyself.' **That is why love is the fulfilment** (or, rather,
the full content, the sum total) **of the law.** It is to the Law as
thus conceived that Paul could apply the epithets **holy, just,**
and **good** (vii. 12).

The precept ' Love thy neighbour as thyself ' has great value
as a test of the quality of moral action, especially when it is
interpreted by the ' Golden Rule,' either in its negative form as
stated by Hillel, or, still more, in the positive form given to it
by Jesus. But in moral philosophy it raises the difficulty that

[1] See Abrahams, *Studies in Pharisaism and the Gospels*, First Series, pp. 18–29.

a love which is commanded, a love which is a ' duty,' is not love in any ordinary acceptance of the term. As we have seen, Paul does not construct his scheme of Christian ethics by deduction from this command. He begins with the grace of God, which implants in men who accept it a new life of the Spirit, renewing the mind, transforming the nature, and bringing about a dedication of the whole personality to the will of God, which is sovereign love (xii. 1-2). Men in whom this new life is active are knit into a unity as close as that of an organism. From that unity, love as a sentiment for humanity is generated, and within that sentiment all duties arise (xii. 3 sqq.), including even the duties of civil obedience. This is true to the spirit of the teaching of Jesus. He accepts the precept of love from the best Jewish teachers of His time, and extends the concept of ' neighbour ' to include the foreigner (Luke x. 30-37) and the enemy (Luke vi. 27-36; Matt. v. 43-48). But the precept is not His starting-point. His ethical teaching begins with ' The Kingdom of God has come upon you.' Men are to receive the Kingdom of God like a child. They then become a family of God, doing the will of their Father (Mark iii. 33-35). Out of that life in the family of God, spring all right relations and right activities among men. They become merciful as their Father is merciful (Luke vi. 36).

The manner of the teaching of Jesus is suggestive, allusive, and imaginative; Paul has more of the manner of the pedagogue; but his approach to morals is essentially that of his Master. We have noticed reminiscences of the sayings of Jesus in the whole section, xii. 9-xiii. 10, and it is evident that Paul had not only yielded to the inspiration of Jesus, but had given careful study to the tradition of His teaching, and based his own ethics on a profound understanding of it. For an example of a different method we may compare the outline of Christian ethics in the *Didache*, or *Teaching of the Twelve Apostles*, which cites the actual words of Jesus much more extensively. Paul, though he does not tie himself to the letter of the tradition, but uses the freedom of the Spirit, comes out of the comparison as essentially better informed, more understanding, and altogether a safer guide to the mind of Christ, than those who made of His teaching ' a law of commandments contained in ordinances.'

xiii. 11–14: THE ETHICS OF CRISIS

And then you know what this Crisis means, you know 11
it is high time to waken up; for Salvation is nearer
to us now than when we first believed. It is far on 12
in the night, the day is almost here; so let us drop
the deeds of darkness and put on the armour of the 13
light; let us live decorously as in the open light of
day—no revelry or bouts of drinking, no debauchery
or sensuality, no quarrelling or jealousy. No, put
on the character of the Lord Jesus Christ, and never 14
think how to gratify the cravings of the flesh.

We have now a short section in which Paul appeals to the
sense of **Crisis** as a motive to ethical seriousness. The early
Church lived in an atmosphere of crisis: a New Age was dawn-
ing; the Present Age was passing away; any day might turn
out to be ' the Day of the Lord.' Paul's earliest extant epistles,
those to the Thessalonians, suggest that at that time he thought
that the Advent of the Lord might come within a few months:
it would certainly come within the lifetime of most present
members of the Church. The same thought is present in 1 Corinthians, and it affects his judgment on ethical problems (see
chap. vii.). It is all the more striking that in this epistle there
is no mention of the imminence of the Advent, apart from these
few verses. The whole argument stands independently of any
such expectation. The forecast of history in chap. xi. is hardly
framed for a period of a few months or years. There is no
suggestion of ' interim ethics ' in xii. 1–xiii. 10. The positive
value assigned to political institutions in xiii. 1–6 stands in
contrast to the depreciation of family life in view of the shortness
of the time in 1 Cor. vii. Clearly the urgent sense of the imminence of ' the End ' was fading in Paul's mind as the years
passed. He dwelt more and more on the thought that Christians
were already living in the New Age, and the date at which it
should be consummated became a matter of indifference. Only
in the present passage the old idea of the nearness of the Day
of the Lord survives to give point to his moral exhortations.

The thought of the coming Day suggests the dark night of
waiting. He had written to the Thessalonians (1 Thess. v. 4–8):
Brothers, you are not in the darkness, for the Day to

surprise you like thieves; you are all sons of the Light and sons of the Day. We do not belong to the night or the darkness. Well then, we must not sleep like the rest of men, but be wakeful and sober; for sleepers sleep by night and drunkards are drunk by night, but we must be sober, we who belong to the Day, clad in faith and love as our coat of mail, with the hope of salvation as our helmet. No doubt this was a favourite theme in his preaching, and it recurs here, with the warning, It is far on in the night, the day is almost here. But the eschatology has become little more than an imaginative expression for the urgency which belongs to all moral effort when it is thought of in relation to the eternal issues of life. The Christian is perpetually faced by a crisis, with the Other World pressing disturbingly into this one. His awareness of that crisis leaves him no interest in the sensual life of unawakened humanity. He must live as becomes one who belongs to the Ultimate Order.

14   The way to do this is to ' put on the Lord Jesus Christ.' That remarkable phrase, no doubt, means in effect, as Moffatt gives it, put on the character of the Lord Jesus Christ. But we must not suppose that it means no more than to follow the example of Jesus as an external standard. In Gal. iii. 27 we have the same words in a different connection: ' All of you who were baptized into Christ have put on Christ.' The reference there is clearly to incorporation into the mystical Body of Christ. Here, where we have not a statement but an exhortation, Paul is urging his readers to live out all that is implied in being a ' member ' of Christ (cf. xii. 5). If we recall that to belong to Christ is to have His Spirit (viii. 9), and that the Spirit gives freedom from the ' flesh,' and newness of life (viii. 4–9), we bring the exhortation, Put on the Lord Jesus Christ and never think how to gratify the cravings of the flesh, into its proper and illuminating context. The life which is appropriate to the New Day is the life of Him who is its Lord, and this life He imparts to those who are ' in Him.'

We may recall how Augustine tells of the impression made upon him by these verses. He was walking in the garden, brooding in despair over his futile struggles to live a good life. ' I kept ejaculating miserably: " How long? How long? To-morrow and to-morrow—why not now? Why not at this hour an end to my depravity? " So I spoke, and wept in bitter contrition of heart; when suddenly I heard a voice from next

door, as of a boy or girl singing over and over, " Take and read;
take and read." I hurried back to where Alypius was sitting,
for there I had left a volume of the Apostle when I got up. I
snatched it up, opened it, and read in silence the first passage
my eyes lit upon: **No revelry or bouts of drinking, no
debauchery or sensuality, no quarrelling or jealousy.
No, put on the Lord Jesus Christ and never think how to
gratify the cravings of the flesh.** I neither wished nor
needed to read further. With the end of that sentence, as
though the light of assurance had poured into my heart, all the
shades of doubt were scattered. I put my finger in the page and
closed the book; I turned to Alypius with a calm countenance,
and told him.' (*Confessions*, VIII. 12, abridged my translation.)

Trinity XIV

xiv. 1–xv. 6: AN EXAMPLE OF
CHRISTIAN CASUISTRY

We have now had a brief but comprehensive survey of
Christian morals in general. But morality in the actual is a
matter of particular applications, and it is here that practical
problems arise. Christian conduct is to be based on individual
insight into **what is good and acceptable and perfect.** On
the other hand it must be guided by the principle of love by
which alone a Christian society can be built and maintained.
Where the society contains individuals at different levels of
moral insight, the clear line of Christian conduct is not easily
determined. ' Act according to your conscience.' Yes; but if
my conscience approves what yours condemns, how are we to
live together in a community governed by love, and obey the
precept, **Keep in harmony with one another**? Paul had
had occasion to discuss at length one such problem in writing
to Corinth, where it was a burning question whether or not
Christians were permitted to eat ' food offered to idols.' His
full discussion in 1 Cor. viii.–x. should be kept in mind in
reading this chapter. The lines which he there laid down he
follows here, in relation to differences of opinion upon vegetarianism and the keeping of holy days. Whether these were
actually burning questions at Rome we do not know. It is
likely enough. At any rate, these were the kind of questions
that were bound to crop up. Similar difficulties, we know,
arose at Colossae (see Col. ii. 16–23). The keeping of the
Sabbath was one of the most obvious marks of the Jew, and

Jewish Christians would wish to maintain the practice. Gentile Christians, on the other hand, would have no wish to adopt a custom both inconvenient and ridiculous in the eyes of Graeco-Roman society. Vegetarianism, again, was a fashionable religious fad. Among pagans, the Orphic and Pythagorean sects practised it. Among the Jews, the Essenes seem to have had an inclination towards it. There was at least one influential Christian who was a practising vegetarian, James the brother of Jesus, bishop of the church of Jerusalem. Abstention from meat may have commended itself to some Christians, because of the extreme difficulty of being sure that meat bought in the market had not undergone some pagan consecration (cf. 1 Cor. x. 25). There was thus room enough for controversy whether or not it had actually broken out at Rome, and, in any case, these instances give Paul an opportunity of showing how a Christian should approach such controversial questions. In xiv. 1-12 he lays down the importance of having reasoned convictions, holding them conscientiously, and respecting them in others; in xiv. 13-xv. 6 he indicates the limits which the principle of love may impose upon the free expression of such convictions.

xiv.

1 Welcome a man of weak faith, but not for the purpose
2 of passing judgment on his scruples. While one man has enough confidence to eat any food, the man
3 of weak faith only eats vegetables. The eater must not look down upon the non-eater, and the non-eater
4 must not criticize the eater, for God has welcomed him. Who are you to criticize the servant of Another? It is for his Master to say whether he stands or falls; and stand he will, for the Master has power to make
5 him stand. Then again, this man rates one day above another, while that man rates all days alike.
6 Well, everyone must be convinced in his own mind; the man who values a particular day does so to the Lord.*

        The eater eats to the Lord,
            since he thanks God for his food;
        the non-eater abstains to the Lord,
            and he too thanks God.

* Omitting [καὶ ὁ μὴ φρονῶν τὴν ἡμέραν κυρίῳ οὐ φρονεῖ] with the Latin version and most manuscripts.

For none of us lives to himself,   7
   and none of us dies to himself;
if we live, we live to the Lord,   8
   and if we die, we die to the Lord.

Thus we are the Lord's whether we live or die; it
was for this that Christ died and rose and came to 9
life, to be Lord both of the dead and of the living.
So why do you criticize your brother? And you, 10
why do you look down upon your brother? All of
us have to stand before the tribunal of God—for it
is written,   11

   As I live, saith the Lord, every knee shall bend before Me,
   every tongue shall offer praise to God.

Each of us then will have to answer for himself to
God.   12

So let us stop criticizing one another; rather make up
your mind never to put any stumbling-block or 13
hindrance in your brother's way. I know, I am
certain in the Lord Jesus, that nothing is in itself 14
unclean; only, anything is unclean for a man who
considers it unclean. If your brother is being in- 15
jured because you eat a certain food, then you are
no longer living by the rule of love. Do not let that
food of yours ruin the man for whom Christ died.
Your rights must not get a bad name. The Reign of
God is not a matter of eating and drinking, it means 16-
righteousness, peace, and joy in the holy Spirit; he   17
who serves Christ on these lines, is acceptable to 18
God and esteemed by men. Peace, then, and the
building up of each other, these are what we must 19
aim at. You must not break down God's work for 20
the mere sake of food! Everything may be clean,
but it is wrong for a man to prove a stumbling-
block by what he eats; the right course is to abstain 21
from flesh or wine or indeed anything that your
brother feels to be a stumbling-block.† Certainly 22
keep your own conviction on the matter, as between
yourself and God: he is a fortunate man who has
no misgivings about what he allows himself to eat. 23
But if anyone has doubts about eating and then eats,

† Omitting {ἢ σκανδαλίζεται ἢ ἀσθενεῖ} with —*A C, Origen, the Peshitto, etc.,
as a homiletic gloss.

xv.   that condemns him at once; it was not faith that induced him to eat, and any action that is not based on faith is a sin.

1 We who are strong ought to bear the burdens that the weak make for themselves and us. We are not to
2 please ourselves. Each of us must please his neigh-
3 bour, doing him good by building up his faith. Christ certainly did not please Himself, but, as it is written,
4   *The reproaches of those who denounced Thee have fallen upon me.*
—All such words were written of old for our in-struction, that by remaining stedfast and drawing
5 encouragement from the scriptures we may cherish hope. May the God who inspires stedfastness and
6 encouragement grant you such harmony with one another, after Christ Jesus, that you may unite in a chorus of praise and glory to the God and Father of our Lord Jesus Christ.

1   Paul makes it quite clear that for himself he has no use for either Sabbatarianism or vegetarianism. Such fads indicate **a man of weak faith,** who has never grasped the liberty of the Spirit. But he is not for that reason to be treated with contempt or suspicion. The Church must **welcome a man of weak faith,** and not make him feel that his fellow-Christians are
2 **passing judgment on his scruples.** On the other hand, the Church has a right to ask from him that he will not **criticize**
5 those who take a more liberal view. Upon all such doubtful
7- questions **everyone must be convinced in his own mind.**
11 That does not mean that every Christian has the right to think just as he pleases. He is responsible to God for his convictions, and he is responsible to God alone. In life and death he belongs to Christ, who, as the primitive confession ran, is Judge of the
6 living and the dead. Thus, whether he keeps the Sabbath or not, whether he eats meat or not, he must be assumed to be acting on a conviction which he has formed 'in Christ,' and he must be respected accordingly. The meat-eater who says grace over his joint confesses that he and what he eats are the Lord's; he eats as a servant of Christ. The vegetarian who says grace over his greens must be allowed to be in the same position. **The eater must not look down on the non-**
3 **eater, and the non-eater must not criticize the eater.**
To both, but more especially to the vegetarian, the admonition
4 is addressed, **Who are you to criticize the servant of**

Another? It is for his Master to say **whether he stands or falls** (cf. 1 Cor. iv. 3–5). **And,** Paul adds, **stand he will** (though you shake your heads over the moral perils of meat-eating), **for the Master has power to make him stand.** On both sides there must be a sense of individual responsibility to God, and a tolerance based on respect for the other man's responsible convictions.

But this may not be sufficient. The ' strong ' and the ' weak ' do not stand on the same footing. The ' weak ' thinks it wrong to break the Sabbath; the ' strong ' does not think Sabbath-observance wrong, but only indifferent. The vegetarian has a conscientious objection to eating meat; no conscientious scruple compels the non-vegetarian to eat it. The more liberal Christian may be quite content to let the scrupulous go his own way, and feel in nowise aggrieved by his scruples. But the scrupulous may feel his conscience to be affronted by the other's conduct. This makes the problem difficult. The argument takes a further step. Paul first frankly states his conviction that **nothing is in itself unclean.** This conviction, he says, he holds **in the** 14 **Lord Jesus**—that is to say, it is something inseparable from his Christian experience. He might have added that such was the teaching of Jesus as understood by Peter and his followers (Mark vii. 14–23; Acts x. 9–16), as he was no doubt well aware. He might equally have appealed to the teaching of Jesus regarding ' holy ' days, for His free attitude to the Sabbath receives strong emphasis in the tradition. Paul's conviction is unquestionably Christian. There is no objective reality in *taboos* of any kind. But, on the other hand, the subjective effects of a *taboo* sincerely believed in may be serious. **Nothing is in itself unclean; only, anything is unclean for a man who considers it unclean.**

We are here on a very interesting and important point. We have seen that Paul makes much of the idea of the Holy as a religious principle (xii. 1). With his clear insight into the meaning of the Christian revelation, that idea has for him become fully rational and ethical. That is holy which is **good and acceptable and perfect.** But, for those who halt on the way, holiness retains something of its sub-rational implications. Holiness or unholiness may inhere in foods or days. Now, in whatever way the Holy is conceived, it commands an enormous amount of instinctive emotion. To the man whose religion is fully ethical, the feeling of having infringed the divine holiness by wrongdoing brings the peculiar horror of the sense of sin. But the same horror is felt by one whose religion remains partly on the sub-rational and sub-ethical plane, if he infringes a *taboo*; if he breaks the Sabbath or eats ' unholy ' food, for example. The fact that the ' holiness ' of the day, or the ' unholiness ' of the food, has no ethical reality about it makes no difference.

Now Paul envisages two men, both members of a Christian community. The one, taking his own enlightened view of the matter, has no feeling whatever about holy days or foods: he **has confidence to eat any food,** and he **rates all days alike.** The other projects his ' numinous ' feelings upon the Sabbath, or upon flesh-meat. As members of the same congregation they are in very intimate relations with one another. Consequently, if the scrupulous Christian sees the other breaking *taboo* in either respect, a flood of ' numinous ' emotion is released. He feels a ' holy horror,' and his conscience is as deeply wounded (to use the language of 1 Cor. viii. 12) as if someone with whom he had close ties committed some gross sin and made light of it. It may be that, in the end, the example or the persuasion of the liberal Christian prevails upon the scrupulous to relax his strictness; to eat meat or to break the Sabbath (cf. 1 Cor. viii. 9-12). If his scruples have simply been overborne, and he still feels the act to be ' unholy,' then grave harm has been done to his conscience. That is what Paul means when he says, **If anyone** 23 **has doubts about eating, and then eats, that condemns him at once; it was not faith that induced him to eat, and any action that is not based on faith is a sin.**[1]

This statement has been disastrously misunderstood. It was once taken to mean that unless a man held the Christian creed, he was incapable of doing right in the sight of God; the virtues of the heathen were nothing but ' brilliant vices.' This monstrous doctrine (which is in clean contradiction to ii. 14-15) is quite foreign to this passage. Paul means that, for the Christian, that which he sees to be involved in his relation to Christ is right, and that alone. If the vegetarian is induced to eat meat, not because he has been brought to realize his freedom in Christ, but by some outside influence, while still feeling inwardly that the thing is wrong, then his action has upon the conscience all the effects of actual sin. This is psychologically verifiable. It follows that the liberal Christian may be

[1] We may compare the saying attributed to Jesus in one MS. of Luke vi. 4: ' Seeing one working on the Sabbath, He said, " Man if thou knowest what thou are doing blessed art thou; but, if thou knowest not, cursed art thou and a transgressor of the Law." '

doing grave harm by claiming a liberty which his conscience fully approves. If so, then the principle of love must limit his freedom. **If your brother is being injured because you eat a certain kind of food, then you are no longer living** 15 **by the rule of love.** It really is not worth while **for the mere sake of food** (which to you is, after all, a matter of indifference), 20 to **break down God's work, and ruin the man for whom Christ died.**

The whole matter, therefore, must be regulated by something more than the mutual tolerance commended in verses 1–12. The question is, What is the Christian life, at bottom? It is living under **the Reign of God.** That expression, in view of 17 its history both in Jewish thought and in the teaching of Jesus, implied the supernatural order of ' the Age to Come,' within which Christians live because they are ' risen with Christ ' (vi. 1–11; cf. Col. i. 12–13, iii. 1–3). In speaking of the **Reign of God,** therefore, Paul is thinking of Christianity as a supernatural life lived **in the holy Spirit.** It is not, like many other religions, like even the Jewish religion in some aspects, **a matter of eating and drinking** (cf. Col. ii. 16–23). Its distinguishing qualities are ethical and spiritual: **it means righteousness, peace, and joy in the holy Spirit.** That being so, Christian conduct **must aim at peace and the** 19 **building up of each other** (as constituent parts of the Body of Christ; cf. Eph. ii. 14–21, iv. 15–16). In the light of this, Paul answers the particular question raised: What is the enlightened Christian to do in the presence of grave scruples on the part of less enlightened fellow-Christians? **The right** 21 **course is to abstain from flesh or wine or indeed anything that your brother feels to be a stumbling-block.** This, Paul adds in 1 Cor. x. 31–33, is his own practice, and it no doubt explains certain actions of his which have been thought surprising (e.g. Acts xvi. 3, xxi. 20–26; cf. 1 Cor. ix. 20).

This emphasis on the danger of putting a **stumbling-block** in the way of the weak recalls certain sayings in the Gospels— Matt. xviii. 7; Mark ix. 42; Luke xvii. 1–2. It can hardly be doubted that sayings like these were in Paul's mind.[1] Thus the two regulative ideas of the discussion—that **nothing is in**

---

[1] The key-word is *skandalon*, translated ' hindrance.' It is not a good or usual Greek word, and the very fact that Paul uses it here suggests that he knew it in the tradition of the sayings of Jesus. The word translated ' stumbling-block ' is its equivalent in good Greek.

itself unclean, and that **to put any stumbling-block or hindrance in your brother's way** is the most un-Christian of all acts—are both part of what Paul had learned from the teaching of Jesus, and the way he develops them shows that he had entered into its spirit.

He does not appeal directly to the authority of Christ's teaching, but he does appeal to His example. He has been pleading with Christians who are ' strong ' in their grasp of the liberty of the Spirit, to limit the exercise of their liberty for the sake of their more backward fellow-Christians. For **we who are strong ought to bear the burdens that the weak make for themselves and us. We are not to please ourselves.** And to insist on our full liberty of action where the conscience of others is wounded by it is simply to **please ourselves,** though we may call it by other names, such as ' the courage of our convictions.' But when it is put in that way, we see at once that it is un-Christian—**Christ certainly did not please Himself.** It is the same appeal that is made in more elaborate terms in Phil. ii. 1–11. Paul saw in the life of Jesus, all through, a continuous act of self-limitation for the sake of men. Such self-limitation is the very principle of the Incarnation. The kind of consideration for others, therefore, which he has been urging has the sanction of the very highest Example.

The upshot of the whole discussion, then, is to show that tiresome questions like Sabbath-keeping and vegetarianism, which may easily split a church, can be solved if both parties keep steadily in view the example of Christ, and the essential nature of the life into which faith has brought them. That is something that holds good for all Christians everywhere. If, however, we wish to apply Paul's particular solution to problems which arise in our own experience, we must be clear what kind of case he has in view. It would, for example, be quite illegitimate to take his maxim, **Nothing is in itself unclean; only anything is unclean for a man who considers it unclean,** to mean ' Nothing is good or ill, but thinking makes it so.' He is dealing exclusively with opinions and prejudices which, though sincerely held, have no rational ground, but are of the nature of *taboo.* He would certainly have said that moral principles are objectively valid; some things are wrong whether you think so or not. He would not have urged mutual tolerance and give-and-take in regard to such matters (see 1 Cor. v. 11). Nor, again, is he thinking of the legitimate differences of opinion which arise when people discuss complicated problems of conduct in the clear light of reason. No doubt many vegetarians in these days would say that their views are not based on irrational *taboo*, but arise from rational considerations regarding the rights of animals, or the hygienic value of a vegetable diet. With such a person I may well agree to differ, with full mutual respect for our convictions, but I see no reason, on Paul's principles, why I should alter my *menu* for the sake of his conscience. Paul's discussion is limited to cases where a conscientious but unenlightened person is haunted by a superstitious fear of some imaginary sanctity attaching to *things*, a fear inaccessible to reason. In such cases the kind and right course is for the more enlightened person to avoid profaning the other's sanctity, even if it means an irksome limitation of his own legitimate freedom of action. Of course, if it were made a rule that, if any member of a congregation professes a ' conscientious objection ' to such and such a course of conduct, that course is forbidden to all other members, then there would be an end of Christian liberty. It is not a rule of discipline, but a matter of individual consideration. And the position is essentially a provisional one; for Paul's hope would clearly be that the scrupulous person should be led, through the tactful treatment he receives, into a more thoroughly Christian attitude to life.

But, while Paul's ' findings ' can be directly transferred only to a restricted range of similar problems, his discussion has brought out certain principles which must underlie all Christian casuistry: that the individual is responsible to God, and to God alone, for his conscientious convictions; that his fellow-Christians must respect such convictions, even when they think them absurd; that, in the final determination of his course of conduct, the individual must have regard, not only to his own conscientious convictions, but to the effect of his act upon the consciences of others. It has also brought out incidentally the principle that thoroughgoing Christianity recognizes no absolute sanctity attaching to things, places, or times. Apparently neither the Puritan Sunday nor fish in Lent would have seemed to Paul to have much to do with the Christian religion, though he would have been most careful not to give offence to those to whom they mean a good deal.

With the appeal to the example of Christ the particular discussion has reached its climax. It now subtly merges in general exhortations which suitably round off the ethical section 3 of the epistle. The transition is supplied by a quotation of Scripture. In bringing forward Christ's example, Paul might most naturally, as it would seem to us, have referred to the evangelical tradition of His life, which, though as yet unwritten, was transmitted orally by Christian teachers (cf. Acts x. 37-41, xiii. 23-31; 1 Cor. xi. 23-25, xv. 3-7). But it is more in Paul's manner to cite Scripture (cf. x. 11-21), because, to his mind, if you can cite Scripture for a fact, you show, not only that it *was* so, but that it *must* have been so, in the eternal purpose of God. To adapt Lessing's famous phrase, ' contingent truths of history ' are then given the status of ' necessary truths of religion.' The particular Scripture cited is not, to our minds, especially apt, but the links of thought in Paul's mind are easily recognized. In Ps. lxix. 9, the Righteous Sufferer appeals to God for help, crying, **The reproaches of those who denounced Thee have fallen upon me.** The Righteous Sufferer of the Psalms, though he was not (in all probability) a Messianic figure in Jewish tradition, was from the first associated by Christians with the Person of their Master. Portions of this psalm are cited several times in the New Testament (the other half of this very verse in John ii. 17), and it is likely that some of them were included in the primitive collection of ' Testimonies ' to which allusion has been made above (note on ix. 32-33). Thus Paul starts from the accepted position that the psalm refers to Christ. It describes Him as being so identified with the cause of God that He endures in His own person the assaults of the enemies of God. Paul connects that with Christ's ' obedience even unto death ' (cf. Phil. ii. 8). Such obedience carries with it the abandonment of any desire to **please Himself**; and so the Scripture meets the point, in a general way.

4   Paul justifies this use of Scripture on the principle, **All such words were written of old for our instruction** (cf. 1 Cor. x. 11). We should say, no doubt, that they were written in intention for contemporaries; but that, since there is a unity in the spiritual history of man, they have an application beyond their original intention, wherever the like spiritual conditions and needs recur; and, further, so close is the unity of the spiritual history represented in the Bible, that there is nothing of permanent religious value in the Old Testament which has not an application to Christ and, through Him, to Christians.

5   The thought of the **encouragement** which can thus be drawn

from the Scriptures—promoting **stedfastness** and **hope**—
leads up to a prayer, to **the God who inspires stedfastness
and encouragement,** that, in view of the possibilities of
disunion with which we have been concerned, He will grant to
the Roman Christians **harmony with one another, after
Christ Jesus;** and the prayer passes into a doxology.

The subjects with which Paul intended to deal in the ethical
section of the epistle have now been disposed of. The following
paragraph, while it is linked to the ethical section, forms also
a fitting close to the whole argument of the epistle, which began
at i. 17. It alludes to themes which have occupied the reader
in earlier chapters, and draws the thought of the whole together
to a conclusion.

xv. 7–13:
THE UNITY OF JEW AND GENTILE
IN THE CHURCH. CONCLUDING PRAISE AND PRAYER

**Welcome one another, then, as Christ has welcomed 7
yourselves, for the glory of God. Christ, I mean, 8
became a servant to the circumcised in order to
prove God's honesty by fulfilling His promises to the 9
fathers, and also in order that the Gentiles should
glorify God for His mercy—as it is written,**
> *Therefore will I offer praise to Thee among the Gentiles,
> and sing to Thy name;*

or again, 10
> *Rejoice, O Gentiles, with His People!*

or again, 11
> *Extol the Lord, all Gentiles,
> let all the peoples praise Him;*

or again, as Isaiah says, 12
> *Then shall the Scion of Jessai live,
> He who rises to rule the Gentiles;
> on Him shall the Gentiles set their hope.*

**May the God of your hope so fill you with all joy
and peace in your faith, that you may be overflowing 13
with hope by the power of the holy Spirit !**

The discussion just concluded developed the theme, **Welcome
the man of weak faith** (xiv. 1). Paul now harks back to this

7 maxim, and generalizes it: **Welcome one another, as Christ has welcomed yourselves.** His next words betray the fact, which he tactfully kept in the background in the foregoing discussion, that the disputes to which he has alluded were very much connected with the tension between Jewish and Gentile Christians. And so, just as at the beginning of the epistle he expounded his Gospel in terms of Jew and Greek, he now recalls that the work of Christ had definitely a double reference: the 8 Gospel was **for the Jew first** (i. 16), and so **Christ became a servant to the circumcised;** but He did so with a double purpose—**in order to prove God's honesty by fulfilling His promises to the fathers, and also in order that the** 9 **Gentiles should glorify God for His mercy.** The meaning of this is clear in the light of chaps. ix.–xi. (and we may note this as evidence that those chapters were incorporated in the epistle in the course of writing, and not as an afterthought). Thus it is through Him that both Jews and Gentiles are **welcomed** into the Church of God. Surely therefore they can **welcome one another.** We may recall that this thought of the unity of those warring sections of the human race, Jews and Gentiles, within the one Body of Christ, becomes the controlling theme of the Epistle to the Ephesians.

1– Having thus come back to the thought of the Calling of the
12 Gentiles, which was the inspiration of his whole career, Paul goes once more to Deuteronomy (xxxii. 43), Isaiah (xi. 10), and the Psalms (xviii. 49, cxvii. 1) for words to move the Gentile Christians to hope, joy, and gratitude and praise to God, for 13 His mercy; and ends with a prayer which gathers up the great key-words of the Christian life: **faith, hope, joy, peace, and the power of the holy Spirit.**

The great argument is ended. Paul set out to lay before the Roman church the **Gospel** which he was eager to preach in Rome, because he was **proud of it,** as being **God's saving power.** He has shown them how **God's righteousness is revealed in it,** by justifying sinful men on the ground of faith alone, and by saving them from the power of sin into a life of the Spirit. He has shown how, though this **righteousness** was promised first to Israel, the promise rightly includes the Gentiles in its scope, and will ultimately be fulfilled for all men. Finally, he has shown them that though the Gospel supersedes the Jewish Law, yet it does not fall away from the moral demands for which the Law stood, but creates its own new morality,

which is **God's righteousness** at work in human lives, because
it is rooted in divine love. That is his Gospel. The Romans
must judge of it. It remains only to speak of some personal
matters.

THE EPILOGUE
(xv. 14–xvi. 27)

XV. 14–33: PERSONAL EXPLANATIONS

Personally I am quite certain, my brothers, that even as 14
**it is you have ample goodness of heart, you are filled
with knowledge of every kind, and you are well able
to give advice to one another. Still, by way of re-
freshing your memory, I have written you with a** 15
**certain freedom, in virtue of my divine commission
as a priest of Christ Jesus to the Gentiles in the** 16
**service of God's Gospel. My aim is to make the
Gentiles an acceptable offering, consecrated by the
holy Spirit. Now in Christ Jesus I can be proud of** 17
**my work for God. I will not make free to speak of
anything except what Christ has accomplished by** 18
**me in the way of securing the obedience of the Gen-
tiles, by my words and by my deeds, by the force of
miracles and marvels, by the power of the Spirit** 19
**of God. Thus from Jerusalem right round to
Illyricum, I have been able to complete the preaching of the Gospel of Christ—my ambition always** 20
**being to preach it only in places where there had
been no mention of Christ's name, that I might not
build on foundations laid by others, but that as it
is written** 21

They should see who never had learned about Him,
and they who had never heard of Him should understand.

This is why I have been so often prevented from visiting 22
**you. But now, as I have no further scope for work
in these parts, and as for a number of years I have** 23
**had a longing to visit you whenever I went to Spain,
I am hoping to see you on my way there, and to be** 24
**sped forward by you after I have enjoyed your com-
pany for a while. At the moment I am off to Jeru-** 25

26   salem on an errand to the saints. For Macedonia
27   and Achaia have decided to make a contribution for
      the poor among the saints at Jerusalem. Such was
      their decision; and yet this is a debt they owe to
      these people, for if the Gentiles have shared their
      spiritual blessings, they owe them a debt of aid in
28   material blessings. Well, once I finish this business
      by putting the proceeds of the collection safely in
29   their hands, I will start for Spain and take you on
      the way. When I do come to you, I know I will
      bring a full blessing from Christ.
30 Brothers, I beg of you, by our Lord Jesus Christ and by
      the love that the Spirit inspires, rally round me by
31   praying to God for me; pray that I may be delivered
      from the unbelievers in Judaea, and also that my
32   mission to Jerusalem may prove acceptable to the
      saints. Then, by God's will, I shall gladly come to
      you and rest beside you.
33 The God of peace be with you all ! Amen.

14   Paul feels the need of a tactful approach to the church of
      Rome. There might well be members of it who would be in-
      clined to resent his presumption in writing as he has done to
      a great church which had been founded and had grown to
      importance in complete independence of his mission, and looked
      to other leaders. So he seasons his dissertation with a compli-
15 ment, and suggests apologetically that he has written only **by
      way of refreshing your memory** of truths already well
      known. Yet even in apologizing he cannot disguise his sense
      of a **divine commission** which gives him the right to address
16 even Rome. He is (as he has already reminded them in i. 5)
      the apostle to the Gentiles, recognized as such by Peter and the
      rest.
      He describes his apostolate here in terms of priesthood. He
      is **a priest of Christ to the Gentiles,** and his **aim is to make
      the Gentiles an acceptable offering, consecrated by the
      holy Spirit.** He has already said that to be members of the
      Church, the Body of Christ, means **to dedicate your bodies
      as a living sacrifice, consecrated and acceptable to God.**
      This is the cult of the Christian religion, **a spiritual rite** (xii. 1).
      In so far as his preaching of the Gospel and his pastoral care
      for the Gentile churches promote this **cult,** he is exercising a
      priestly office. The sacrifice he offers is not any material thing,

but the consecrated **bodies,** or personalities, of his converts. Later on, when he stood before the prospect of martyrdom, he wrote to the Philippians: **Even if my life-blood has to be poured as a libation on the sacred sacrifice of faith you are offering to God, I rejoice** (Phil. ii. 17). It is in this truly spiritual sense that the Christian ministry is a priestly ministry. To deny its priestly character is to belittle its spiritual worth. Ministerial priesthood in this Pauline sense does not exclude the priesthood of all believers; for each individual Christian is called upon to dedicate his body as a living sacrifice. But the minister who brings men to Christ, and instructs and trains them in Christian living, is making that sacrifice possible, or helping to make it more real and complete. As the sacramental system of the Church developed, the priesthood of the minister came to be more particularly connected with his administration of the sacrament of the Lord's Supper. Since that sacrament, as conceived by Paul, is **a participating in the** (mystical) **body of Christ,** it gives a fitting visible form to the **spiritual rite of** self-dedication, and the minister's part in it similarly gives visible form to his priestly relation to the Church. It is when the self-offering of the Church, in association with Christ's own sacrifice, is forgotten, or pushed into the background, that the abuses of sacerdotalism arise.

By way of corroborating his claim to a **divine commission** 17 as apostle to the Gentiles, Paul now permits himself to speak of the actual work which he has done—not as a personal achievement, but as that which **Christh as accomplished by me.** 18, That his mission has been powerful and effective in the Gentile world is a fact which no one can deny, and he offers his record to the Roman church as part of his credentials. He has taken the eastern provinces of the Roman Empire as his sphere of work, exclusive of those places where other Christian missionaries have been first in the field; and his work in this sphere is now finished, since he has preached **from Jerusalem right round to Illyricum.**

The province of Illyricum comprised, roughly, the western part of the present kingdom of Yugoslavia, and as Paul regularly uses geographical terms in their official Roman application (as Achaia for Greece, and Galatia for the composite province which included Lycaonia and part of Phrygia), he probably means the province, and not those Illyrian districts which had been assigned to the province of Macedonia. Whether Illyricum is given as the inclusive or the exclusive limit of the area covered is not clear. The explicit narrative of the Acts of the Apostles brings him no further west than Macedonia, but its account of his journeys is certainly not exhaustive. As we have seen (Introduction, p. 18) this letter can be placed at the point represented by Acts xx. 3. On a reasonable scheme of chronology there would be ample time between his departure from Ephesus (Acts xx. 1) and his arrival in Greece (Acts xx. 2) for an extended tour. According to Acts, ' he left Ephesus to journey to Macedonia, and after passing through those parts and exhorting them at length, he arrived in Greece,' and so came to Corinth, where this letter was written. It may well be that the journey thus vaguely described carried him farther west than he had been before, perhaps as far as the borders of Illyricum, possibly over the frontier.[1]

At any rate, Paul means that he has now adequately covered the area of the eastern provinces, and that leads him to speak of his next step. When he wrote 2 Cor. x. 16 (perhaps some two years before this) he was already planning to **preach the Gospel in the lands that lie beyond you,** i.e. west of Corinth. That plan has now taken shape. He is about to extend his mission to the western provinces; and as Christianity has already reached Italy, he will go to Spain. On his way he will pay Rome a passing visit. **I am hoping to see you on my way there, and to be sped forward by you after I have enjoyed your company for a while.** The expression **to be sped forward means** more than appears on the surface. In 1 Cor. xvi. 6, 2 Cor. i. 16, he speaks of the Corinthian church **speeding** him on his journey to Jerusalem, on an occasion when he was going as an official representative of the Gentile churches, or of the churches of Greece in particular (see p. 232 below), to take their contribution to the relief fund (see verses 25-27 below). That is to say, the church of Corinth was to make itself responsible for his journey, and to accredit him to those to whom he was going. The author of Acts has used the word with the same kind of implication in xv. 3, where Paul and Barnabas go to Jerusalem as the accredited delegates of Antioch. A similar usage crops up again in 3 John 6, where Gaius is enjoined to **speed on their journey** certain servants of the Church, clearly with the implication that he is both to accredit them to the next church they visit, and to defray their expenses. Thus the expression seems to have been almost a technical term

24, 28

24

[1] See P. N. Harrison, *The Problem of the Pastoral Epistles*, p. 117.

with a well-understood meaning among missionaries. Paul is hinting that he would like the church of Rome to take some responsibility for his Spanish mission, so that he can start work in the west with their moral support at least, and possibly with some contribution from them in assistants or funds. If this is so, we can see a special reason why he took pains to give the Romans a clear and fully argued statement of his position. They might be prejudiced against him by misrepresentations. It was a matter of practical moment to him that they should understand and accept the doctrinal basis on which his missionary preaching rested.

The journey to Spain via Rome cannot be undertaken at once, 25- because Paul has an urgent piece of business to attend to first— 27 namely, the winding up of his relief fund for the church of Jerusalem. This enterprise occupied much of Paul's thought during the later years of his ministry. Many years before, when he was a minister of the church of Antioch, he had been sent as a delegate to Jerusalem to take famine relief to that chronically poverty-stricken church (Acts xi. 27-30). Either on that occasion or later, he had made a ' gentlemen's agreement ' with Peter, James and John, whereby he was to be free to conduct his mission to the Gentiles without interference from the headquarters of Jewish Christianity. In return, the 'pillars' of the Church stipulated that he should ' remember the poor '—in other words, that he should undertake to raise funds for the support of the impoverished community at Jerusalem.

Their poverty was perhaps partly the result of persecution; but, even without this additional cause, it is hardly surprising. The Jerusalem church contained from the beginning many poor and few rich. Filled with a sense of their unity as ' brethren,' they instituted a system of partial and voluntary communism. But they carried it out in the economically disastrous way of realizing capital and distributing it as income. (Acts ii. 44-45, iv. 34-v. 5.) So far as we can gather, no practical steps were taken to replace the capital thus dissipated; and when hard times came, the community had no reserves of any kind. When this happened, it was fortunate that a new centre of Christianity had come into existence in the wealthy city of Antioch. True, it contained many Gentiles, who, since they did not accept circumcision and the Law, must be regarded as rather inferior Christians; but it was only right that they should have the opportunity of showing such self-denying generosity as the rich Christians of Jerusalem had shown before the economic depression set in. So the poor ' saints ' of Jerusalem thankfully accepted their alms. The Gentile Church began to expand, under Paul's vigorous leadership, and Gentile converts soon promised to outnumber the Jewish Christians. Now among the Jews, the piety of the Dispersion was very profitable to Jerusalem. Why should not the Gentile Christians, if they wished to be recognized as the Dispersed of the New Israel, follow this excellent precedent? The ' saints ' would thus continue to enjoy the prestige that accrued from the virtue of voluntary poverty, and could attend to their religious duties without troubling about such worldly affairs as earning a living, while the Gentiles would win merit by contributing to their support.[1] That this was the light in which the average Jewish Christian, at any rate, saw the matter is highly probable.

When the proposal was made to Paul, he readily accepted it. It was in fact the only kind of proposal he could have accepted as the price of the recognition of his mission. He was quite clear that members of the Christian Church must accept responsibility for one another in the sphere of economics as well as in spiritual matters. He laid this obligation upon his churches, and, as we have seen, he commends it to the church of Rome (xii. 13). But we may note that, warned by the example of Jerusalem, he advised that money given for the support of the poor should be earned (Eph. iv. 28), and that no one who refused work should be entitled to the dole (2 Thess. iii. 10). Thus Paul accepts the principle of Christian communism, while putting it on a sound economic basis. Since the sharing of resources is the economic expression of the unity of the Body of Christ, it must, of course, extend beyond the limits of the local community. To induce the Gentile churches to feel responsibility for the poor Jewish Christians of Jerusalem was to find an effective expression for the unity of the two wings of the Christian Church. We have seen how the argument of this epistle ends in the thought that Jews and Gentiles must **welcome one another** in the fellowship of Christ's Body; and we can understand why the raising of the relief fund for Jerusalem became such an important concern for Paul. It was a great gesture in the interests of the unity of the Church, threatened with an irreparable breach through the bad feeling between Jewish and Gentile Christians.

We learn something of the methods adopted, and the progress

[1] See W. L. Knox, *St. Paul and the Church of Jerusalem*, pp. 284 sqq.

made, in 1 Cor. xvi. and 2 Cor. viii.-ix. Here he reports to Rome the position at the moment. **Macedonia and Achaia 26 have decided to make a contribution for the poor among the saints at Jerusalem.** That it has the grace of a free and voluntary **decision** on their part he emphasizes. Nevertheless, it is only the fulfilment of a moral obligation. **If the Gentiles have shared their spiritual blessings, they owe them a debt of aid in material blessings.** The spiritual blessings of which he speaks are those of the ' Israel of God,' now extended to the Gentiles (see ix.-xi.). The Jews within the Church are, so to speak, the trustees of these blessings, and through them they have come to the Greeks of Macedonia and Achaia. As a plain matter of fact, the church of Jerusalem was the mother-church of Christendom; and, however Paul had to fight its representatives for his freedom and that of his churches, he retained a deep piety towards those through whose witness the Gospel had first been given to the world. He would have felt it to be a disaster if his mission had been disavowed by the 'pillars' of the Church (cf. Gal. ii. 2), or if the Gentile Christians had been cut off from communion with Jerusalem. But the outward sign of such communion is the sharing of needs and resources, and if Jerusalem is in need, Christians everywhere should feel responsible for her. Paul does not add that for him it was not only a moral obligation, but a contractual one, in view of his agreement with Peter, James, and John; although, indeed, after the way in which he had been treated since the agreement, he might well have felt that the contract had lapsed. But even so the moral obligation remained. It was on this ground that he had appealed to Macedonia and Achaia—as well as to Galatia (1 Cor. xvi. 1) and evidently Asia, though these are not mentioned here.

That it had been difficult to raise a substantial sum is clear. No doubt there were anti-semitic prejudices to overcome, and in any case there were few wealthy members of these churches (1 Cor. i. 26). Most of the money had to be laboriously collected in small weekly sums (1 Cor. xvi. 2). But at last the fund was complete. Paul was at Corinth, and had arranged to meet the delegates of the contributing churches and to journey with them to Jerusalem. The delegates are named in Acts xx. 4. Macedonia is represented by Sopater of Beroea, and Aristarchus and Secundus of Thessalonica; Asia by Tychicus and Trophimus of Ephesus; Galatia by Gaius of Derbe and Timothy of Lystra. No Achaian delegates are mentioned. Probably Paul himself was accredited by Corinth as the special representative of the province.

The original plan was for the party to sail direct from Cenchreae to Palestine, but the discovery of a Jewish plot decided Paul to travel overland—an inauspicious beginning for an errand
31 of conciliation. It is no wonder that Paul begs for the prayers of the Roman Christians **that I may be delivered from the unbelievers in Judaea.** But this was not his only anxiety, he was by no means sure that his gift would be accepted by the Jewish Christians in the spirit in which it was offered. He had spent several years in preparation for what he intended as a decisive gesture of unity. But the tension between him and the extreme elements in Jewish Christianity had not decreased, and he feared it might all be a failure. The Romans must pray **that** his **mission to Jerusalem may prove acceptable to the saints.**

As a matter of fact, everything went wrong (Acts xxi.). James was guardedly friendly, but rattled by the aggressive attitude of ' tens of thousands ' (so he said) of Jewish Christians incensed against Paul and all his works. He persuaded Paul —or, rather, ordered him—to make a demonstration of his faithfulness to the traditional ceremonies of the Jewish religion. Paul, ready to do anything to disarm prejudice, complied. Whether the effect upon the Christian Jews would have made any difference to their attitude we cannot say. For the non-Christian Jews took matters into their own hands. The presence of the Ephesian delegates in the city was made a pretext for a charge of defiling the Temple. Paul was nearly lynched, rescued by the Roman guard, and ultimately sent to Rome as a prisoner. The course of history, therefore, has given a deep colour of tragic irony to this section of the letter. The man who writes to Rome, full of far-reaching schemes, who is planning to visit the capital on his way to remoter fields of enterprise, was brought to Rome worn by years of imprisonment, in chains, his hopes disappointed, his active career at an end.

33   An ancient letter, like a modern one, usually ended with good wishes for the recipient, and greetings to friends. The good wishes were often given the form of a prayer. Paul follows this custom, and, before proceeding to greetings, closes the body of his letter with a short prayer commending his readers to **the God of peace**—the expression, no doubt, being determined

by the thought of the menaced unity of the Church which has
been in his mind since xv. 7.

xvi. 1-2 [1]: AN INTRODUCTION FOR PHOEBE

xvi.

Let me introduce our sister Phoebe, a deaconess of the 1
church at Cenchreae; receive her in the Lord as 2
saints should receive one another, and give her any
help she may require. She has been a help herself
to many people, including myself.

By way of postscript Paul adds, before sending greetings, a 1
few lines to introduce to the church of Rome a **deaconess of**
the church at Cenchreae, who must probably be supposed to
have come across the Isthmus to Corinth in order to take ship
for Rome. The terms in which Paul writes are familiar from
examples of letters of introduction among papyri of the period.
Such letters of introduction were evidently widely used among
the early Christian communities. Paul in writing to Corinth
asks sarcastically, **Do I need, like some people, to be com-**
mended by written certificates either to you or from
you? (2 Cor. iii. 1). The necessity of a proper introduction for
persons less well known than he is obvious. A church must
know that a stranger arriving and seeking hospitality as a fellow-
Christian is a genuine member of the Christian society, and
not a parasite or a spy. In a satirical work of the second century [2]
there is an amusing account of how an impostor made a very
good thing out of the generosity of simple and credulous Christian communities.

Phoebe may have been going to Rome on business of her own.
The Greek expression Paul uses in describing her as **a help to** 2
many people has a shade of meaning something like ' patroness
of many,' implying probably some measure of wealth or social
position. Perhaps she was making the journey at her own
charges in the service of the Church. In any case, we are, no
doubt, to suppose that she would carry the Epistle to the Romans,
and deliver it at Rome. Private persons had to make their own
arrangements for the conveyance of letters. Only officials and
their friends could make use of the imperial postal service.

---

[1] The notes on chap. xvi. proceed on the assumption that this chapter is an integral
part of the Epistle to the Romans. Arguments for and against this view will be
found in the Introduction, pp. 12-18.
[2] *De Morte Peregrini*, attributed to Lucian of Samosata.

It would be interesting to know more of Phoebe and of her place and functions in the church of Cenchreae, but we are ill informed about the ministry of women in the early Church. The term by which she is described (*diakonos*, with no feminine termination) is a very general term. In this epistle it is actually applied both to the civil magistrate as **God's servant** (xiii. 4) and to Christ as **a servant to the circumcised** (xv. 8). When Paul uses it of the Christian ministry it is again usually in a quite general sense (e.g. 1 Cor. iii. 5, Col. i. 23, 2 Cor. xi. 23, Col. iv. 7). Only in Phil. i. 1 does he seem to apply it to a particular order of ministry in a local church; though the use of corresponding verbal and abstract forms in Rom. xii. 7 (there rendered **practical service**) may perhaps imply something of the same sort. We may assume that, whatever the 'deacons' were at Philippi, that Phoebe was at Cenchreae. In the (probably post-Pauline) First Epistle to Timothy (iii. 8–13), deacons are a recognized order, and something is said of their qualifications for office, but nothing of their functions. But we may fairly suppose that the order of deacons which emerges in the second century, with special charge of the more secular side of the Church's affairs, had its origins in Paul's own time; and that it then included women as well as men.

xvi. 3–16: GREETINGS TO FRIENDS IN ROME

3 **Salute Prisca and Aquila, my fellow-workers in Christ Jesus, who have risked their lives for me; I thank**
4 **them, and not only I but all the Gentile churches as**
5 **well. Also, salute the church that meets in their house. Salute my beloved Epaenetus, the first in Asia to be reaped for Christ. Salute Mary, who has**
6 **worked hard for you. Salute Andronicus and Junias,**
7 **fellow-countrymen and fellow-prisoners of mine; they are men of note among the apostles, and they**
8-9 **have been in Christ longer than I have. Salute Amplias, my beloved in the Lord. Salute Urbanus, our fellow-worker in Christ, and my beloved Stachys.**
10 **Salute that tried Christian, Apelles. Salute those**
11 **who belong to the household of Aristobulus. Salute my fellow-countryman Herodion. Salute such**
12 **members of the household of Narcissus as are in the Lord. Salute Tryphaena and Tryphosa, who**

work hard in the Lord. Salute the beloved Persis; she has worked very hard in the Lord. Salute that 13 choice Christian, Rufus; also his mother, who has 14 been a mother to me. Salute Asyncritus, Phlegon, Hermes, Patrobas, Hermas, and the brothers of their company. Salute Philologus and Julia, Nereus 15 and his sister, Olympas too, and all the saints in 16 their company. Salute one another with a holy kiss. All the churches of Christ salute you.

On Prisca and Aquila, see Introduction. The occasion on 3–4 which they risked their lives for Paul is not known to us, though it is an easy conjecture that it may have been during the troubles at Ephesus a year or two earlier, when they and Paul were together for the last time so far as we know. The gratitude which **all the Gentile churches** feel towards them was well earned, not only by their devotion to Paul, but by their important services in connection with the establishment of Christianity at two great centres: Corinth (Acts xviii. 2–3) and, still more, Ephesus (Acts xviii. 18–28), even if there were not further services unknown to us.

The Church that meets in their house. In order to 5 understand this expression (which recurs in 1 Cor. xvi. 19; Col. iv. 15; Philemon 2) we must recall that ancient religion, both pagan and Jewish, was very largely conducted on a family basis. Similarly we hear of whole households becoming Christians together (Acts x. 44–48, xvi. 15, 30–34, xviii. 8; 1 Cor. i. 16). The household included, not only members of the family (in our sense), but also slaves and dependants, who were members of the *familia* (in the Roman sense). Such a household very naturally became a unit in the Church. If it was a large household, the head of it influential, and his premises commodious, it would be natural for neighbours who were Christians to attach themselves to it as members of the *familia* for religious purposes. Thus, while the household, or *familia*, of Aquila and Prisca as a civil unit might consist of their children (and perhaps other relations), their slaves, employees, and tenants, it included as a religious unit both Christian members of the civil household and also their ' brothers in Christ ' who met at their table for the Lord's Supper. At death these ' brothers in Christ ' would have the right of burial in the family vault. Several of the ' catacombs,' or early Christian cemeteries, of Rome can be shown to have developed out of such family burial-places. Moreover, as the archaeologist De Rossi showed, several of the ancient *tituli*, or parishes, of Rome can be connected with particular cemeteries, and may well have grown out of the domestic churches which used the family burial-places. This family element in its organization was congenial to the idea of the Church as **God's own household** (Eph. ii. 19) or **the household of the faith** (Gal. vi. 10), and of its members as children of God and brothers of Christ (Rom. viii. 16–17, 29); and its central rite, the Lord's Supper, took over something of the family character of the Jewish Passover.

5   **Epaenetus.** See introduction. The majority of MSS. describe him as the **first to be reaped for Christ in Achaia.** This is clearly wrong; the first converts in Achaia were the household of Stephanas (1 Cor. xvi. 15). All the best MSS. read ' **Asia.**' At Corinth the senior members of the church evidently held a position of authority. If Epaenetus was still in Asia he would, no doubt, be in such a position at Ephesus. But, apart from the possibility that his private affairs may have taken him to Rome, it would not be surprising to find that a distinguished member of the church of Ephesus had been sent to Rome on Church business.

7   As **Andronicus and Junias** were Christians before Paul, who was converted (on a reasonable chronology) not more than four or five years after the Crucifixion, we must connect them with the primitive church at Jerusalem. As they were Jews bearing Greek or Graeco-Latin names, they would naturally belong to the Hellenistic group whose leaders were Stephen, Philip, and their associates. Like others of this group (Acts viii. 4–5, xi. 19–21), they became missionaries, or **apostles** in the wider sense. In the stricter sense ' the Apostles ' were the Twelve appointed by Christ Himself; or the Eleven of them who remained faithful, together with Matthias who was appointed in place of Judas. But the Acts of the Apostles gives the title also to Paul and Barnabas (xiv. 14). Paul (1 Cor. xv. 5–7) seems to distinguish **the twelve** from **all the apostles** as a wider body. He gives the title also to delegates of churches (2 Cor. viii. 23). He also accuses missionaries of the Judaistic party opposed to him, of being **spurious apostles, masquerading as ' apostles of Christ '** (2 Cor. xi. 13). In the *Didache*, or *Teaching of the Twelve Apostles*, travelling evangelists are called ' apostles.' It seems clear, therefore, that the title was widely given to persons properly commissioned by the Church to preach the Gospel. In this sense, Paul and Barnabas

would be generally recognized as ' apostles.' But Paul claimed that he was an 'apostle' in the stricter sense, by direct appointment from Christ (Gal. i. 1), on a level with Peter and the rest of the Twelve. He appears to have understood their recognition of him to imply that they acknowledged this (Gal. ii. 7–9), but it does not appear to have been universally admitted.[1]

Our present point, however, is that among the wider body of apostles Andronicus and Junias were **of note.** It may even be that they had some hand in the founding of the church of Rome. In calling them his **fellow-prisoners,** Paul may, but does not necessarily, mean that he and they had been in the same prison together. But if the conjecture is justified that they were associated with the Stephen group of the Jerusalem church, we may recall that it was members of this group that founded the church of Antioch, in which Paul ministered, and that he was acquainted with Philip, another member of the group; so that his association with these two may have been of very old standing. We may note that the second name might equally well be the feminine *Junia*. In that case, Andronicus and Junia would be husband and wife working together as missionaries, like Aquila and Prisca. Chrysostom, preaching on this passage, saw no difficulty in a woman-apostle; nor need we.

Amplias is a familiar abbreviation for *Ampliatus*, which, 8 indeed, is the form of the name read here by the best MSS., and should be adopted in the text. For a possible identification of this Ampliatus, see Introduction.

For **the household of Aristobulus** and **the household of** 10 **Narcissus,** see Introduction. The expression, **such members** 11 **of the household of Narcissus as are in the Lord,** may be illustrated from an expression which is not unusual in early Christian sepulchral inscriptions: a Christian head of a family will erect a tomb *sibi et suis fidentibus in Domino*—' for himself and those of his household who believe in the Lord.'

Rufus. If this is the Rufus (as suggested in the Introduction) 13 who, as Mark tells us, was a son of Simon of Cyrene, we may pertinently recall that ' men of Cyprus and Cyrene ' founded the church of Antioch (Acts xi. 20). It is quite possible that Paul met the Cyrenian Rufus there, together with his mother. This however is speculative.

The formula, **Salute one another,** is one which Paul uses 16 also at the close of 1 and 2 Corinthians. It is another way of

---

[1] See W. L. Knox, *S. Paul and the Church of Jerusalem*, pp. 363–371. I should not however assent to all his conclusions.

putting a general greeting to all members of the particular church addressed. To the Thessalonians he says, **Salute every one of the brothers with a holy kiss** (1 Thess. v. 26), and to the Philippians, **Salute every saint in Christ Jesus** (Phil. iv. 21). In all those four epistles the general greeting takes the place of greetings to individuals; here it supplements them.

In his greetings to his correspondents, Paul usually associates with himself friends who are with him, or churches with which he is at the moment in touch. Thus, writing to Corinth from Ephesus (1 Cor. xvi. 19–20), he sends greetings from **the churches of Asia,** as well as from Aquila and Prisca, and **all the brotherhood,** which probably means all members of the church of Ephesus, unless it means a group of immediate companions of Paul. It is probable that **all the saints,** in 2 Cor. xiii. 12, are similarly the members of the local church, as they must be in Phil. iv. 22: **All the saints salute you, especially the imperial slaves.** Thus it is something exceptional when Paul writes, **All the churches of Christ salute you.** We are probably to understand by that, all the churches of Paul's mission-field. He might feel himself competent to speak for them, as their apostolic founder and leader. But it may be that their greeting was more direct. Paul was at the moment, as we have seen, in close touch with the churches of Galatia, Asia, Macedonia, and Achaia, over the business of the relief fund, and it may be that their delegates had already assembled (Acts xx. 3–5 does not make it clear whether they joined Paul at Corinth or first at Troas). In that case, they may have authorized Paul to send the greetings of the churches they represented. In any case, however, it is highly probable that he had acquainted the leaders of his churches in these provinces with his plans. They must have known that he had definitely decided not to return to work among them (cf. Acts xx. 25), but to extend his mission westwards, and it is likely that they were aware of his approach to the Roman Christians. They would be glad to associate themselves with this approach, and they would send their greetings, not only with the feelings of respectful attachment which provincials certainly felt towards the capital of the Empire, but with a desire to give Paul their backing in his appeal to the Roman church. Paul, on his side, would wish to send such greetings, both because the exceptional position of the church of Rome made it a fit recipient of friendly homage from all provincial churches, and also because of his anxiety that the Romans should make common cause with his

Gentile mission. Thus the exceptional expression, **All the churches of Christ salute you,** is well accounted for in a letter to Rome at this particular juncture of affairs, whereas if these greetings were addressed to Ephesus it would remain unexplained.

xvi. 17-20: A FINAL WORD OF WARNING

Brothers, I beg of you to keep your eye on those who stir 17 **up dissensions and put hindrances in your way, contrary to the doctrine which you have been taught. Avoid them. Such creatures are no servants of Christ our Lord, they are slaves of their own base** 18 **desires; with their plausible and pious talk they beguile the hearts of unsuspecting people. But surely not of you! Everyone has heard of your** 19 **loyalty to the Gospel; it makes me rejoice over you. Still, I want you to be experts in good and innocents in evil. The God of peace will soon crush Satan under your feet!**

20

The grace of our Lord Jesus Christ be with you.

After the general greeting, we might expect the greetings from individuals to follow, if any were being sent (cf. 1 Cor. xvi. 19-20; Phil. iv. 21-22). It would appear that Paul did not at first intend to name any individuals, but to close the letter. It was his custom, after dictating a letter, to take the pen in his own hand and add a brief personal message. Thus, in 2 Thess. iii. 17, he writes: **The salutation is in my own hand, Paul's; that is a mark in every letter of mine. This is how I write. ' The grace of our Lord Jesus Christ be with you all.'** Again, in Col. iv. 18: **This salutation is in my own hand, from Paul. ' Remember I am in prison. Grace be with you.'** In 1 Cor. xvi. 21-24 the autograph conclusion is a little longer, and in Gal. vi. 11-18 it runs to eight verses, and contains, in place of a brief admonition, a somewhat full re-statement of the main appeal of the epistle. In view of all this, we may perhaps take it that verses 17-20 correspond to Paul's usual epistolary conclusion, ending with the formula which with slight variations he uses in every epistle, **The grace of our Lord Jesus Christ be with you.** We may suppose that he has taken the pen from the hand of his amanuensis to add the brief admonition and ' grace ' in his own handwriting, which, as he tells us in 2 Thessalonians, was the invariable **mark** of an authentic letter from him.

The fact that he now feels himself to be in more direct contact with his correspondents may help to account for the unexpected change of tone which every reader must notice. Throughout the epistle he has been scrupulously ' correct ' in his address to a church to which he is a stranger. We miss in this epistle what we may call the pastoral note which is characteristic of letters written to his own churches. He writes, in the main, as one stating a case, and apologizes for anything that might seem like giving instruction to people **filled with knowledge of every kind,** or advice to people **well able to give advice to one another** (xv. 14–15). But here at the end of the epistle the 17 pastoral note breaks in. The tone reminds us of the Epistles to the Galatians and the Philippians. He knows, or has reason to fear, that the sort of people who have disturbed the peace of his own churches are at work in Rome. He has carefully avoided controversial references to them in the body of the epistle; but when it comes to the final admonition, he cannot refrain from an appeal to the Romans to beware of them. In 18 making the appeal, the strong feelings of his own bitter conflict with such disturbers break through. He denounces them as **no servants of Christ,** but **slaves of their own base desires.**

Who they were, we can only conjecture. Paul's chief adversaries were Jewish Christians of the extreme party, who dogged his steps to persuade his converts to adopt Jewish practices. His controversy with this party lies behind the *apologia* for his own position to which the main argument of the epistle is directed. But he has, with evident intent, avoided expressions of hostility to them. His argument ends with a plea for unity between Gentile and Jewish Christians. He would hardly be likely to spoil the impression by an outbreak like this against the Jewish-Christian extremists. Besides, to call these Jewish Christians ' slaves of their own belly ' (the expression which Dr. Moffatt has politely paraphrased) would be grossly unfair. We may compare Phil. iii. 18–19, where he speaks of **enemies of the cross of Christ,** and declares, **Destruction is their fate, the belly is their god, they glory in their shame.** We know that Paul had trouble, not only with the extreme Jewish party in the Church, but also with people in the Gentile churches who practised and defended immoral licence in the name of Christian liberty (see 1 Cor. v. 1–13, vi. 12–20). The language, here and in Philippians, would suit such tendencies better than the propaganda of extreme Judaism, and they were equally disruptive. They may have been associated with quasi-gnostic speculations **contrary to the doctrine which you have been taught,** such as cropped up a little later at Colossae. Similar doctrinal aberrations seem to be hinted at in Acts xx. 29–30, in the speech attributed to Paul at Miletus a few weeks after the date of this letter—a speech which has a better claim than most of the speeches of Acts to represent what Paul actually said, since it belongs to a section of the work where the use of the first person implies that its author was an eyewitness. But we can have no certain knowledge on this point. Whatever the particular threat to the Church's unity and health may have been, Paul pleads with the Romans to beware of it in much the same terms as he might have used to any of his own flock. Apparently the disturbers, like some of those at Corinth (1 Cor. iii. 18–20, &c.), laid claim to superior ' wisdom.' **I want you,** says Paul, **to be experts** (' wise ') **in good and innocents in evil.** (Had he in mind the warning of Matt. x. 16?) If they persevere in their far-famed **loyalty to the Gospel,** then the evil will be crushed by the power of **the God of peace** (cf. xv. 33).

xvi. 21–23: GREETINGS FROM FRIENDS AT CORINTH

Timotheus my fellow-worker salutes you; so do my fellow-countrymen Lucius, Jason, and Sosipater. 21
I Tertius, who write the letter, salute you in the Lord. 22
Gaius, my host and the host of the church at large, 23 **salutes you. Erastus the city-treasurer salutes you; so does brother Quartus.**

The letter is now concluded, but, by way of postscript, Paul adds greetings from some of his companions. **Timothy** is well known. The other three cannot be certainly identified, though it has been suggested that Lucius is Lucius of Cyrene (Acts xiii. 1), Jason, Paul's host at Thessalonica (Acts xvii. 5–9), and Sosipater, Sopater of Beroea (Acts xx. 4). There is nothing to be said for or against the two former identifications. Both names are common, the latter being used as a Greek equivalent for the Hebrew Jeshua or Jesus. It is not impossible that Sosipater is Sopater, one of the relief fund delegates. If so, Sopater, like Aristarchus (Col. iv. 10) was a Jew. Timothy was a half-Jew (Acts xvi. 1), Trophimus a Gentile (Acts xxi. 28–29). The delegation was evidently mixed. We cannot say why these three are singled out to send greetings. Possibly they had some connections with Rome.

22   At this point the amanuensis, Tertius, who must be supposed to have taken up his pen again at verse 21, adds a greeting from himself, perhaps thinking Paul has finished. But Paul has greetings to send from three more friends. The first is Gaius (1 Cor. i. 14), at whose house Paul is staying; he is described as being also **the host of the church at large,** which may mean that his house is the meeting-place of the Corinthian church, or simply that he kept 'open house' for all Christians. The second is a municipal official of Corinth, **Erastus the city-treasurer,** whom it is interesting to find as a member of the Christian Church. The third is an unknown Quartus, who, again, may have had some connection with Rome.

xvi. 25–27: THE DOXOLOGY

25 **[Now to Him who can strengthen you by my Gospel, by the preaching of Jesus Christ, by revealing the secret purpose which after the silence of long ages**
26 **has now been disclosed and made known on the basis of the prophetic scriptures (by command of the eternal God) to all the Gentiles for their obedi-**
27 **ence to the faith—to the only wise God be glory through Jesus Christ for ever and ever; Amen.]**

At this point (as verse 24) some MSS. insert the 'grace,' but they are certainly wrong. The better MSS. give a long doxology. Its theme is that the divine plan of salvation, though it was attested by **the prophetic scriptures,** was, in its full scope, a secret until the coming of Christ. It was then revealed, and became the subject-matter of the Gospel, or preaching about Jesus Christ. It thus became known to the Gentiles, who believed and obeyed the Gospel. In virtue of the Gospel, therefore, God **can strengthen** the Roman Christians to overcome all temptations and opposition; and, for all this, Paul praises **the only wise God.** All this however is expressed very obscurely.

The idea of the secret purpose revealed in Christ is most prominent in the later epistles (see Col. i. 24-29, ii. 2-3; Eph. iii. 1-13). But it is not unknown to the earlier epistles (see 1 Cor. ii. 6-7, xv. 51); and in this epistle we have the allusion in xi. 25. The idea, however, is not so prominent in this epistle that we should expect it to form the theme of the concluding doxology. Moreover, the involved style, though slightly reminiscent of that of Ephesians, is not like that of this epistle, or indeed like Paul's style in general. There is ground for the suspicion that it is not an original part of the epistle at all. While some MSS. give it here, some give it at the end of chap. xiv., some in both places, and one after xv. 33. One extant MS., as well as others which we know only from citations, does not give it at all. It is very probable that when the last two chapters were removed to make the epistle more suitable for general reading in church, the shortened edition was supplied with a solemn ending in the form of a doxology composed on the analogy of Eph. iii. 20-21, and embodying certain Pauline ideas familiar from the later epistles. Subsequently, scribes copying the epistle had before them both the shorter recension ending with xiv. 23 + the doxology, and also the longer recension ending baldly with the postscript xvi. 21-23. It was a happy idea to transfer the doxology from its old place, where it was not needed if the epistle was copied in full, to the end, where something of the kind seemed to be called for. See also Introduction, p. 10.

GENERAL INDEX[1]

ABBA, 144-6
Abraham, I., 42f., 64f., 68f., 87-92
Abrahams, 213n.
Adam, 99-102, 117, 123f., 129, 136-7
Adoption, 143-7
Advocate, 158f.
Agape. *See* Love
Ambrosiaster, 21f.
Amos, 56
Amplias, 16f., 241
Andronicus (and Junias), 240f.
Antinomianism, 70, 105, 113-17
Apostles, 240-1
Aquila. *See* Prisca
Aristobulus, 16, 241
Aristotle, 38, 61, 131f.
Assurance, 152, 157, 217
Augustine, 127, 216f.
Aurelius, Marcus, 151

BACON, FRANCIS, 51
Baptism, 105-9, 111f.
Blood, 79
Body, 110f., 140-1, 143, 199f., 202f.
Body of (Christ), 108, 120f., 139, 202, 216, 234
Bousset, Wilhelm, 178

CHARACTER, 96
Charity. *See* Love
Christ-mysticism ("in Christ"), 99, 104-8, 113, 135-42, 151
Church, 107f., 120, 172, 174-6, 190f., 231, 239-40
Circumcision, 64-8
Claudius, 15-16, 20
Clement (of Rome), 20f.
Communism, Christian, 233f.
Conduct (right), 117f., 197-200, 217, 223-4

Conscience, 23, 61-2, 77, 81, 159, 217, 222-3
Consecration, 115-18
Covetousness, 128, 212-13

DALMAN, G., 128
Deacons, 238
Death, 101f., 108-11, 140f.
Death (of Christ), 96-100, 106, 108-11, 120-1, 208
Dedication, 113f., 117
Determinism, 170-1
Deutero-Isaiah, 25, 39, 181
Domitian, 15, 17

EASTON, B. S. 65n.
Election, 155
Endurance, 96
Epaenetus, 12-13, 240
Ephesus, 12-18
Epictetus, 162, 203
Eschatology, 216
Esdras (2), 25, 44-6, 62, 65, 102
Experience, religious, 25-8

FAITH, 37, 41-5, 79-80, 92, 154, 174, 175, 177-8
Faithfulness (of God), 48, 67
Fall (doctrine of), 123-4, 129
Family, 239f.
Flesh, 129, 135f., 141
Freedom (of God), 168-72

GALATIANS, EPISTLE TO, 23
Gentiles, 227-8, 230-5, 244f.
God (as Father), 146f.
Gospel, 179f., 191, 246. *See also* Paul, (Gospel of)
Grace (of God), 28, 48, 75, 80, 103, 118, 214

HABAKKUK, 41f.
Hadfield, J. A., 132, 201n.

[1] I owe the compilation of the Indices to the kindness of Mr. James W. Stewart, to whom I wish to express my thanks.

INDEX OF SCRIPTURE REFERENCES

OLD TEST.

APOCRYPHA AND PSEUDEPIGRAPHA

NEW TEST.